Alex Bonham was raised in the the arts before travelling overland in 2008. She now lives in Auck and a pack of dogs, and campaig all-ages-friendly city. She has two Master's degrees: one in Law, the other in Drama, and she is currently working towards a doctorate on the Playful City. She was elected onto Auckland Council's Waitematā Local Board in 2019.

Play and the City

How to Create Places and Spaces to Help Us Thrive

Alex Bonham

ROBINSON

ROBINSON

First published in Great Britain in 2021 by Robinson

Copyright © Alex Bonham, 2021

1 3 5 7 9 8 6 4 2

A CIP catalogue record for this book is available from the British Library

ISBN: 978-1-47214-480-5

Typeset in Times by Initial Typesetting Services, Edinburgh
Printed and bound in Great Britain by Clays Ltd, Elcograf S.p.A.

Papers used by Robinson are from well-managed forests
and other responsible sources

Robinson
An imprint of
Little, Brown Book Group
Carmelite House
50 Victoria Embankment
London EC4Y 0DZ

An Hachette UK Company
www.hachette.co.uk

www.littlebrown.co.uk

This book is for Andy, Charlie and Olivia: the play experts

'It may be a bit of effort and you may not want to go, you may not know anyone there but you should go because you will probably have a good time. I forced myself to go to the party, met some people who became friends that would last forever and some of the conversations I had led to some great business opportunities. Good things always happen. Secondly, you should go because if someone has worked to put on an event, it really sucks if people pull out at the last minute. And one day the invites won't come in. You'll be really depressed that no one invites you to things any more, that people don't want to hang out with you. Don't even wait for an invitation. Start organising things yourself. Good things will happen and you'll have a good time. And if the party sucks, you can leave. You get to go home and you lost a little bit of time, but you put yourself in a place where awesome things can happen. Always go to the party.'

Jimi Hunt, author and co-founder of
mental health charity Live More Awesome

Contents

Contents

Introduction: The vital importance of play for all ages

The best first date of my life started at an inline skate store at Marble Arch, when I was living in London. Once equipped, we set off gently through Hyde Park. Picking up speed, we crossed to Green Park and into St James's. A short section on pavements got us on to Embankment Bridge, and then down to the South Bank. We glided eastwards until we made it to the Tate Modern, and there we lay on our not-too-sweaty backs staring at The Weather Project in the Turbine Room. It looked like a giant orange sun.

We were playing, basically. Rollerblading is aerobic: you move your body, which feels good, and you move at speed, which is thrilling. Doing things that you don't normally do and submitting to an adventure with no clue where you are heading is exciting. I was twenty-seven or thereabouts and I felt like a kid again. It is easy to associate play with childhood, when kids shake rattles, dress up, whizz around on little trikes, or paint pictures with bold, bright brush strokes, but this isn't the beginning of a person's play journey – nor is it the end.

It is well established that children play, but babies also play, and so do adults. Through their play people develop the physical, cognitive, social and emotional skills they need. It is not uncommon that as they get older they are encouraged to take life more seriously. This is a mistake: the more people play and enjoy their activities the more skilled and productive they become.

Humans are unique in that we play the whole way through our lives. We are wired to learn through play. When human babies are born, they are a bit different from other animals. They are not wired to get moving on their first day, like newborn deer, for example. Human babies' brains have huge amounts of brain cells, but a lot of them are unconnected. What this means is that we humans come into the world highly adaptable and flexible. When we do something that is useful for our survival – like eating something delicious or working as a team – chemicals are released that make us feel good. What *feels* good probably *is* good for us, nine times out of ten (as long as no manipulation, social or chemical, is involved).

When we do something that puts our survival at risk, like drinking polluted water, or getting too close to the edge of a cliff, we feel very different sensations that divert us away. That we are motivated by our enjoyment or loathing of aspects of the world around us may be built into our cellular building blocks. Single-cell organisms also reach for what is good for their survival and recoil from things that damage them. They have sensors and possibly a sense of what feels right or wrong. Single-cell organisms can and do also reach out for each other and work together as teams. It makes sense for their survival but I wonder if they are also enjoying each other's company at some basic visceral level. Some scientists have theorised that play, this reaching *towards* pleasure and other things and beings to work with, and moving *away* from pain and existential threats, is a motivating force for all life forms. Perhaps it is our particular enjoyment of collaboration and play and our enthusiasm to extend ourselves and try things that are novel that has made the human race so successful.

Research work in epigenetics reveals that the environment people grow up in can turn parts of their genes on or off, so the way that brains connect up then depends to a large degree on their play and interplay with the world around them. Everyone plays, but the way they play depends on the culture in which they live and the contacts that they have. Where, and how, and by whom a child is raised makes a huge impact on who they are, what they can do, and how they behave. We don't stop playing when we grow up; we just don't usually call what we are doing play. As our civilisations – and the way we spend our time – evolve, it is our capacity for play, our delight in novelty and desire to win when faced with diverse challenges, that help us to adapt.

For many adults this exploration of the new and whimsical is more mental than physical. Our ability to converse, to communicate intangible ideas and to tell stories is one of the human race's superpowers. The process of articulation is an exploratory act, unlocking new ideas and knowledge. This puts new power into the phrase 'putting your mind to something'. By making the effort to explain something to someone else we also get a better handle on a concept ourselves. If you teach, they say, you learn twice. Listening is key too – the interplay of ideas that reveal new things. Conversation is active. This comes through with play scripts, which are mainly made up of words to be spoken. When putting on a play, the actors will work out all the 'actions' that lie beneath the words, and what they are trying to do to the person they are speaking to – please them, shame them, persuade them, etc. Status can shift a lot in conversation – you can raise people up or put them down. In some comedy scenes, the goal is to top the other person. This is a bit like being in the pub trying to tell the best anecdote. Anyone who likes to chat and banter likes to play!

We enjoy experiencing playfulness with those we love and respect. Our friends are very often the people we like to play with, and it is often the people we play with (in a sports team, or a drama club, or meet at the pub) who become our friends. When we arrive in a new school or city, it is often through playful activities that we can start to build our networks. Having close relationships with others, or even a network of light ties, does more for our longevity than exercise, healthy eating, giving up smoking. Statistically, if you are obese, you can more effectively improve your life expectancy and sense of wellbeing by having lots of social interactions, than by losing weight.[1] Play and sport can be so effective for combating mental health issues that some doctors in Europe prescribe art and fitness classes instead of therapy or drugs.

Families who play together, stay together. We love our relatives for many reasons, but we love the best those that are fun, who have time for a chat, who enjoy crosswords and pudding, who will pretend to be a horse for the little ones, who play card games with you, come to your performances and yell support from the sidelines of the football pitch. We are delighted to discover grandmothers entering high-diving competitions or going to dances. We appreciate people who have a sense of humour. Why then do many adults seem to like playfulness in others while seemingly feeling shamed out of play themselves?

Adults *need* play. Play is essential for wellbeing – which is why you need this book because play is both about expanding what you can be, and the utter joy that can be obtained from submitting to the moment. Life isn't always easy, and taking a step outside the daily grind can be essential for morale. You may have lost the contract, but at least you have been selected to do a solo in the choir! You may feel overwhelmed with tasks, but dressing up for '80s week at the gym is so much fun you realise you can face the in-tray after all. Each small win releases a little bit of natural chemical happiness into your body that energises you to carry on. There is value in taking time to smell the flowers.

Even when things are going well, it is important to take a break and 'do the opposite' – something dramatically different from what you normally do. We love pretending to be something we are not, at music festivals, in fiction, in the Vauxhall Pleasure Gardens, at the Venice Carnival, or on a night out. Princess Diana, rumour has it, dressed as a man and snuck out for an evening with Freddie Mercury and Kenny Everett to spend the evening in the Royal Vauxhall Tavern, and pronounced it the best night of her life.[2] Her mother-in-law, Queen Elizabeth II, also escaped the palace for a night out on VE Day in 1945, dressed as an army officer, and did a conga through The Ritz. For her, too, 'it was one of the most memorable nights of my life'.[3] For the rest of us, when it comes to a special night out, we dress up and expect to be treated like a prince or princess. Restaurants allow everyone an opportunity to be master rather than servant, and the cinemas and dance halls of the 1920s and '30s called themselves The Majestic, the Palais, or the Coronet to remind us that everyone should be treated royally, at least sometimes.

In this book I will explore how very broad the scope of play is, and how our ideas about play change over time. Play is ubiquitous across cultures and has survival value at an individual and societal level. Our sense of humour and love of chat and novelty is shared with only the most intelligent of species. If play is so valuable though, I ask, what is it that holds us back from playing and how can we address those challenges? I will also demonstrate how play, cities and survival are so profoundly linked. Does the way we play impact on our chances of survival? And if so, can playing differently improve those chances? Ultimately, I hope to tease out your playful side and encourage you to make your cities more enjoyable places to live, despite the various challenges we are all facing. Along the way will be loads of suggestions to bring some fun into the city to suit both shy and confident players of every type. I am hoping that this book will encourage you to enjoy play for its own sake in a way that suits you. If you enjoy life, chances are your children and the people around you will, too. You may find in many cases, despite your fears that you cannot, may not play, that you are allowed. The door is not locked. It just takes a little courage to turn the handle. This book is by no means comprehensive, but I hope it strikes a chord.

Part One:

Play and You

1

Play and pleasure: which is which?

Play is ubiquitous in our lives in different contexts and we all have an understanding of it and yet it is curiously hard to define. Play is not pleasure exactly, but they often come together. It is much easier to define pleasure. It is the happy feeling you get when chemicals are released in your body in response to your senses – touch, sight, hearing, smell and taste – taking in something good. Our senses bring all sorts of bad things to our attention, too, of course. We instinctively try to avoid or protect ourselves from nasty smells, sharp thorns, deafening noises and discoloured food. Our eyes, nose, ears, taste buds and nerve endings are forever negotiating our surroundings.

We can feel pleasure when we play. Various cocktails of chemicals are released when we win, when we give and receive acts of love and friendship, when we are praised, and when we are engaged in new, exciting, even risky endeavours. We are rewarded with good feelings about actions and behaviours that are good for the survival of the species and punished with bad feelings about things that are likely to lead to our destruction. Sex, at its best, feels great. Eating good food feels great. Exercise feels great (once you've got warmed up). Wearing nice textiles that don't scratch your skin is great; love and friendship make you feel great. We enjoy beauty, nature, music, sport, going for a bike ride. Doing these things takes effort, but they are intrinsically rewarding. They are enjoyable in themselves, whatever anyone else thinks. If you want to be happy, get out there and do what you enjoy.

Play seems to be an active reaching towards pleasure where the outcome is uncertain. Drinking alcohol isn't exactly play but can encourage it by reducing tensions and lowering the inhibitions that act as a barrier to play. Physical activities like sport or dancing are ways to release chemicals in a healthier, natural way that put you in the cheerful expansive mood that makes it easier to be social. However, there is less pleasure if one loses badly, or nobody wants to be your partner. Play is a bit like a wrapped-up parcel. Satisfaction is hoped for, but not guaranteed – but it is fun finding out!

Johan Huizinga,[1] a Dutch medieval historian writing just before the Second World War, argued that play had no economic aspect; but games often involve prizes, and gambling is ALL about money. Gambling draws more economic activity than any other form of discrete recreational activity. While ideally play is intrinsically motivated, it is nevertheless the case that prizes can be a great motivator for play (as much as work). As people become more experienced at a particular form of play, the prize element can become a more important factor than the joy of the game. Then the way they play adapts – systems develop: tricks, shortcuts and efficiencies are found, so as to gain the largest rewards for the player themselves at the lowest risk. For some, adding a financial element can spoil the fun of the game.

Huizinga felt that desire to win, or what he called the agonistic instinct, lies at the heart of human motivation and success.[2] The term agon referred to a trial or contest in Athenian society. In an agonistic culture the 'best' would be determined by the winner, whether it be in athletics, an argument or the answer to a riddle. Like the old joke asking how fast you need to be to run away from a lion (answer: faster than someone else running away from the lion) success is often not absolute, just relative. Con-test means 'with witnesses'. Tests are conducted openly, ideally, and the winner is the best on the day. Huizinga argued that this competitiveness could bring the best out of all players and yet he also observed the agonistic instinct generally ended up in decadence and corruption: playing the system.

To add to the monetary aspect, we invest a huge amount of money and resources into play – which means that people make a lot of money out of it. The salaries of top football coaches in American

4

colleges dwarf those of most lawyers and surgeons. Dabo Swinney of Clemson Tigers in South Carolina made $9.3 million in 2019 for coaching the college football team.[3] Why? Perhaps success on the field brings in more donations from wealthy sponsors and alumni. Perhaps football is just really important to lots of people, as something they have participated in, as something they connect to, and for its broader allegorical value, to demonstrate viscerally that for everyone in life there are ups and downs however hard you work.

One might observe that the Covid recession has started to bite not because of a failure in the harvest, or over oil or industry, but because people are unable to spend their money on tourism and the non-essentials, the things they enjoy. We underestimate the extent of the 'fun dollar' to the point where we don't even use that term (discretionary spending barely hints at fun in my view), but it is huge. The tabletop board and card game industry aimed at the dedicated 'gamer' market (not including children's games and toys) was worth $1.2 billion in the USA and Canada alone in 2015.[4] In New Zealand, more money flows through tourism than through dairy. Then there is theatre, the visual arts, music, novels, TV, crafting, sports equipment, eating out, clubbing . . . the list of essential non-essential businesses goes on and on. Of course online shopping has boomed – in itself a form of play – will the outfit look as good on us as it does the model? Is the book a good read? We hope but don't know. We reach for pleasure but it is a gamble. It is fun partly *because* it is a gamble.

Play is tricksy. It is fun! – although not everyone enjoys it all of the time. It doesn't matter – except that in certain moments it feels like it matters more than anything. Doing something 'in play' can be used as an excuse for saying or doing something that you didn't really mean. Or, alternatively, for doing what you want and saying exactly what you mean and then putting it down to drink or 'just playing!' It can strengthen relationships, or test them. Play is associated with power games and game theory, and yet also with mucking about. Play expert Brian Sutton-Smith put his finger on it: the only thing consistent about play is its ambiguity.

It is not uncommon to be unsettled by other people's play, particularly if it is accompanied by hysterical laughter. In drama fiction we connect the desire to play and win games with the most terrible deeds: *Game of Thrones*, *House of Cards*, Len Deighton's spy series *Game, Set and Match*, the list goes on . . . Let people get away with some sort of silliness, some think, and you will only encourage worse behaviour in time. Play is amoral and can easily slip into chaos. No wonder some people are uncertain about it. Many a parent would prefer their children play without them. '"I would rather stick spoons in my eyes than play with my kids," said mother of two' in the *Daily Mail* (admittedly after a few weeks of stressful lockdown). It is not uncommon in adulthood to lose touch with play, and to find imaginative play a drain, forgetting that playing with peers in an activity that engages you is very different from playing with someone at a different age and stage with different tastes and different gaps in their knowledge and skills that they yearn to fill.

What play does seem to do is allow us to extend ourselves while leaving some room for retreat. We can take on a new challenge in play and give it our best shot, honing new skills while claiming that 'it is just for fun'. Keeping the stakes low can be enabling. Conversely, professional 'creatives' can find the pressure to do something new and playful stultifying. Through play, we can experience personal growth, increase the store of reliable knowledge, and establish and improve societal structures from which we can take the next step (and improvise more fun things to do). Don't underestimate play, play expert Dr Stuart Brown advises, it has survival value, even though it is risky. He argues that play must have survival value BECAUSE it is risky; what we gain from it in building our personal and societal capacity more than makes up for the risk and cost. And yet all this may still not capture what play looks like or why it might appeal!

Play looks different to different people. Dr Brown, who is an American psychologist and academic, reckons that most adults fit into eight play personality types – jokers, kinaesthetes (people who like to move), explorers, collectors, storytellers, competitors, directors and artist/creators. For him play is a state of mind. Something is play if you think it is, and can start with as little as a smile. Play is the grease that allows people to enjoy living in close proximity to each other.[5] Play makes urban living enjoyable – and without it perhaps impossible.

Play and pleasure: which is which?

French anthropologist Roger Caillois also thought that play could take different forms. He travelled around the world looking at different cultures, and observed that the way a society played could tell you a lot about what sort of society it was, as well as the challenges it faced. The play was a way to work through or tackle problems. In agrarian communities with lots of farmers, many of the rituals and festivals are about rain and fertility. In places where women are homemakers there are more dolls. In cultures where child mortality is high, children would even play at burying their dead. As the culture changed so did the play. What remained consistent, he reckoned, are four components of play that by themselves, or combined, would stimulate that excitement in your stomach that we associate with fun activities: simulation, chance, competition and vertigo.[6] All have survival value.

Simulation At its simplest, this is pretending to be someone or something else, like dressing up or playing at cops and robbers or princesses. Simulators in arcades with moving chairs and dashboards make it easy for us to play at being pilots, or dinosaur hunters. Simulation can also be more subtle: it can involve copying what other people do as a way to learn or perform better. We may cover a song or repeat someone else's words. Trying to simulate something can be helpful even when theoretically impossible – pretending to be a tree or flowing water can produce a mental shift. You could say that simulating one thing – a scene from real life, an emotion or a concept – with paint, or wood, or light, is what art is all about. All of us sometimes 'fake it till we make it', dressing to 'look the part' as we take on a new role. We assume a confidence we may not feel as we learn the ropes until the happy day when we realise we know what we are doing. Simulation then is a fun way to develop capacity.

Chance Whenever something is uncertain, there is an element of excitement. Opening a door, when you don't know what is behind it, is to take a chance. The same goes for pressing a button when you don't know what it does, or going on a blind date. Games are fun only if you don't know whether or not you can win. Flirting is fun for the same reason. Gambling at the casino is exciting because you don't know whether luck will be with you or not, whether you will end the evening rich or with empty pockets. Smartphone newsfeeds are compelling not because all the content is interesting but because they are modelled on fruit machines, where sometimes you win and often you don't. Games of chance are useful in developing the capacity to manage risk, both emotionally and practically. Insurance companies and betting shops are remarkably similar in the way they work.

Competition In a competition the aim is also to win, but there is a greater focus on merit and skill. To win a running race (or a rugby game or a spelling bee) is to be acknowledged as the best. For all the competitors, the competition is a way of finding out their strengths and weaknesses, and where they sit in the pecking order, which in turn determines what opportunities become available to them. Most of us like to win (or come close) and be acknowledged for our strengths. Winning releases the chemical dopamine, which feels glorious. Losing leaves a visceral feeling of failure that can be very disheartening, and which we must learn to recover from. Knowing where our talents lie and being able to find other small wins in play can be very helpful in this recovery process. Competitions can generate excitement and focus the mind. They can bring out the best in people, and/or stress them out completely but they do motivate progress.

Vertigo This is that rush you feel when you are slipping, spinning, sliding or rushing through the air but just about avoiding falling on your face. It is the feeling you get when you go skydiving, or jump from a high board at a pool. Vertigo is enjoyed by babies being thrown in the air, and dancers spinning in each other's arms. There is an element of vertigo in imagining falling, walking on a tightrope, looking down from the top of a tall building or even up to the rafters in a grand cathedral. The thrill of vertigo, the release of adrenalin, raises levels of alertness which makes us feel more alive. Experience of dangerous play enables us to cope better and make good decisions when in immediate danger. Moving at speed can make us feel we are reaching our goals – and this winning feeling releases dopamine – a double hit.

All these four aspects do add an element of fun and excitement to an activity. While pleasure is not guaranteed, engaging with play ups the chance of having a very good time.

Activity: Vertigo

What you need A public wall.

Method Walk along it without falling off.

Variations

- Slide down banisters.

- Run down flights of stairs.

- Spin your child around by their wrists until you can't do it any more. Go the other way.

- Try Scottish country dancing and spin with your partner.

- Spin your partner anyway.

- Have a go at the swings, slides and flying foxes in the playground (If they are strong enough).

- Climb a tree.

2

Playing to learn

It is pretty well established that playing is a way that kids (and young animals) learn. We play to learn from others, through copying, testing and exploration, both what we can do, and what we *may* do. We also learn from others more experienced than ourselves from what they say, and more importantly by what they do. Stuart Brown writes about how the way we play develops over time. It is interesting to consider how much we continue to copy, test and explore as a way to learn our whole lives through.

Copying and attunement

Copying to learn

One of the most important ways that children play is by copying and learning about call and response. Babies are wired to be interested in faces, and adults are wired to find babies adorable. It starts, as so many relationships do, with a meeting of the eyes. The distance between the eyes of a baby on the breast and their mother's face is, helpfully, a baby's best focusing distance. When they are not feeding, babies copy the facial expressions of people looking at them and attempt lots and lots of different expressions. We have all, I am sure, broadened our smiles at babies to encourage them to smile back to us.

Parent and child in particular take cues from one another. They are not just copying, but modelling the interplay of conversation: one person says something while the other listens and responds in a way that acknowledges what has been said, while also introducing something new. First efforts at replying are far more like random mur-murings and gurglings than real speech, but obligingly parents will continue the 'pretend' conversation anyway. In time, the child grasps a few key words and the conversation begins to make sense. If a child communicates nicely then the response is appreciative, if it is rude or destructive then the response will be negative: Mummy or Daddy will say no. The offender can see their impact and backtrack, apologising, perhaps trying to find out what they did wrong and how they can make things right or at least return to favour. It is through this person-to-person interplay that children learn how to pick up social cues, which enables them to venture into new territory because they know how to recognise danger signals that demand retreat.

By adulthood, picking up social cues is second nature, and we become used to the dance of conversation, venturing opinions and modifying our views according to the response. It is rare for more than a slightly hardening expression to be required to put us on notice. Humans are one of the few species that blush, that feel the shame of other people's disapproval. Not only do we feel, but we are constantly communicating our feelings, which makes us easier to please. It also suggests that over time we have evolved into a world where pleasing others, and letting others know how to please us, is a normal thing. Pretending things are OK when they are not might then be a mistake as it makes it harder for others to know if their behaviour is off. The way we behave is informed by the standards of behaviour that we picked up from our parents, teachers and friends as kids. Through our play and interplay we learned how to live within a particular place, time and cultural context and that provided a value framework as a benchmark. However, being able to pick up social cues can help us move between and adapt to groups that do things in different ways. Kids need social play. 'Cats deprived of play-fighting can hunt just fine,' writes Stuart Brown,[1] 'What they can't do – what they never learn to do – is to socialise successfully.'

Copying to teach

One of the oldest ways to teach is for someone proficient at a task to model it. The children of the San people in Africa are encouraged to watch animals and copy what they do.[2] Teaching by rote is a less interesting way of getting children to copy so as to learn. I remember my fellow pupils and me marching around the schoolroom at the age of seven or eight, chanting our times tables (it was the 1980s, a time of good old-fashioned teaching methods). Children in schools do still copy letters and rote learning is still quite common in Asian societies, where even university entrance exams can be multiple choice.

This approach may have fallen out of fashion in Western schools that value critical thinking, but there are still times when learning something by copying might be helpful: in science and cooking, but also, counter-intuitively perhaps, in the visual and performing arts, at least to get started. Italian Renaissance artists worked like this. The artist's workshop would have housed not just the lead painter but also his apprentices and assistants, who were there to learn. They started by drawing copies of symbols and designs, then, in time, went on to more complicated scenery and drapery, then hands and faces. It was this constant practice of copying two-dimensional images that revealed how to copy from life. All these copies would form the basis of a portfolio of inspiration for them to use – and copy – in their later careers. When a master painter signed a painting, he was not necessarily authenticating that he had painted the work, but that it had reached his standards – in other words, it was a sufficiently good copy. It was art as a brand. (If you fancy this approach, it is possible to join art classes in bars, where each week participants are invited to copy works of the great masters while knocking back a glass of wine.) Classical ballet and instrument classes also often begin with copying exercises, so as to learn the basic steps. This is necessary so that the performer can understand the shared language of the art and know what to do in order to fit in with everyone else. Copying is not a bad thing. There is something rather enjoyable about moving in sync with other people, or watching groups of dancers move in sync with each other.

Copying as a strategy

Our penchant for copying may be key to the human race's survival. Go back fifty thousand years, and there were a number of different types of hominids, human-like creatures, walking the earth, with slightly different characteristics. The Neanderthals had larger brains and larger bodies, and were more individually able, but *Homo sapiens* were chattier and friendlier and more up for sharing skills and discoveries, and copying each other's successes. It seems that in nomadic societies to this day, groups meet up to share food and knowledge, shift groups, dance, talk and have a laugh. Joining in and doing what everyone else is doing is not only fun, but it also allows us to learn new things quickly. Copying saves an awful lot of time and energy that would be expended on trial and error.

Unsurprisingly, copying is rife in manufacturing. High Street fashion follows the catwalk collections, while new toys and gadgets are copied and sold cheaper than the branded original. New technologies steal concepts from old technologies. Microsoft used the metaphor of a desktop with files and folders to make the personal computer interface more intuitive. Cars have relatively similar dashboards, a steering wheel and footbrakes, so that when people hop in a different make of car they can still drive it.[3] Individually we may not push the knowledge dial that far ahead, but by sharing what we've got, and by taking on board and repeating what we've seen or learned through conversation, printing and now the World Wide Web, we can all benefit from the hivemind and collaborate our way to extraordinary feats of innovation,[4] a process we enjoy more generally than swotting up alone.

While we may not think of ourselves to be particularly copying others as we go to choir, a tea dance, or to the pub, or as we drink tea at each other's kitchen tables, what we are doing has been done many times before. Singing songs together that other people have written, dancing steps correctly so that your partner can follow, even the etiquette for chatting over a drink in a tavern or at home, as people have done for millennia, are all ways of joining in that have involved at some point a bit of watching, copying, learning and attunement. This desire to grasp, and attune to the world around us, can become so instinctive that we take it for granted, and only notice ourselves doing it when we are in a new and strange environment.

Pretending

If, when we are *copying* others, we are trying to do something that has been done before so that we can learn how and join in, when we are *pretending* to be others we want to either mimic the person concerned, or try on their role for size, taking on their status along the way. Little kids like to pretend to play Mummy and Daddy, or Kings and Queens, or soldiers or doctors. My mother has a story she loves to tell of one nativity play in which the text was not tamely recited but devised by the children. 'How's our Jesus?' asked young Joseph, sitting down to his tea a couple of years after the birth. 'He was a right little bugger all day,' replied Mary. Cue, hilarity from the audience. Not only is pretend play an opportunity to *act* differently, it is an opportunity to be *treated* differently. Dress as a princess in a long gown, brush your hair and move gracefully, and your more indulgent parent, at least, might start treating you as one. Put on a soldier's outfit, raise a stick and say, 'Bang!', and you are inviting your parent to die dramatically and noisily on the kitchen floor.

Whether you ultimately like these reactions or not is moot. It is interesting to put on roles to see what impact you have. For shy, isolated or autistic children, school drama projects with scripts can be a way to step out of the private worlds in their heads and learn the different ways that people act towards and respond to each other. Children observe and represent what they see in writing and drawing and performance all the time. Trying out and having people accept them in a role suggests to young people that this is something they could actually be.[5] It is interesting that acting (as in pretending) is the same word as acting (doing something for real). Perhaps it is no coincidence. You learn how to act so you can learn how to act. And sometimes learning how to perform another person by copying their voice and movements can bring fascinating insights into who people are, what motivates them, how they go about life.

Harriet Walter, the English actress, has had a long and varied career on stage and screen. In preparing for a performance she tries to unlock her character by using a number of different 'keys'.[6] Some of them start with the inside of the character, imagining their feelings and goals, but she also uses the physical language and biographical

15

keys, which are all about starting with how a person appears on the outside, and working inwards. For some actors, simply putting on a costume can be a trigger to a deeper transformation. Copy someone else's movements, clothes and voice, and you begin to walk in their shoes. By pretending to be someone else you can feel different too, more confident, more comfortable in your skin. The most basic mask is one's face. You may smile when you are happy, or you can smile and make yourself feel happy. Reading the room and copying other people's behaviour is a good start for fitting in; obviously dressing the same, stalking them, and so on, is going too far.

Copying and attunement are helpful for learning but we also need to test, to try things for ourselves. We are drawn to new things and new experiences, and we find them exciting. Part of this excitement is fear – new things are risky – and so we test, engaged and alert, to see what happens. We find out how things work, and we work out what makes an impact on the world around us. Testing and finding out are practically the same thing. We can test ideas out on each other, critique a news story or a movie and prepare for the future in our imagination, but nothing beats real-life experience.

Testing

Back in the Paleolithic days, when people were nomadic, they would find new plants and not know if they were poisonous. Most members of the tribe stuck to what they knew – followed the existing menu, if you like – a few would try tiny amounts to see what would happen to them. This may have been the wise elders of the tribe, the medicine men or women, or perhaps slaves. If they didn't get sick, then others would try. New opportunities to test were made possible when food had been affected by the elements, the sun or fire. Meat that had been cooked by wildfire or dried in the sun might have tasted better and hinted at how it could be prepared or stored. As knowledge about foods increased, there would be more and more foods on the menu to copy, and less testing required. Knowledge about which foods and plants were poisonous was useful, too, and children were taught to copy their elders in not eating them.

Obviously, there is always a good deal more testing at the boundaries of what is possible/impossible and what is certain/uncertain. The frontier is exciting, because beyond the edge is the unknown, where old rules may not apply. The scientific process sets a framework for tinkering in an organised fashion to find out new things. The knowledge frontier is explored at the edges of the known world, with information gathered under the sea, in space or at a tiny atomic level, with innovative research tools, and shared with the networked community of scientists in laboratories and universities testing, testing, testing new ideas, new theoretical frameworks, new ways to build structures, new vaccines, new forms of energy, new foods.

It is no surprise then that testing starts from the very earliest moments, when the whole world is uncertain to us. Babies seem to flail about, moving for the sake of moving. They make aimless offers that are rewarded with pleasure and information when their fists grip something that they can put it in their mouths and taste-test. Toddlers test themselves and the world around them constantly. They delight in objects, in visual contrast, in new tastes, in finding out how high up the furniture and onto the bookcase they can climb. They may not be sure what they are doing, or what things are for, as they clash saucepan lids together, but they are having a fine time working it out. The only innate fears babies are born with are a fear of loud sounds and a fear of heights (which is why parents are advised to cover electrical sockets). Kids will try new things to see if they can do them and demand their carers observe and feedback on their new skills (Look Mummy! No hands!). They delight in their progress – passing each test, each milestone.

We test things to check that they work, and when something doesn't seem to be working as it should, we challenge ourselves to make it work. We will have a play, have a fiddle to try and get it sorted. Kids will tap, twist, tinker and bash things to see what happens. When we buy a new piece of equipment or a game, it is not unusual to try and figure out how it all works by adopting a similar process. What if I do that? Or that? Looking at the instructions can be perceived as a last resort, cheating even. Some games are designed to be so explorative that they don't have instructions at all: working out what you are supposed to do *is* the game. We get the same sort of satisfaction when we mend something and make it work. We have triumphed over the obstacles and can move forward! We win! We test because we are curious. We test things to be sure about them – new foods, the depth of a lake before diving in, the strength of a tree branch before we climb on it. Testing has survival value.

The child will not only attune to but test the social world around them. Parents set down rules and boundaries, and children, who are constantly growing in both stature and capacity, see how far they can stretch these boundaries and flout the rules without getting into trouble or losing their parents' approval entirely. Children test each other, to measure the quality of their friends, or their own power, and to see whether the frameworks they have been brought up in apply universally. For young people who are just starting to date, testing is essential: testing the relationship, the other person and one's self. Agonising questions over how long to wait before calling someone back, what to wear and how to negotiate the transition from just friends to something more are the trials of youth.

Tests are a way of finding out more about something, or about the capabilities of someone, but they do more than that too. Tests can have a transformative impact on the thing or person being tested. They push people on to the next stage of whatever they are doing, and they can motivate people to work to ensure that they lead the pack, or at least are not left behind (back to Huizinga's 'agonistic instinct' – the desire to win). Public challenges give people a rare chance to demonstrate their mastery and be acknowledged in a world that doesn't like braggers. Audiences admire and encourage those with talent willing to put themselves forward. The ongoing popularity of the shows *Grand Designs*, *Dancing with the Stars* and *The Great British Bake Off* underscore that it is not conflict or cruelty that draws us in as much as the display of mastery at an activity that seems to most of us to be very difficult. Ordeals which require hard choices that test character are so compelling to us that they are at the heart of most plays, novels and films that we enjoy.

Tests reveal character.[7] In the Victorian period, competitive sport like football, rugby and boxing were encouraged in schools and in the military, to develop not only physical strength and fitness, but also moral character: resilience, teamwork, good humour, determination, selflessness. One look at today's sports pages indicates that these values haven't really changed. Once a challenge is taken up, there is a pressure to complete the task – whether it be training for a marathon or an ocean swim, putting on a theatrical performance, getting elected or giving up something for Lent. The language of challenge reframes tests of endurance and self-discipline as something fun, rather than difficult, painful or tedious. The social aspect reframes peer pressure as supporting friends. But the pressure is still there, enough to motivate some effort! Being able to demonstrate graciousness in victory or defeat is all part of the test. This can be hardest of all.

There are stakes in play. Tests rank participants in sport and in the academic world. When people do well new opportunities may be offered them. For young people, exams and displays determine who is worthy of going up to the next level. In the feudal medieval period, a squire's performance in the jousts might determine whether he became a knight, with salary, lands and improved marriage prospects. In the USA, performing well in academia or sport or the military can be pathways to a university scholarship and improved career and marital prospects.

Testing is connected to the concept of interplay. If testing involves subject and object (man with new radio), interplay is subject, subject with the two sides impacting on each other. There is interplay in the interaction between people, between people and things and between people and places and systems. Interplay is at the fore on a first date when both parties are sussing out and trying to impress each other. Interplay is fun in an exploratory way, opening up opportunities for more fun, while simultaneously deepening the bond between the players. This can work in a lively, friendly conversation – which is probably how adults spend the most time playing – but also between a person and an enabling object, such as a tool, a computer or a car, or for many small children, particularly fine sticks. It may seem crazy to suggest that people develop loyalties to machines, but they absolutely do.[8] It makes sense – and has survival value – to develop an appreciation, even affection, of things, and systems, physical, cultural and political, that are useful to us in our tasks and projects.

The city is an enabling structural system writ large. It is physical, tangible and when it functions well facilitates individual and societal success and progress. We become attached to people and places and, by extension, the city itself because it offers opportunities to connect, to work and do what we want to do.[9] Our pleasure in interplay is what enables us as a species to collaborate and to create.

Evolving play

We interplay in the present and also with the past, or at least with ideas from the past. Creativity, according to musician Anthony Brandt and neuroscientist David Eagleman, is taking old ideas and breaking, bending or blending them to create something that is new, but not so 'out there' that people can't get their heads around the concept. We learn to dance by copying the teacher's steps, but the more we are able to attune to the music and other dancers, and as our repertoire of moves gets larger, the more able we are to get creative on the dance floor when we mix these moves up, or mash different elements together to do something new.[10]

Evolving play to make a game better is quite normal. When kids play, they rarely sit down and establish all the rules of engagement but instead develop them over time. They create new games and meld different ones together. Artists and academics are encouraged to use other people's ideas. Sports' rules change to become more exciting, led by the industry; movies become more spectacular, video gaming more immersive – both pinch ideas, and employees, off each other. Structures in academic thought keep shifting, one article at a time. Legal systems are designed to evolve, to try and improve outcomes for people and to meet the challenges of the present and future, either led by politicians or pushed from the bottom up. Change too much too quickly though and no one will follow, on the dance floor or anywhere else.

Sometimes creativity is spawned by a misunderstanding or a mistake. Even if the story about the boy who picked up the football to create rugby is apocryphal there are certainly real occasions when mistakes turn out well. Alexander Fleming, investigating the antiseptic properties of body fluids, discovered penicillin mould after he forgot to put his petri dish in the fridge and it picked up a penicillium spore. When he returned, he noticed the effect the spore had on bacterial growth. What is interesting is that Fleming still worked in error. He didn't move away from the old idea that he was looking for antiseptics, and it took other scientists to make the leap that penicillin could be used to combat a wide variety of bacterial diseases. Nevertheless, embracing mistakes even when they lead to other mistakes can set the quest for knowledge in new and fruitful directions. Because he took notes on what he observed others could build on his work while taking a new perspective. A playful curious mindset takes the bigger picture and worries less about achieving a certain outcome than appreciating and working with what is there. Ideology and theories are only good if they work in practice.

Sometimes the vision is right but the early work is wrong. In 1980, Steve Jobs heard that Xerox was developing a desktop software system called Smalltalk. One of his designers, Bill Atkinson, was able to watch a presentation and assumed the Xerox team had developed a functionality that it hadn't. Confident that something had already been achieved, Atkinson set out to duplicate it, and ended up pioneering the desktop software that has made the Mac ubiquitous with the personal computer. A bit of peer rivalry no doubt served as a motivator here, too.[11] Having a vision for something really cool can focus the mind, even if you don't know at the beginning of the project how that can be achieved. It's how NASA got their man on the moon.

Evolving play, evolving cultures

As Caillois noted different cultures play in different ways. In the '60s American anthropologist/theatre-maker Richard Schechner wondered whether the tail could wag the dog. In other words, if people could play at doing things differently, could that change the dominant culture? Schechner's research into play, ritual and performance led him to think that the theatre could be used as a form of social problem-solving.

Theatre workshops could serve as 'play laboratories' and be used to deepen understanding of all types of knowledge and research,

21

including psychology, politics, social work, history, and the arts.[12] In the 1960s Schechner in California, Jerry Grotowski in Poland, and Augusto Boal in Brazil led participatory theatre workshops as a way to examine behaviour and reshape it with actors and non-actors. The work was presented by Schechner as a positive and exciting alternative to therapy and therapeutic drugs – and by Boal as a way to empower the oppressed. (Interestingly, Boal himself felt that in South America people feared the cops in the streets while in the States they feared the cops in the head.) The work, however, was similar in both places. Boal's theatre of the oppressed worked in this way: by taking turns to assume roles of players in conflict situations, and re-enacting them, drilling down into particularly difficult moments where choices are made, or harm is escalated, participants could watch and experience them at a remove. This gave perspective that helped them deepen their understanding of the issues and stimulated the participants to try doing things differently. If any of the participants could see a better way forward, he could tag out a performer on stage and take over the scene. The idea was that we learn more from seeing, doing, copying and working through solutions than from reading theory.

Pretending to deal with a situation well can be the first step towards actually dealing with it well in real life. The idea evolved into business training. John Cleese put out a series of videos that demonstrate how staff do things wrong (think *Fawlty Towers*) and also how to do things well. Copy the bad, get a laugh from the audience, then demonstrate the good, to be copied in turn. We learn. Trying something 'just to see' in play can be an excellent strategy to put a new idea into action without having to commit to wholesale change straight away. One can see how this 'trial, error, reflection, and try again' approach can absolutely work in other areas where there is conflict and progress needs to be made. It is not a million miles from cognitive behavioural therapy.

Caillois also conceptualised play as a dynamic way to progress. He described the original jolly impulse of play as *paidia*, or improvisation, that in time establishes rules, *ludos*. As play becomes gamified, some of the intrinsic delight in making things up as one goes along is lost, in favour of the extrinsic pleasure of winning and getting rewarded in some way. Any interplay between people, or between people and things, or systems, begins as exploratory and improvisatory, and becomes increasingly structured as time goes on. A good game has a structure but leaves room for improvisation, or chance. Balancing structure and improvisation is also key, in my view, to creating cities that are dynamic, interesting and innovative and also safe to live and do business in.

The game of football was improvised for centuries before the rules were codified in the nineteenth century and then became increasingly set in stone – but there is still room for improvisation on the field and by fans singing and bantering in the stands. Actors rehearsing a stage play will try doing a scene in different ways, to explore which movements work and make an impact before establishing how they will play it each night – but they will still continue to look for new details throughout the run so the performance stays interesting. Scientists will look for proof for their theories until they establish a solid enough framework to be relied upon in the development of new theories, which expand knowledge further.

This dynamic has been conceptualised by other play theorists as a wheel.[13] Anticipation at a new task; surprise (or uncertainty) in starting out; pleasure in enjoying some wins; understanding how the play works; strength (the work in developing mastery); poise (the play has become easy) and then anticipation again. It is easy to see how this might play out in a ballet class, or learning to ski, or even beginning a relationship. What I love about this image is how it incorporates the idea of vertigo at the beginning, and then at the end poise or balance, and a desire for a new challenge. In fact, you could probably apply this analogy to any learning project. The key thing is that if you do not have to do new things then you stall and get bored. You could say that when something becomes conceptually easy but still takes physical effort, and is part of the structure of your day, then it has become a chore that can only be relieved by adding in an improvisatory element (this could be as simple as listening to the radio or daydreaming). If you have no structure or discipline at all, though, life can be chaotic and stressful, and it is hard to make progress.

You could go further and say that this dynamic applies to the whole human project. Justice, religion, politics and commerce, Huizinga felt, were all rooted in the fertile soil of play, particularly the desire to win (by being better than everyone else).[14] Our systems of parliament and justice are structured as a battle of wits, with different perspectives, rather than an inquisition into one truth. Our representation of justice is vaguely reminiscent of the old game blind man's buff: a blindfolded statue of justice holds a sword in one hand and scales in the other. But with these institutions – as in any form of structured play or work – when a newcomer wants to change that structure, it can be deeply unsettling for and resented by those who have learnt how to work the system (or play the game) as it stands. Can systems play us? Perhaps.

Bringing play back into everyday life

Being forced to do something a new way can be alarming – improvisation is a tool brought out in times of crisis. Forcing oneself to improvise, though, can be a great way of increasing one's abilities and knowledge, is fun and helps you avoid getting stuck in a rut. How do you force yourself to do things differently? The inventor of lateral thinking, Edward de Bono, developed the Six Hat System[15] to improve the way management teams made decisions. All too often, he felt, someone would have an interesting idea and someone else would shut it down. Companies got stuck, and in a fast-moving world, getting stuck was the beginning of decline.

De Bono's idea was that there are six different ways to think about an issue:

- White Hat thinking is about gathering information (what you know you know)
- Red Hat thinking connects to gut feeling and emotions (what people want to do, or don't want to do)
- Black Hat thinking is about picking holes in an idea
- Yellow Hat thinking is seeing the upsides and opportunities
- Green Hat thinking is about creating new ideas and solutions
- Blue Hat thinking is thinking about thinking – setting a structure around how the meeting proceeds and what is to be tackled.

The Blue Hat is generally worn by the chair. Instead of sticking to their comfort zones, people around the table would be expected to step up, take their Black Hat off and put their Green Hat on, and consider how to make the company 'lighter' or a product 'more cosy', even if it made them feel like an idiot. Instead of squashing ideas before they began, the chair could demand everyone consider their business from a bizarre perspective. The value in it was that it was interesting (slightly alarming perhaps) and discussions could reveal opportunities that could be explored in a positive way.

Brian Eno called these oblique strategies. Invited to work with David Bowie on an experimental ambient music album in 1976 in Berlin, Eno developed a series of cards with strange provocations on them. When rehearsals were getting stuck, he would pull out a card instructing people to 'change instrument roles' or to 'emphasise the flaws'. The musicians found it alarming and destabilising, but trying to obey these problematic instructions took them to places musically that they wouldn't have otherwise found.[16]

In academia, the term used is 'problematising' the subject. It is worth problematising cities and setting oblique strategies to see them afresh. Just as we take the city for granted, and need to attune our senses or play the city in some way to become more aware of what is in front of us, city councils can take existing systems and plans for granted, too. They can get themselves stuck filling in the potholes in the existing system and find it too difficult to ask whether they need the road at all. There has been a series of books anthropomorphising cities, like *Consuming Cities*, *Happy City* and *The Well-Tempered City*, to jolt us into reconsidering what a city is and needs to be. So in this book we ask these two important questions: what does a playful city look like – and how can you play the city?

3

What is a game?

A game's structure has only four defining features, according to professional game creator Jane McGonigal.[1] There should be a clear goal. There should be rules, which create limitations on how to meet the goal. There should be feedback, so people know how well they are doing. Finally, engagement should be voluntary (putting your hand up for the mission is what differentiates a game from a compulsory chore).

Games can be tremendously diverse. A game can have one player or many, pitted against each other or invited to work in collaboration against the game. A game where people play against each other can be as simple as Pooh sticks – dropping twigs into a stream from a bridge, and seeing which one appears on the downstream side first – while a slot machine is a simple example of the person pitting themselves against the game. The goal is to get the wheels to line up a number of matching symbols, and you have to choose to press the lever to play. The limitation is that all you can do is press the lever – nothing else. The spin of the wheels and the final resting place of the symbols is the feedback, determining whether you win or lose. There are also enormous multiplayer video games, which allow both competition and collaboration, like Minecraft. Games are generally more engaging when other people are involved – the greater the degree of commitment the players have to the game, the more people get out of it and the more impact it has.

The **goal** determines what is most valued in the game. In a game like Monopoly, the goal is to make the most money and bankrupt one's opponents. In a game like chess or Risk the goal is to conquer and colonise the board/world. A field game, in which players need to drive the ball across the pitch into each other's territories and shoot goals, is a visceral physical version of that. A sweet game like Chatter Matters is about getting the most points by being the most engaged family member. A game like Pandemic is about saving the entire human race from disease.

The **rules** limit the approaches that can be taken which determine how the game is played. The limitations can inspire creativity, strategic thinking, and/or physical strength and often some improvisatory scrambling. An Escape Room demands the application of problem-solving skills, creative thinking and teamwork by limiting the approaches to escape. For example, you are not supposed to punch a hole through a wall. If you are playing football, then stamina and physical effort are required, as will be a degree of aggression. The restrictions on movement within the field demand strategy and teamwork. Board games, in which players have to try and dominate the board, also develop strategic skills. These are often set out on grids or maps, such as chess, Risk, Pandemic and Settlers of Catan. In some games, the pieces or participants have different roles and skillsets, for example field games, chess, Pandemic and Dungeons & Dragons. The art is ensuring that all the pieces, or players, work together to win. In chess, a single player has command and control over his pieces, while in Pandemic players have to learn how to collaborate in real life, which includes the discipline to hold back and listen.

Feedback comes from the score that is tracked on a board or called out by players. The score matters, because it defines how well each player or team is doing, and ultimately who wins. The tracking element of who is doing well is not so clear in complex games like chess. The key indicator of success is to win, but there is a sense of progress that comes from blocking attacks, forging ahead and staying in the game. Consider that a good tennis game is a close one, and a close tennis game is often a long one.

Does the game need to be **voluntary**? This point is arguable. On the one hand, a player does have to take action to play. On the other hand, a lot of pressure can be placed on an individual to do so. With lights, beeps, music, movement and the chance of some sort of reward, the slot machine is making a strong offer. Once you put the money in, there is no going back. Similarly for up-and-coming football players or pop stars, once they have signed to a particular team or label, they have to play whether or not they feel like it. For them, play is work – it is the spectators, who might work 9–5, who are at play. For many children, too, field games are compulsory. Does that make their Saturday football game not a game? As Stuart Brown says, it may depend on one's own perspective and state of mind. Depending on your enthusiasm, work can feel like a game, while a game, ostensibly voluntary, can feel like a chore. When math classes are gamified they are still compulsory for children, which makes them work, but perhaps a more engaging sort of work. There is also evidence to suggest that once you have to do something it is easier emotionally to submit to it. In some countries some forms of play are compulsory. Is that torture or a blessing? What is true, though, is that whether willing or reluctant, most players must commit to and play an active role in the game, or the game itself will fall apart.

What is also true is that just because something works like a game, it doesn't make it a game that is always fun to play! As games often reflect the cultural system in real life, one can extrapolate that some societies don't work for everyone either.

What makes a game good to play?

Success leads to a sense of pride and satisfaction, but the best games are enjoyable whether the players are winning or not. Monopoly and Risk often end in tears, because they are brutal wars of attrition that continue until only one player is left in the game. Early losers can only sit on the sidelines and watch, or go and do something else. No one likes having to fail slowly or getting kicked off the table. Players may not particularly enjoy being destroyed or tricked by their friends and lovers. No parent, admit it, really enjoys playing Monopoly. Game designers recognised in the late twentieth century that what people most wanted from a game was a bit of a challenge that was fun to play with their friends. They wanted opportunities within the game for social interaction and to finish the game without anyone feeling excluded, or hopeless. They wanted games to end within a reasonable time and to move at a reasonable clip.

A game is fun if it challenges you mentally, physically or creatively: if it is too easy and/or predictable, then it will be boring. The risks create tensions that stimulate laughter. An engaging experience includes surprises and points of excitement. This could be a dramatic reversal of fortune (like going down a snake in snakes and ladders or winning tokens off other players), it could be a forfeit or challenge, it could involve bluffing or it could be inherent in the strategic work and tension of leading a campaign, as in chess.

Rivalries are a great way to improve the performance and engagement of competitive people. In fact, a good rival can be more helpful than an ally. John McEnroe and Bjorn Borg were fierce rivals on the tennis courts. Borg was older, the established champion, cool, sexy, in control. John McEnroe, on the other hand, was volatile and rude, and regularly lost his temper. The two of them went head-to-head in the 1980 Wimbledon Championships final, widely considered the best game of tennis ever played. The fourth set tie-breaker extended and extended until it was won by McEnroe 18–16. Two sets all. Borg would win the final set, but if he'd won the battle, he didn't win the war. His five-year run as champion would end the following year with McEnroe lifting the cup. They played each other fourteen times in various finals, winning seven times each. They took tennis to another level, delighted the crowds and became lifelong friends. When people play their best, everyone benefits.

Secondly, games are designed to promote improvisation and human interaction. This is inherent in the game of charades, and in its devilish offshoot Cards Against Humanity, that are full of memorable moments of unexpected silliness, of unlikely melding of ideas and, in the case of charades, the emergence of unexpected talents (as Uncle John reveals that not only can he sing but he can also do it while gargling water and standing on one leg). In a poker game, the play comes also from the rituals that accompany the game, the betting and banter. A good structure can hold up lots and lots of different forms of play. Some games, like cribbage, even develop their own vernacular, 'two twos are four and the rest won't score'. Sports games are special because of the chants and Mexican waves. A good game makes life a bit more like a movie. It condenses the good bits and reveals parts of people's character that are normally hidden. There are successes and failures, but everyone (hopefully) makes it to the end with friendships a little bit closer than before.

Thirdly, these new games are also designed to ensure that everyone can enjoy the game, even if they are behind. In them no one 'loses' early and must leave the game; in fact, they are designed to give unlucky players a hand up. Triggers in the game mean that people doing well are slowed down, while people at the back get boosts. In Settlers of Catan, the rolling of a seven means that any player with more than eight cards must put half of them back into the store. These adjustments increase the chances that an underdog will come through, and this uncertainty (and greater equity) makes for a better game.

Finally, the temporal element. To ensure you create a game that is really fun to *play* you need to consider its pace, length and rhythm. Music has a beat; Shakespeare's verse has a regular metre to prevent the play from sagging. Novels and films often maintain tension and pace by limiting the time the protagonists have to achieve their goals. In a movie, you want set-piece moments where there is some showing off. Good games should be sufficiently elastic to allow for banter, but also drive forward towards the finishing line. Instead of continuing for hours like Monopoly, Risk or Scrabble, this new breed of games is designed so the endpoint is reached within an hour and turns don't take too long. Turns might involve all players in some positive way, too, reading out scenarios or collecting cards. Timers also have a role to play.

In real life, projects are often shaped according to these rules. Students study for a set period and then are examined. This way, the work gets done and students must engage with it. City infrastructure improvements may well finish on time and on budget if there is a major event coming for which they must be complete. The urban improvements in Auckland for the America's Cup yacht race of 2021 were mainly achieved, even despite Covid.

Do the opposite

I was taught one of the most important lessons about making play engaging by the hugely talented American clown Ira Seidenstein. Ira is a genius at playing the fool: he has a doctorate to prove it. He is also the teacher most likely to make students feel deeply inadequate. Smart, tough, talented and terrifying. The contradictions within him were only the beginning – being contradictory seemed to be the essence of 'clown'. One of his exercises involved wearing a clown nose and coming out into the performance space. There you had to say: 'Yes, yes, yes, yes', and then, at a signal from the director, start saying: 'No, no, no', then 'Yes, yes', then 'No', then 'Yes' and so on and so on. It was hilarious – ridiculous but hilarious – to see someone changing their mind and being in conflict with themselves. Changing direction – on stage, with a football, in a car – is more fun than going in a straight line.

Another exercise was 'do the opposite'. An actor would strike a pose at random, which he would use as a launching point for an improvisation, pretending to play the oboe, for example. Then Ira would cry 'Opposite', at which the actor would immediately reinterpret his physical posture and pretend to be, say, eating a sword. Watching someone pretend to play an oboe is quite interesting, as is watching them pretend to swallow a sword or down a yard of ale. What is delightful – and masterful – is watching an actor flip between multiple ideas. Ira wasn't full of contradictions, I realised, as much as an indicator of infinite possibilities.

Another practice in theatre is to 'play against'. If a character in a play gets terrible news, then the actor may choose to react as though they were not bothered. If another character discovers that their lover, thought dead in an aviation accident, has been found alive, the actor may choose to look pissed off. The curious thing about playing against the feelings that you would expect someone to feel is that it often results in much more realistic performances than going down the more obvious route. People are complex beings.

Play is full of contradictions. In play, you can say the thing you really mean, or you can say things that you don't mean. Play can be really low-stakes, or it can feel like the most important thing in the world. It is nice for play to be challenging, but it is also nice to win. If work has been really hard, then it is nice to play easy – perhaps prepare a meal you know you can cook, or knit something simple. If work has been really easy, then you may be chafing at the bit to do something that stretches you and where the stakes are high, like mountain climbing. We like to feel a sense of progress, so some failing is OK, as long as there are some wins too. Certainly, playing board games with my nine-year-old reminds me that losing once is OK but losing twice or three times in a row is disheartening. For grown-ups, too, one major crisis can be coped with, but two is very difficult. Evidence suggests that most homeless people have faced two major life crises, whether it be job loss, relationship breakdown, health issues or addiction. Perhaps losing repeatedly makes it very hard to identify with succeeding. It is notable that countries with prisons that offer opportunities for inmates to engage in projects in which they can feel success – whether it be further education, carpentry or other trades skills – end up with a lower recidivist rate than systems that are overwhelmingly punitive.[2] All of us have the capacity to take on many different roles over time.

The more broadly we think about play, the less play seems to be about a certain activity and the more it seems to be about diversity, opposites and having a change. We like contrast (and even colours that contrast well: blue and yellow are more appealing together than blue and green). In Japan they have a phrase: 'Do not forget your beginner's spirit.' It recognises the value of the enthusiasm that comes with beginning something new. Any activity that is new feels a bit like play: fun in the beginning, then a bit hard as one grapples with the basic steps, and then fun again as we learn enough to show off or to mix things up.

If you spend the week in an office looking at a screen, hanging out at the urban farm learning regenerative gardening is fun. If you spend a week on a building site, getting involved in a gaming project online may be just what you need. That might be why the plumbing work in the plumber's own houses takes a while to get done. Work in comedy, and you may spend your downtime watching snooker – certainly I know that comedian David Mitchell used to watch a lot of it. Work in a hospital, and you may turn to stand-up like Jo Brand. Work and play feed ideas and energy into each other – both the Renaissance princes and the Victorians celebrated the good all-rounder.

What we are into shifts. Dangerous play tends to become less appealing as we move into middle age, while gardening becomes increasingly enticing. Giving ourselves permission and time to take up new hobbies, to remain curious and to maintain and begin new friendships takes effort, but it is stimulating and makes us happier. Happiness and wonder make us better people, more likely to be generous, more likely to be hopeful and more likely to keep going when things get tricky.[3] There is evidence to suggest that even non-risky play keeps our skills honed, and our brain and body developing. James Suzman's *Work*[4] argues that the activities we expend our energy on shape who we are, literally, and our descendants too. Generations and generations of developing tools and cultural pursuits is what has turned early hunched hominids into the highly able modern human society of today. It seems that the projects that we engage in, because they inherently delight us or because they matter to the people around us, shape our characters, our bodies and our minds.[5] How we work and play makes us what we are as individuals, and as communities too.

Trends in play

People pay much more for things that are new. New technologies and designs are expensive for a reason – the costs of developing a new product and bringing it to market come at the beginning of the process, while old products just need to be replicated. And many products and ideas that are partly developed by inventors and companies never make it to market at all. A drug trial may be unsuccessful or feedback from focus groups negative. Their costs have to be covered by the good ideas that do make it through. A new product has to be innovative enough to attract attention, but not so 'out there' that no one understands what it is for. Some of the world's most desirable creations, like the iPod, the miniskirt and New York's High Line, were met with disbelief at the design stage, but fortunately enough people were feeling the excitement to push on through.

But what is the value for the customer in testing objects that may turn out to be rubbish? New is uncertain, while tried is tested. Putting more value on untested things seems odd. There is a competitive aspect to this: to be the pioneer, the first to know, the first to have, or the first to go where no one has gone before. Winners are ahead of the game, losers behind the times. When people buy premium products they are paying a lot, but for the competitive person there is kudos in having the new toys – even if they don't catch on – as it sends a message to the world that they are so successful that they can afford to waste some resources on folly. Yesterday's news makes fish-and-chips wrappers, and yesterday's fashion can be found in a charity shop, unworn. Most products lose value once the wrapping is off. It is the wrapping that makes the quality of a product uncertain: valuing wrapping then is the triumph of hope over experience. It is odd.

Play activities go in and out of fashion, but just because a game is unfashionable does not mean that everyone stops, or should stop, enjoying it. It is crazy not to do something that is new and exciting for you just because other people have been there and done that. It can sometimes be prudent to wait a little for prices to come down. The wheel of time and new contexts make the play fresh once again, and you will bring your own take on it. Of course by then the fashionable set will be on to the new thing. *C'est la vie.*

There is pleasure in taking a gamble on an unknown quantity. Trying new things is fun. It might work out, or it might not, like a slot machine. Watching a football match is more exciting if you don't know the result. We like to consider uncertain futures too. When we watch a science fiction movie or a thriller, we fantasise about crisis situations and think about how we might act in them. We engage with new things to prepare for a future that we don't yet know, and we develop skills in play for which we currently have no use – but might later.

The idea of what play *is* shifts over time. Go back a hundred years, and people made their own fun more – they were in bands and orchestras, they were members of clubs or they played at home. Now we seem to enjoy play vicariously as consumers, while the active 'players' – musicians, sportsmen, actors – are paid for their 'work'.

While in the past we *had* to sew the children's clothes and bake the bread, these activities have now become a form of recreation. Having a sourdough starter is a sign of affluence rather than poverty.

New forms of play can freak older folk out – like pirate radio, gaming or following people online – but even waltzing was considered outrageous in its day. The more important issue, when people indulge, is whether they are well, happy and able to balance their play with their life. The evidence suggests that while kids are facing lots of challenges, play is more likely to help rather than hinder. Though there is a lot of moral panic about kids being on screens too much, it is the kids who are digitally savvy who have an advantage in the modern world. Who would have thought, twenty years ago, when media studies were regularly dismissed as nonsense, that there would be such a career as a social media influencer?

It is through play that we develop new ways of living. There is a trickle-down effect with play ideas.[6] Play pioneers, usually young adults, develop a new fun activity because it appeals to their desire to crack a puzzle, give themselves a thrill or otherwise amuse themselves, and in the process they extend what is possible. As one sort of play challenge is realised, new challenges and opportunities are opened up.

Take the example of flight – something that humans have long wanted to be able to do and have imagined in myth and fiction. Pioneering aviators in the Edwardian period wanted to build planes that worked for the thrill of becoming airborne. As the technology got closer to success, competitions with cash rewards stimulated extra effort. Challenges and competitions make the basis for great stories, told by the newspapers, that celebrate the people involved and inspire others. Success is emulated and embraced by early adopters who want to have a go. These people evolve the play into something new, testing the limits of the technology and imagining new uses for them (aerial acrobatics, racing, exploring). As the popularity of the activity grows, corporations take the idea, then refine, scale and promote the play as a saleable commodity or an experience. They will offer this to adults, both for its inherent qualities (the joy of flying) but also as a tool for another profitable form of play (importing flowers, letterwriting, war or leisure activities like sightseeing/tourism). They may also market a version of the play to children (toy planes/books on flying adventurers) that stimulate their imagination, and things come full circle. By the time that air travel became ubiquitous, the pioneers had turned their sights to the moon. Similarly, in computing, what pioneers in New Age California in the 1960s, '70s or '80s could only imagine is now part of our everyday lives, changing how we play once again.

It is not unusual for an idea to be realised in play first: the Aztecs, it is thought, invented the wheel for children's toy carts without using carts themselves, being totally impractical for the rugged mountainous land in which they lived. Engineers are not surprised that toys can be sites of invention – new ideas can be tried out on a small scale where little is at stake.[7] Whenever I check in on my journey's progress on Google Maps, I can't help thinking of Harry Potter's Marauder's Map.

4

Why don't we play (more)?

If play is so much fun and helpful for developing our skills, our character and society itself, why don't we spend more time doing it? There are a number of reasons:

Play has a cost. It can be expensive, as a trip to a theme park will demonstrate, but even cheaper play – like being in a sports team or a band, or learning ballet – means fees for subscriptions, extra coaching, uniforms, entry fees for competitions, exams and so on. Play also takes up time which could have been spent studying or working to pay off the mortgage. Work can also be weirdly addictive and feel more reliably rewarding and easier than play. Going out for a drink with mates has a cost. Of course you could socialise at home and organise a party but then you'd have to clean the house . . . which leads to the second point.

Play may feel effortless when you are in the zone, but **it takes effort**. Going for a run may release endorphins, but not everyone enjoys the first mile as their muscles warm up. Cycling is great, but if your journey begins with an uphill stretch there will be a strong temptation to take the car or the bus. Going to a play rehearsal at the weekend means getting dressed, organised and out of the house, when you could be on the couch watching TV. Even calling someone up for a chat might seem too exhausting. After a long day at work it is easy to slump when you get home. It is now so easy to consume play through screens that we are at risk of losing our play muscles, and perhaps, as individuals, getting stuck. It is extraordinary how difficult it is to actually go and do the things we really *want* to do. Like Chekhov's eponymous *Three Sisters* who want to return to Moscow, we can talk repeatedly about our desire to do something, and never take the steps necessary to further our plans and make our dreams come true.

Perhaps the most important but least acknowledged barrier to play is that **play is risky**. The flip side of play being exciting is that it can be terrifying. Sometimes the risk is real and physical: climbing high up a tree, catching a wave at a beach with a strong rip, or doing sports like snowboarding, rugby or gymnastics where there is a chance you (or someone else) could land on your head. This barrier can be mitigated with helmets, reef shoes for sea swimming or following safe practices. Often, though, the fear is connected to ego and too shameful to be acknowledged: a fear of being judged a failure as you have a go at a new sport or a new challenge. This anxiety can be felt intensely. I have taken my daughter to a ballet class where she was too terrified to join in. I was encouraging and didn't let on that when I signed up for a fencing class with people half my age, I fled too. As Stuart Brown notes,[1] so many adults are shamed out of playing, or from doing things they enjoy or consider important, because they worry that other people might think those things are silly and their goals naïve. We worry that we are not good enough, we don't know what to do or how to reciprocate.

Sometimes **we don't like the play on offer** and this might be because we don't identify with the values at the heart of the culture we live in. For some a child beauty pageant is a celebration, for others it is deeply unsettling. Sometimes we don't like the play that is on offer because we would rather do something that is supposedly for another group. Sometimes the way that the play is managed feels cruel and frightening. It is sometimes hard to get out of something once we've started even if the play has become unpleasant. Peer pressure can be helpful sometimes, not always. In this section I will first look at the darker and more dangerous side of play.

The dark side of play: Cheats, spoilsports and crazy stuff

As we have seen, we get a kick out of challenges, even dangerous ones. Dopamine rewards wins – which, when applied to catching fish or to bringing down a deer or boar for the tribe to eat – is also pro-social. Endorphins are released to reduce the pain of physical injury and to enjoy effort (necessary for tracking that deer down and then dragging it home). Endorphins boost sex hormones, appetite modulation and immunity. We enjoy the noradrenalin (fight or flight response), acetylcholine (released to activate muscles) and serotonin[2] (regulates anxiety, happiness and mood) that come when it is necessary to be vigilant (perhaps we are being hunted ourselves). We enjoy surprises. This is helpful, because if we suddenly feel some sort of unusual threat we become more interested and more vigilant, which releases a bit of adrenalin followed up by a dopamine chaser if we get through.

Anthropologist Richard Schechner noted that play mode is very close to survival mode. 'Play allows kinetic potential to be maintained not by being stored but by being spent ... Crisis – the sudden and unstinting spending of kinetic energy – is the link among performance, hunting, ritual and play ... together they comprise a system through which the animal maintains its ability to spend kinetic energy irregularly, according to immediate, even unexpected needs.'[3] Rugby, football and boxing all stimulate this sort of crisis excitement. Risking one's life, or pretending to do so, releases adrenalin, serotonin and dopamine. Children love to be chased, young people like to drive fast. Joyriding presents a dark vision of the playful city: dangerous, but undoubtedly a real buzz.

Even watching sport – or car chases, free falls, gunfights or monsters – on the screen or at a stadium activates these chemicals vicariously. Our bodies respond positively to the need to act dynamically for our own survival, for real and in play. Our brains prepare for future crises – who knows, perhaps we will have to defend our kids from murderous zombies sometime in the future. Video games facilitate exploring strange places and finding secret portals. The viewing figures for *Star Wars, Game of Thrones, Peaky Blinders* and *House of Cards* suggest we also enjoy films about forbidden love, murder and (in the case of *Star Wars*) fighting back against the oppressive Empire state. Fortunately, violent video games, horror movies and crime novels do not lead to criminal behaviour. Indeed, there are far more hours going into game play now than ever before, and crime statistics are going down. Fortunately also, our bodies send messages to say when we have had enough, that our stomachs are full, say, or that we have had enough TV or gaming. Most of us enjoy the play, and then we do something else.[4] For some though, this intense play can be too much, too real. Horror movies stop being entertaining and cause nightmares.

The value in pushing the boundaries

What is allowed or not allowed is defined by laws and regulations, but also by cultural norms, and sometimes the division between what is right or wrong is fluid. When you are a kid, the rules keep changing and the boundaries shifting. Some rules are considered more important than others. Some are hard and fast, some depend on what is culturally appropriate at that moment, while some change depending on your size and age. Some rules exist just because the adults said so. Breaking a rule can be a way to find out whether the rule actually applies.

There are the adult rules, and then there is what my son calls the 'children's law'. These value systems do not always align. I wonder how much tension children hold negotiating between the established 'rules', the cultural conventions of their peers, their own fears, values, desires and ever-developing capacity, and the instinctive desire to push boundaries. My friends and I spent a significant portion of our childhoods laughing hysterically over our low-level rule-breaking, like talking after lights out, sneaking cake from the dining hall or trying to find a way into the basement tunnels at school (there were exciting rumours about priest holes and treasure). Laughter bubbled up – whether we got into trouble or got away with things, *just*. So many outcomes are uncertain it is no wonder this tension needs to be released. No wonder, too, that children seem to respond well to some order and routine.

These kinds of minor transgressions are not only memorable in a way that ordinary life is not, but they also bind us together with our friends, building trust and loyalty, creating stories and legends that we can laugh about years after the event. Laura Armstrong's play *Posh* is based on the premise that bad behaviour in Oxford University drinking clubs is all about creating stories and bonds of complicity to hold the perpetrators together through their adult life. Mad pranks on a Saturday night with your mates do exactly the same thing – creating stories of extraordinary experiences and shared complicity, the retelling of which can become more important for the group than the experience was at the time.

A lot of these transgressions involve copying adults to experience being in their world, and they are crimes only because of the age of the perpetrators, who the law desires to protect. Loud music at parties shows a lack of consideration for others, rather than an intentional assault, at least until the neighbour comes over in distress. These crimes may involve the appropriation of and/or damage to public assets, but the victim – or any sense of wrongdoing – is perhaps obscure. In many cases those most in danger of damage would be the students themselves.

Cheating

No one wants to be called a cheat, and yet no one wants to be called a goody-goody either. Cheating can ruin the game, and most would agree that fairness is important and that the innocent should be protected from harm. However, to obsess with the rules is to be a square and miss the bigger picture. Clearly, if it is someone on your own side who cheats that is very different from someone on the other side who cheats. 'Win at all costs' is still the spirit behind some of the more aggressive competitive sports teams. The All Blacks rugby team, Australian cricket team and Russian Olympic teams are lauded in their home countries but considered terrible cheats by sporting commentators on the 'other side'.

Our response to rule-breaking is nuanced. Johan Huizinga reckoned that while people may not like cheating, they preferred a cheat to a spoilsport who ruins or stops the game. The documentary *Icarus* tells the story of an amateur American cyclist who approaches the Russian Olympic team's doctor, ostensibly for performance tips, and they become friends. Ultimately, the doctor blows the whistle on the Olympic doping operation, flees to the USA and spends the next few years keeping his head down. Other Russian athletes have blown the whistle on their colleagues, and while there was condemnation of the cheating and Russia was excluded from the games, it was notable that when 'clean' Russian athletes were given permission to compete under the Olympic flag, the whistleblowers were not amongst them.

We may also feel that sometimes breaking the rules is necessary in order to allow more people to join in or to do something extraordinary – like walk a tightrope between the Twin Towers in New York. Breaking the rules comes with risks, but perhaps sometimes the risks are necessary. We certainly have a soft spot for mavericks and outlaws – if their hearts are in the right place and the system is unfair. Pretending to be criminals in play is also much more fun than being the good guys.

It can also be tempting to break the rules for our own benefit if we think we can get away with it. Play takes effort and playing well takes lots of effort. Herbert Simon and William Chase made the case in the *American Scientist* magazine nearly fifty years ago that there were no instant chess masters. They suggested that it took players between ten thousand and fifty thousand hours to gain that level of skill. Malcolm Gladwell applied this idea more broadly and called it the '10,000-hour rule'.[5] To become a master of anything takes resources, time, enthusiasm and luck; to be well rewarded for one's efforts even longer. It may seem easier to cheat, to take performance-enhancing drugs or do a job off the books. Feeling that you are *above* the law also has a status dimension that is visceral, whether one is a canny cat burglar, a crooked businessman in a Savile Row suit or a seventeen-year-old who has blagged their way into a bar to see their favourite band.

A certain degree of cheating is also encouraged by economic and cultural forces as the smart choice. Our senses may be designed to trigger the release of pleasurable chemicals when we do something that is good for us, like eating when hungry or helping each other out, but we can release them directly with the help of chocolate or a tab of Ecstasy. We may enjoy looking beautiful, and we know we should exercise, eat well and sleep well, but why go to bed early when you can use make-up or surgery? Because you are worth it? While cheating can be very tempting, and great fun, it can also bring anxiety. Is it worth it? You are taking a risk. Moreover a cheat's pleasure is fleeting; you can't own and feel happy in your success long term in the way that you can when you have worked for it.

The right to play

Sometimes it seems that some forms of play are considered appropriate, even desirable, for some people and not for others: for men but not women, for adults but not children or youth, for some races or classes of people but not others. All of us probably have a childhood memory of a time when we were excluded or not allowed to join in. These memories are painful. Read the news or social media for too long, and it will seem likely someone out there hates us. It is all very well encouraging people to go out and do something new but we do not want to experience rejection or criticism. While the debates are often about systems and governance, at an individual level these uncertainties are felt as social cues that suggest whether we are welcome in a place or not.

Play and belonging

Throughout history pressure from the powerful to convey that lesser types should know their place has been set against pressure from some brave souls demanding the right to join in. Some play activities enjoy higher status than others, and some people disdain and try to restrict the play of others because that play is considered particularly damaging, wasteful, elitist or tasteless.[6] A day at the races is somehow respectable because the event is old-fashioned, while gambling on the slot machines is thought problematic. Social orthodoxy in the West determines that alcohol and sugar are respectable, but drugs are not. This can build resentment between groups (including between young and old) and obscure empathy and understanding of the real issues with regard to gambling, alcohol addiction and so on.[7]

It might make groups double down their commitment to their tribe and their forms of play. At the extreme end of this you get the

Millwall chant: 'Everybody hates us and we don't care.' This is not a million miles away from the approach of the gay rights movement to own insults, and reassert them – boosted with the accoutrements of play, costumes, music, performance – as markers of pride. Ideas of what is normal shift and most of us are pretty relaxed now about diversity. Those who suffered injuries in the battle for equal rights will have a shared bond that the rest of us do not. If one is not rainbow, it is OK not to be invited to the Pride March after-party.

The intense pleasure in the rituals of the football game or cricket match is steeped in expressing group identity: identity of place, of class, of the tribe. This is not all bad. That the same core things happen each week gives a sense of belonging, and everyone knows what they are supposed to do. They wear the appropriate clothes, they know the words of the songs. For those football fans, Saturday afternoon is about being part of something bigger than oneself and making an impact. It feels like anything can happen (except what happens is usually what has happened before). While you must be completely loyal to your team, and are obliged to insult the enemy across the terraces, generally the two opposing sides have more in common than not, sharing a love for the game.

Paradoxically, football, despite its oppositional nature, stoking up passions and excess that can sometimes spill over into violence, can be a way of reinforcing the status quo. This again may not be an awful thing. There is always going to be some system, and it may be wise to find the joys of living within it. On the other hand, the status quo can sometimes be deeply inequitable, underscoring that some people belong while others do not. It is disappointing to discover that there was a women's football team in the nineteenth century, before women were banned from FIFA and excluded for decades before they were allowed to play once more. Some British boxing tournaments a century ago banned African fighters because they were likely to beat their white opponents, which did not fit the cultural narrative that white people were superior.[8] In recent discussions about rugby it seems that the 'harden up and be a man' culture that is necessary to be one of the boys isn't entirely great for the alpha male players' long-term physical or mental health either.

Play, power and identity

Portuguese dictator António de Oliveira Salazar famously relied on the three Fs – football, Fado (a genre of Portuguese song) and Fatima (Catholicism – Fatima was a local Saint) – to encourage people to come together, to enjoy themselves (or take out their frustrations) on the pitch, through music or in prayer rather than consider challenging what was a deeply inequitable macho system. Leaders and regimes that feel insecure may discourage improvisation, free thinking and new forms of play by removing artists, academics and jokers, and insist on participation in highly structured forms of play instead, like rallies and military parades, sporting spectacles or mass weddings in stadiums as is said of North Korea. While there is certainly pleasure in doing things as a harmonious group, when play is performed in a way that maintains the status quo it can be oppressive. Choosing to join in or not can be a matter of politics as well as taste: doing things the old-fashioned way is a more conservative take, while embracing new forms of play is more liberal and progressive. We may well wonder then whether our play will get us into trouble, politically, legally, physically, socially or culturally.

Doing things a certain way is often connected to a sense of national identity. In Japan, there is an interesting dualism. On the one hand, Japan is a dignified and proud nation that respects its past. On the other hand, it is a country that was defeated by the United States, and still has US Army bases on its soil. Japan was obliged to copy Western systems, to become expert at creating and exporting the goods the West wanted. Japan, and indeed other Asian countries, are very good at copying new technologies and refining them. There is many a second-hand car dealer who will find it hard to recommend any car company above Toyota. On the other hand, Japan remains attuned to its culture and painstakingly protects its own old ways of doing things.

In Japan, the practice of traditional cultural art forms is not simply about the outcome but about the process, the correct *way* of doing things, as it was for the Italian painting assistants. For example, to learn the tea ceremony is to learn a well-established choreography, in which every move is anticipated, done cleanly and in the correct order, with an air of calm effortlessness. To become a master of cooking, pottery, kimono making or calligraphy is to take years, perhaps decades, of study. The masters of these artisanal arts are considered living national treasures. They cannot be usurped by the younger generation with their new ideas, because new ideas are not correct. What is correct is the old way, and that has to be copied. Of course, there have always been tensions about this and exceptions to the rule, but culturally this assumption holds. Japanese cities are so fascinating because so much effort is made by everyone to maintain their culture.

In New Zealand in the last few decades there has been a revival in *tikanga* Māori, the Māori way of doing things, that incorporates traditional weaving, *kapa haka* (ritualised group song and dance performance – which includes the war dance the *haka* performed by the All Blacks before a game), tattooing and wood carving, among other things. All these crafts embrace a spiritual and cultural element, and a correct way of doing things which young students must copy. White New Zealanders are becoming increasingly attuned to *tikanga*, incorporating greetings and prayer into business meetings and the opening of events. Increasingly Māori design is making its way into libraries, changing rooms, architecture and even the interior design of new underground stations in Auckland. The traditional designs are done by Māori, easily identifiable as Māori and shift the sense of identity and storytelling of the city – away from British colonial, or post-war 'could-be-anywhere', but Auckland, or rather Tāmaki Makaurau.

Nevertheless there is still some awkwardness. To say that only some people, like Māori, can produce certain public art can feel exclusional. On the other hand, for people outside a cultural group to take elements of what has long been the less powerful group's cultural practices and use them in a different context, however creative and fun the outcome, runs the risk of accusations of cultural appropriation. If a cultural ritual has become renewed because it is also an act of resistance to a pervading dominating rule, the point is that it represents an alternative value system and way of doing things put forward not theoretically by academics, but enacted and re-enacted by a particular group of people who very much want to have their own place in the world acknowledged. It is probably not the goal that either the practices themselves or the values can be cherry-picked and incorporated into the mainstream culture or business. Public art plays a role in re-enforcing the stories that we tell each other about our values and how we got here. Public art is a form of conversation between the city and its people. We like to see ourselves in it. This is the very reason that is used to justify the importance of more indigenous art in a colonial landscape, but immigrants also want to be part of the narrative and have a role in the team. Finding the balance can be tricky.

Dressing up and adorning oneself is fun, particularly at parties, but there was a huge outcry in recent years when headdresses based on those worn by indigenous American leaders became popular as a dress-up at music festivals. People, perhaps surprised by the criticism but not intending offence, stopped doing it. In New Zealand, tattoos are very popular across society but the *moko*, the traditional Māori facial tattoo, is only worn by Māori. There are very few exceptions, and all those who bear their stories on their face must be deserving of it. It is moving onto shaky ground to recontextualise a symbol of something particularly honoured by another society. If someone was making replicas of the Victoria or George Cross and people wore them in nightclubs in Shanghai, I am guessing this would cause offence too. To copy, without attunement, is to insult.

At Auckland University, a young student from Beijing proposed exploring Chinese folk dance for her thesis. Her intentions were good, but she was advised to be careful in her approach. In China, folk dance is more than a playful form of exercise; it has been a way for minority groups, who were otherwise relatively powerless, to assert their cultural identity as separate from that of the Han majority and Beijing. This feedback from supervisors made one consider parallels elsewhere. Could this desire to assert cultural identity, physically, but politically safely, be the reason why traditional Scottish and Irish entertainments (like ceilidh and music and the Highland Games) are so much more widely supported and appreciated than their English equivalents (cheese-rolling, folk music and morris dancing)? The Scots may be ambivalent about the English embracing their culture, but I would wager that more English people would be comfortable and confident at a ceilidh than skipping round a maypole. There is a red-blooded vigour and fire in Scottish dancing and folk music, which is harder to find in the English equivalents. James I of England may have come from Scotland, but power has been located in the south of England for a long time, and there is a continued resistance to that. It will be interesting with the shifts in Europe and Britain's place in the world, and even within the United Kingdom, to see if there will be a stronger sense of what it is to be English when England is more alone. The olde English pub, a bit of banter and a pint of beer have become strongly linked both to UKIP and to Boris Johnson's administration, which also focuses on resisting European power. Time will tell.

Choosing homogenous vs diverse societies

It is perhaps not surprising that people find it easier to hang around with the sort of people they grew up with, who share similar values and do the same sorts of things. The feedback is better understood. Where we may flounder with people brought up in different cultures – acting overly or insufficiently courteously or suspiciously – life is easier with people we understand – we know whether we are welcome or not, and we act accordingly. The feedback we receive is possibly also more positive on the whole. Research suggests that babies respond more positively to people who look like them. We make friends when we have something in common. By picking up social cues, we gravitate towards people who seem to welcome us. It is often noted that places with high taxes and a strong community focus, like Japan or Denmark, are also very homogenous racially. The anthropologist Robert Putnam found that neighbourhoods in the USA are more connected when they are homogenous too.[9]

Good manners and the ability to pick up social cues make living close to each other possible. For neighbours, that balance between friendliness and intrusiveness must be carefully managed. It is easier to pick up cues when we share the same culture. Getting it wrong can be threatening. Privacy is essential to human dignity, as is the choice over how far we will interact with someone or at all. We don't think about it much, but most of us would probably prefer strangers to have no particular opinion of us at all. Not being judged is part of the appeal of being in a city. It is easy to take this for granted until we attract unwelcome interest. People do not like feeling forced into sociability. As Jane Jacobs wrote: 'The more common outcome in cities, where people are faced with the choice of sharing much, or nothing, is nothing.'[10] People are much happier when they have porches or front gardens outside their windows, as it creates a buffer zone that allows them to control their interactions with the outside world. People do not want others to glance through their windows and judge their decor or level of tidiness. People do like to talk to neighbours on the street, but the further away from the private realm of the house one is, the less intrusive and thus more welcome, usually, small interactions are.[11] It is the same in the pub. Being close to the bar is a signal of openness to new interactions, while sitting at a table is a signal that one wants to be private. Being able to know when to say hello, when to talk and when to move along quickly denotes that one is a safe person with whom to engage. Getting these things right and picking up lots of very light, positive feedback makes life infinitely more enjoyable for both sides. Putnam discovered, all things being equal, that diversity is not so good for social networks unless some effort is put in to draw people together through the provision of sports facilities, community centres and so on.[12]

Before we conclude that we are better off sticking to our own, there is also research to suggest that it doesn't take much contact with someone outside of our known group to warm to them. Anyone who learns another language, or reads a novel or sees a movie will understand that there are lots of ways to think about the world, and that we can identify with people regardless of their setting and background. We may want to have something in common with our friends, but we don't want a clone. Diverse groups achieve more, even if (or because) they don't always see eye to eye. Groups are often more successful when they choose goal harmony over team harmony.[13] Our whole academic system of learning is based on wrestling with ideas and making them better – thesis, antithesis, synthesis. Bringing more ideas and perspectives to the table increases the pool of knowledge, even if it means problematising matters, rethinking values and working a bit harder. In the end there is generally more diversity of skills within a particular group than between them. This diversity is a good thing because we bring different qualities to the group. We don't have to be very close to our colleagues or collaborators. In fact, sometimes a little distance helps.[14] Just as we get used to and even start to enjoy bitter tastes as we get older, we also learn to appreciate the value of humility and diplomacy as the price of greater success and experience. When the goalposts shift, that can renew the game. Life is more interesting when we don't stick to our silos and instead engage with people outside our own fields and share notes.

A good way to bring people of different heritage, race or class together is the shared project. People who play together often forge social bonds that endure well beyond the football field or the drama club or the fighting unit.[15] This could apply to schools, community events or clubs and nature restoration projects – as it may have applied to creating massive temples or giant heads on Easter Island. Playing together and working together reveals shared values and shared pleasures, as well as differences. We are wired to attune one-to-one – this is sometimes called code-shifting, when we try and talk each other's language to promote better understanding and connection – and so the more we come into contact with people who are different from us, the more we like them and appreciate their perspective and the less we fear them. Facing challenges together can build respect. Over time new groups align together that break the old boundaries, with shared interests, often in play.

The opportunities to engage in shared projects and enjoy shared spaces arguably should start in childhood. There is sometimes resistance to that idea but it can be overcome. In 2019 the *Guardian* reported on a developer who had tried to keep the children who lived in the social housing out of the playground built for the children of home owners. The outcry was enormous and all the children were allowed in – and rightly so.[16] Meanwhile the West-Eastern Divan Orchestra in Israel has demonstrated over twenty years how young people across religious communities can play together. Deyan Sudjic, former head of the Design Museum, has noted that there is evidence to suggest that more tolerant societies are more successful. This may flow both ways.

Successful societies may mean that people who are more confident, connected and prosperous are actively working together, and therefore more willing to share with and be tolerant of each other. There is some evidence to show there is less racism when the economy is good, there is lots of work and enough to go round.[17]

The challenge of joining in

Sometimes it is right to assert that you can do something even if you don't fit current stereotypical norms. Over the last two hundred years women have been fighting to be allowed to do what men can do, those born in one class have been pushing to do what those in another class can do, while immigrants have been fighting to be allowed to do what the majority can. A desire for equal rights applies to play as much as work. Blind auditions for orchestras have been successful in balancing gender participation. The private clubs that continue to restrict access to women or people of specific racial groups are on the decline, and that is, I would say, generally a good thing. Women and people of colour are fighting hard to play more roles in films and they are making progress. This matters for everyone, because they are the role models for our children. When Tracy Edwards led a team of women in the Round the World Yacht Race, she demonstrated that women could and should be able to participate in sport (and play), too. Not only did they complete the course they also won two sections of it. The idea that only men could play at this game changed forever.

Legislation is not in itself enough to change norms: there also needs to be good leadership. The Civil Rights movement in the USA ruptured the status quo in America in 1972.[18] The segregation of schools was being challenged in the courts, and in two cities judges ordered that the kids be educated together. The outcomes were very different. In Detroit, the Ku Klux Klan blew up ten school buses and the judge received death threats. In Louisville, Kentucky, however, many influential families supported desegregation and the dissenters held their tongues. Five years down the track, the Louisville judge was guest of honour at a banquet celebrating the scheme's success – the kids in Louisville were doing twice as well as those in Detroit. Equity seemed to build trust and success. The more we know of each other, the more we attune to each other. Kids would be educated together, would play sport together and would fall in love with each other.

People seem to have followed the lead of, or copied, the person, or people, they felt was the better authority. And to a large degree, this came down to trust. It is counter-intuitive to copy, or follow, someone who is not attuned, who you do not trust. It is also perhaps difficult (or, considering cultural appropriation, unacceptable) to copy someone who doesn't like or trust you. Bringing people together to talk, work, play and learn from each other builds trust and can lead to good things. If people can bring different perspectives and skills to projects, they make the outcomes better for everyone. In the 1920s, European music and African spiritual music came together to form Jazz in America. Compare this to the separationist efforts of Nazis in Europe and hours of Wagner. What would you rather?

The key perhaps is to shifting social norms. Betsy Levy Paluck is a psychologist at Princeton University specialising in how leaders shift social norms so as to change behaviour. In one project, Paluck looked at high schools and how they addressed bullying. In her study, she found that many students did not like the bullying culture but accepted it as normal and believed that it was better to accept incidents of bad behaviour rather than actively disobey the unwritten cultural rule against sneaking. Schools that had the best chance of stopping bullying involved a variety of leaders – academic, sporty, arty and counter-culture groups – to support a process to discuss and address the issues and shift ideas of what was acceptable. This included a school assembly where students were supported to speak up and be heard. Establishing that not just the teachers but the cool kids wanted the school to be a kinder place was a turning point. With diverse leaders championing a change in direction, social norms can shift dramatically in a positive way.[19]

Impostor syndrome

If people who are overconfident in their adoption of new identities can be criticised for cultural appropriation, those who lack confidence may suffer from impostor syndrome. One of the paradoxes of learning through copying is that when people start emulating the person they want to be, or take on a role, they are not yet a master of it. In the workplace, high status, desirable or challenging roles can be stressful. It is not uncommon for people to feel impostor syndrome,[20] that they have no right to be there and that they will be found out and ejected. This is particularly so if they belong to a group around which hover stereotypes about competence (or lack thereof).

However, if we don't go out and try to take up opportunities, the greater risk may be a smaller life. Reinventing yourself is not always easy. In the final *Star Wars* film, the lead character Rey seems to yearn for permission to break with her roots, to be the person she wants to be and to choose the family she wants over her natural one. This permission is granted her, but she must still wrestle with internal conflict that she is an imposter. Conversely, I know people whose working-class parents consider the middle-class values espoused by their offspring as a sort of betrayal. We learn by copying, and we begin with our parents, family and neighbours, the people we are close to and who we, hopefully, love and trust, but it is also reasonable to be influenced by people from all walks of life that we admire. Doing jobs we are suited to and that we enjoy must be desirable. Could society be structured less like a ladder and more like a web, that rewards different forms of works more equitably and in which no one feels left behind?

Everyone should be able to participate in activities that they enjoy and matter to them and not feel obliged to spend all their time doing things that others believe are more appropriate. Being happy, being connected and getting satisfaction out of life raises one's status and dignity. One should be happy in one's skin and forge one's own identity. Why shouldn't someone from Peru be great at martial arts? Why shouldn't a Mongolian have a passion for Mozart? And unlike most status symbols, the more people who are enjoying themselves, the merrier it is for everyone.

5

Easing yourself back into play

So far we have raised a few issues around why you don't want to play, and looked at why you still should. The answer then is to keep your senses alert; to proceed, while keeping an exit strategy; to pick up social cues and to aim to fit in without moving too fast. Be polite and warm but not over-effusive at the start (don't give too much away while working out the lay of the land).

Keep the stakes low. Being courteous to a fault can both avoid offence and reduce implications of intimacy. Accept invitations. Move towards people and activities you enjoy, even though this may scare you the most. Work out discreetly how you can join in. Find out more about the other players. Observe (you probably do this instinctively).

Children are very aware of status, groups and the leaders who decide who can join in. Watch small children come into a new play space, and you may find that a number of them stay on the sidelines, watching and working out how the play works before entering the arena. That's quite normal. A wonderful kindergarten teacher, Rebecca Ward advised those children to ask *how* they could join in, instead of *can* I join in, because when you ask the latter the answer is so very often 'No'. This was less about the qualities of the particular child asking and more about how all kids value their play. They didn't want someone new to come in and take it over or mess it up. Asking how to join in communicated to the existing group of players that the newcomer wanted to fit and understood they weren't in charge. By being submissive they raised their chances of being welcomed and accommodated. This and 'How can I help?' are very useful phrases, however old you are. For adults at a drinks party, hefting around a bottle of wine as a prop is a good way of entering a group of people engaged in conversation, because one is offering one's services rather than butting in. Of course, after a little while, when the newcomer is attuned, their status may rise.

It is also normal for kids to cling to safety and, on their first day at playgroup or ballet class, those who do not want their parents to go will literally cling to them. Being a bit nervous about a new venture is not weird. In fact, gauging the play first is eminently sensible. Wait too long though, and they may never play at all. We disengage their hands from our clothes, let them be distracted by a cheerful teacher, and duck out, hoping for the best. Sadly, in play, as in life, nothing is ever quite certain, however much we would like it to be. Even as adults, we still get daunted at the thought of engaging in certain activities. We might be terrified by public speaking, or of being forced to dance or play tennis if we think we won't meet the required standard or won't be welcome. We may be nervous about the unwanted relationships we may encourage. If someone does something for us we will be obliged to reciprocate. And vice versa.

When we do want to connect, to contribute and to reciprocate, sometimes the rules are obscure. This can be difficult for natives as much as newcomers in class-stratified Europe. Consider the number of social guidance books written through history. There has long been a terror of getting it wrong. We want to be aware of shifting social norms.

Joining in, but moving with caution, may also be wise on social media – an area that is developing its rules of etiquette as it goes along. Social media has exponentially increased the influences we can draw on to share play ideas and build on other forms of play. Affordable film-making technologies and sharing platforms have changed us from consumers of content to co-producers of it, but there are still tribes, silos, identities and uncertainties about who can participate and what can be said. Being able to critique online offerings has also turned us into gatekeepers of others' success, which is so satisfying that we can wade in with our approval or disapproval with minimal independent fact-checking or deliberation. Affirming someone else's value judgements makes just as much, if not more, of an impact as offering up something original ourselves.

Social media can be incredibly positive and also destructive. It is not a million miles away from the Roman circus which can lead to glory or death based on a show of hands up or hands down. The backlash to an inappropriate remark made in jest can be career ending. In this pioneering form of play, where the rules are uncertain, being attuned to social cues *and* one's sense of ethics is as important as ever.

Making time

Sometimes you are so exhausted that play has to be pretty simple. More like a cheat. The good news is that watching other people play can also be restorative, so turn off the news feed and embrace some feelgood TV contest like *The Great British Bake Off*, a tennis match or a TV drama. Fit tiny dashes of play in and between other activities. Smile. Do a little dance by yourself when the kettle is boiling. Getting your body moving cheers you up and makes you more alert. Take the extra seconds to ask those people you interact with how they are. Listen to music or fun audio when you cook. Pick up a novel before you go to bed at night. Make time for some light relief – it is a tonic. Eat well, rest well. Smell the flowers.

At some points in the week you will want to play more actively – and if even a few hours feels too much, you may be working too hard. This may be just the way things have to be, but if you have options try and work a bit less. Make time for board games with the children, for dinner parties, or date night. Going for a walk in the park after dark turned out to be a rather exciting new activity during Covid. In New Zealand it is really common to ask people to bring food or dishes to dinner parties. This is a godsend – it massively shares the load. The time-poor, cash-rich guest brings the fancy cheeses and wine, while the starving artist brings along a great salad. My cousin's wife Abbie is incredibly strict about what everyone brings to ensure everything is covered. It's a good system and makes life so much easier. It helps that she is a primary school teacher.

Time off needs to be designed back into the middle of the day as well as into the end, and perhaps into the middle of the week too. Sometimes a bit of cultural pressure can help to ensure that we all set aside time for lunch or hobbies. This might mean returning to a daily structure that limits how long we work, and a weekly structure that ensures there are days when we don't work. Perhaps work mobiles need be turned off at 6 p.m. and not turned on till 8 a.m. For those without steady work schedules planning play (not to mention child-care, or any sort of social life) becomes infinitely more difficult. The gig economy can be brutal.

The best way to make time for play is to plan ahead and mark it in. In France, the right to a private life is well established, and it is standard to work a 35-hour week and take at least an hour off for lunch. In 2010, UNESCO declared French gastronomic meals a part of the intangible Cultural Heritage of Humanity. People eat at the same regular time as each other and eat well, which is better for wellbeing. They return to work refreshed and stimulated, because a shared lunch provides opportunities to share ideas, laugh and strengthen social ties. The French value relationships with other people, and that takes time.

Activity: Do lunch

What you need Three friends and a restaurant.

Method Invite three friends from your workplace, including someone from a different department, to lunch somewhere nice and convenient. Book it. Send a formal invitation. Take an hour off for the meal. Do this at least once a week. It will be the time you have all your best ideas.

Variations

- Meet one friend or seven, or any number in between. They can be from anywhere.

- Contact a business associate and take two hours off and go somewhere fancy you have never been before. It will be good for future business. (Even if it isn't, it is fun anyway.)

Restricting hours can actually make people more productive at work *and* play. The 48-hour work week became common in New Zealand relatively early on – there weren't many skilled tradesmen, so they had bargaining power! After years of recession in 1893, it was decided to reduce hours further, introducing half-day holidays on Saturdays for everyone but domestic servants (the wealthy had to eat of course). This stimulated sport, recreation, picnics at the beach and, of course, rugby. During the Great Depression in the 1930s baking company Edmonds moved to the 40-hour week, as did Kellogg in the USA, in order to reduce the wage bill without laying off staff. In a few years they were able to pay people the same as before their hours were reduced. The less time we spend working, it seems, the more we get done. In addition, lower earnings could be mitigated, because families had more time to tend their vegetable gardens, make their own clothes and make their own fun. These days in New Zealand the general limit is 40 hours[1] and in France 35. Luxembourg, the most productive country, has an average workweek of just 29 hours.[2] Facing another recession, this may be a very good time to go to a four-day week.

Andrew Barnes, head of Perpetual Guardians, a trust firm in Auckland, persuaded his company to do just that in 2018.[3] He had read that Brits were only productive for two and a half hours a day. If his staff could work a bit harder for four days, then in theory they could be more productive than they had been in five. If they could, he would gift them the fifth day (still paid). Two university researchers reported that productivity per day went up by a quarter and engagement went up 30–40 per cent. Stress levels dropped 15 per cent, and people said they were better able to handle the workload. They worked better as a team and did less personal admin in the office. Social media use dropped by 35 per cent. The gift of a day changed lives, wives spent more time with husbands, fathers with kids, or allowed people to upskill, stay fit or do private projects. The change levelled the playing field between men and women, and meant 20 per cent fewer cars going to work. It is ironic that despite so many labour-saving devices created in recent centuries we still spend so much time doing work or chores.

Activity: Make time for the fun stuff

In a nutshell Try and get all your work done in work time so that you can fit fun stuff in during your non-work time. Presenteeism is such an issue in countries like Japan that people actually die of overwork. This is not good for anyone, particularly you. If you are healthy, engaged, rested and happy, you are more likely to do better at work than someone stressed, tired and overworked. You are also less likely to become upset by colleagues, which is helpful.

What you need Some self-discipline and discretion.

Method Start no new tasks after 4.40 p.m. and start finishing up. At 4.50, if you haven't been able to finish, make a note of where you are and do no more. Tidy up your area. File things. Cleaning up at the end of the day is very calming and makes it easier the following morning. At 5 p.m., go!

Tips

- Prioritise what needs to be done before going on to other work.

- It can be more productive to chunk the day up into sections. If you can organise meetings with hour-long gaps between them you get the variety that is energising. Use morning tea and lunch breaks as another way to chunk up the day and spend the time with a colleague, not on the web.

- Stay off social media during the day and leave it for the commute on the bus.

- Unsubscribe from unnecessary emails.

- Organise something that you have to be at for 5.30 p.m. Having something to look forward to can be energising the whole day through. This includes work drinks on Thursday or Friday. Go.

Of course we do not, could not and should not accept every recreational offer that comes our way, however well meant or exciting-sounding. We know, conceptually, that we will be missing out on the vast majority of human experiences, but in the city there can also be a sense of failure of our own judgement over which offers to accept and which to decline. The noise provided by media, marketing and the millions of people around us reinforces the idea that we often get it wrong. It appears that we are not so good at anticipating what will make us happy; however, we are capable of noting the things that are making us happy in the present time. It sometimes takes something like Covid to remind us that a bit of exercise, the occasional hello at a safe physical distance, a chat with friends and a new book are quite sufficient to get us through the day happily. Trying out new experiences is fun but inherently risky. The goal is to balance doing things you need to do and things you definitely like to do with some new experiences, so you don't get overwhelmed or bored, or with a lingering sense that things could be better.

Activity: Saying no nicely

In a nutshell If you know how to avoid and retreat from risky or chaotic situations then you may well feel more confident to get involved in the first place.

What you need Ideally a trusted friend to practise on.

Method Prepare what you want to say in advance for various different situations.

1. Saying no to a dance: 'I'm sorry, I'm exhausted/sweaty/ parched. I just need to sit this one out.'

2. Saying no to going out when you like the person: 'That sounds fun but I'm afraid I am already busy on Friday. Can we do something another time?' OR if you don't want to encourage the person but respect them: 'That sounds jolly and it is nice of you to ask but I am exhausted by Friday/things are quite busy at the moment.'

3. Saying no to a date: 'No, thank you, I am completely asexual' OR 'No, thank you, I am holding a torch for someone else I'm afraid.'

---

4. Saying no to going on further after a date: 'I won't come but I had such a good time, thank you' OR 'It is a bit late for me, I did enjoy meeting you.'

5. Getting out of a dangerous activity: 'This is too much for me. Enjoy it you lot. See you at the pub later.'

6. Saying no to sex without a condom – the trick here is to establish the need for condoms while your knickers are still on.

7. Ending a telephone call quickly: 'I won't keep you. Take care. Bye!' OR 'I will get on to it. Thank you for calling, bye NAME.' The trick is to start strong and don't cut back on the pleasantries. 'How are you? What can I help you with?'

Tips

- Be brief, clear, courteous and cheerful. You are allowed to say no. It is no big deal.

- If someone is really not getting the message then ghost them.

- If you are concerned for your own safety then ask for support, friends, family, authorities as necessary.

Variation Taking rejection well is also important. 'No worries' covers most situations. Again, be brief, clear, courteous and cheerful. People are allowed to say no. It is no big deal (and even if it is it won't help to let it show – go find, or call, a reliable friend or family member and enjoy time with them instead).

Adopting a play mindset

Making time is the first step towards more play, but there is still the need for courage to take that step out of the house and into the great unknown. Most people are not judging you or criticising your play choices. Really, if there is anything more adorable than seeing seniors dance together or hold hands as they walk down the road, I want to know. Who remembers the prank in which a secret camera recorded people on a high street playing hopscotch on some chalked-on markings? You had to love the people who had a go. A sense of humour and a willingness to play makes us more lovable, not less. There is a perception that lovable people are less effective as leaders, but this is not true either. Lovable people can be the most effective leaders and bring out the best in their teams.[4] And isn't that the sort of leadership we want? Someone who is human, fun, kind and encourages you to do well?

Some people are so naturally confident or excited about an activity that they don't seem to mind being a beginner, and that is absolutely fantastic. If this is not you, make sure you are well rested, well fed and keep the stakes low at first. While high-stakes action is quite fun when someone else is feeling the heat, it is less fun if you are the person having to perform. If the pressure is off, you can relax. It can be encouraging to remember the dictum that no one is looking at us because they are far more concerned with themselves. So why not do things that we are really into – whether guilty pleasures or serious hobbies – that we could think of as play but perhaps don't, that are not controversial or risky at all. Exercise is a really good way to raise morale, energy levels and makes it easier to sleep – all of which set us up better for work and play. What sort of physical activity do you genuinely enjoy? If you want to get fit but feel awkward about your body don't go hard. If you have given birth at some point, perhaps choose an exercise class for mums only.

Activity: Get physical again

In a nutshell Exercise releases chemicals that make you happy because exercise is good for you. It is so easy to get into sedentary activities and as the years go by it can get less and less appealing to get fit (especially if one has never been good at sports). Losing strength in one's forties or fifties has ramifications for one's well-being in later years. It is worth getting back into it at any time.

What you need Low expectations and a truly lovely gym/dance/sports instructor.

Method Many gyms are filled with super-fit people but there are lots of people out there with varying abilities. Pick an activity you can bear, a class at your level and a teacher who seems kind and onto it. No point doing exercise and getting injured.

Tips

- Sometimes the best options are not in the gym or a specialised sports facility but in the community centre, on the roads with a bicycle club or in a dance hall.

- If you've never liked running you probably won't like it now. Try something else.

- For many a little bit of pressure can help. Paying upfront is one tactic. Gyms encourage attendance by getting new members to pay in advance or to lock themselves into a year-long subscription. Simultaneously acknowledging one's physical flaws and getting into Lycra gymwear to address them is a daunting package. Gyms play on our reluctance to waste money to give us a nudge in the right direction. Unless the experience is absolute agony it can be worthwhile giving it time. I used to go out dancing in the evening. Asking, or waiting for, partners was daunting but I forced myself to have three dances before I could go home – by that time the nervousness had worn off and I was having a grand time.

Once you are suitably set up for the play activity that you are really interested in but feel shy about, do involve someone else. Having a friend there (it doesn't matter whether a good friend or an acquaintance, as long as both parties commit for a period) can get people through the first terrifying moments, or sessions, of a new class. You don't have to spend the whole time in each other's projects. Finding people to do things with means the fun things happen and a world of unexpected opportunities opens up. Who knows what they will invite you to in return?

What sort of player are you?

Everyone likes music and stories, but not necessarily in the same genres. Some people like baking cakes, and others like running marathons, some like playing pranks on people, others prefer to preach. Psychologist and play expert Stuart Brown has a theory – which he admits isn't scientifically based, but in his experience seems to be accurate – that there are eight different play personalities. They are the joker, the kinaesthete, the explorer, the collector, the storyteller, the competitor, the director and the artist/creator.[5] You may recognise yourself in there.

These play personalities give some idea of the breadth of the diversity of play, but these categories are probably not comprehensive. Most of us might be a mix of these, and our play personalities may shift over time. Perhaps Brown is missing cultivators, those people who love to care for others – the children who care for their toys who become healers and matchmakers? Or problem-solvers, those who love to work things out, whether it be crosswords, murder mysteries or complex human phenomena (like neuroscience or cities)? Where fits the fishermen and deer stalkers, the hunters and killers? In the past, the prime meaning of sport was to go out killing things, and my son has spent many a happy hour trying to create bird traps in the garden.

One could also say that every one of Brown's play personality types has a foil – jokers/organisers, kinaethetes/sloths, explorers/traditionalists, collectors/declutterers, storytellers/readers, competitors/fans, directors/followers, creators/destroyers, artists/audiences. People enjoy so many different things and that is fantastic. When you get lots of people with different passions and playful projects in the same place, there is a correlated rise in creative, inventive, playful projects, from giant stone structures and music machines to centrally heated glasshouses and automatons. These achievements, initially motivated by pleasure, can trigger ideas and applications that will impact the world, from engineering to computing.

The joker

The joker has been around since the dawn of history and is the most basic and extreme player. He is encapsulated in various mythologies as the trickster god, Loki in Norse, Anansi in West African folklore. Shakespeare's Puck is a close cousin. He happily disrupts and plays tricks. Modern-day jokers will photobomb, drop false eyes in glasses of Guinness, create and share comedy memes, and/or set up complicated pranks to confuse or frighten friends and other innocents. Disassembling and reassembling a friend's car in their bedroom is one example (my grandad's mates did this to someone else in the RAF during the war – anything to take their mind off death presumably). Arguably too, learning to laugh in the face of an annoying prank can help us prepare for remaining calm when real adversity comes along. The more difficult life is the more we need to laugh. We need the jokers.

The kinaesthete

Kinaesthetes need to move. They are the runners, jumpers and fidgeters who can't sit still. They get a huge kick out of moving about and can find exercise addictive. Joy and survival go hand-in-hand. Walking helps you think. Superbrains like nuclear physicists Niels Bohr and his student Heisenberg, and Daniel Kahneman and his colleague Amos Tversky, all walked for hours in the countryside to get their brains thinking and to engage in conversations without unwanted interruptions. Many of us, when faced with a difficult problem, may walk to clear our heads.

We know that exercise is good for our health and most of us get some pleasure in moving around if we can be comfortable doing it, whether it is having a walk, a run, a cycle, a dance, a swim or racing down a ski slope. Increasingly life is quite sedentary but we need people who can move and are strong – to be our firemen and police service, to do physical labour. In hunter-gatherer societies not everyone goes on the hunt, but it is necessary that those who are young and fit do. If we could all use our cars less and cycle more, we would use less carbon and become more beautiful and cheerful (why not?).

The explorer

All of us start off as explorers, but some of us stay curious for life, wanting to go further, find out more, feel more and experience more. Explorers like to travel, both abroad and closer to home. There are armchair travellers too finding out about other places, or dimensions, or to expand their fields of knowledge. The researcher in the lab devising experiments is an explorer without leaving the room. Urban explorers are often out on foot, a notebook in hand, actively aware of what is going on around them and making discoveries. The explorers are the pioneering adventurers that lead the way. Sometimes of course it may be wise for explorers to turn back, but we always need people who are keeping their eyes open. The explorers – including scientists, naturalists and engineers – are picking up the cues from the world around us that we need to change course.

The collector

The pleasure for the collector is in having the best, the most interesting and the most complete collection of a certain thing, or a collection of things that create a whole, like finding the furniture for a home. There is a thrill in the chase, and a pleasure in holding the objects close. One can also collect intangible things like memories, contact details, photographs. Collectibles can be incredibly beautiful, like paintings or feathers. There is probably some survival function in this, displaying our precious things to prospective mates like magpies. One can collect stamps, paintings, Pokémon cards, antiques, even properties. The more you have in your collection, the more satisfying systemising it and finding meaning within it. People who obsess a little about their collection of antique farming tools can become mines of esoteric but sometimes useful information. The rarer your collection the more valuable it becomes. Collections can be status symbols indicating disposable wealth. By their nature, collections are often about having more than you currently need. This can have a survival function for squirrels and jays, who stow away nuts for future eating – and for their human equivalents gathering tins, flour and toilet paper in case of emergency.

The storyteller

Storytellers like to tell stories and make meaning of what has happened or is happening. They might use words, the stand-up mic, the radio, the printed press, a blog, or they might tell stories visually using art, photos, infographics or maps. In the nineteenth century John Snow was not just a great doctor but a great storyteller, using maps that made it easy for people to understand how cholera was spread by the water supply. Stories are an engaging way of sharing what is going on and to connect people to a place, to ideas and to other people, dead and living. If games replicate a value system, so do stories. This is more overtly the case in religious parables but the author Christopher Booker argued that there are only seven plots that echo infinitely the power of love, redemption, courage, vanquishing evil and warning about the pride before the fall etc.[6] Stories encourage, illuminate and put things in perspective, whether it be in conversation or a great work of fiction. Telling our stories helps hold us together.

The competitor

The competitor loves to win. The competitive kinaesthete will not just go for a daily jog, they will sign up for a marathon or a 24-hour endurance cycling event. The competition hones the mind, provides something to work towards and gives an opportunity to show off. Peer pressure can help people reach another level, which is exciting for both participants and spectators. The appeal can lie in the glory, praise and prizes and the intrinsic reward of self-respect. The most competitive of all will work towards an elite level, perhaps to represent their country in the Olympics, to wear the yellow jersey in the Tour de France, to get a Michelin star, to build a new business into a multi-million-dollar company, perhaps to become prime minister. This gives the opportunity to be part of the elite club, to mix with the other movers and shakers, the actors, the rock stars, the aristocracy, the rich. The competitor is valuable because they are willing to work hard and are always looking to do things better. If they are decent and honest everyone can benefit from their success. If they don't, however, they can cause more problems than they solve.

The director

The director enjoys planning things and making things happen. They are the matchmakers and choir leaders, party throwers and business leaders, the campaigners and local politicians. Directors can come from all parts of society, and the best leaders encourage others to be leaders as well. It is fun to be in the driving seat but good leaders also need to work hard and smart to make sure that the project is successful and, as with competitors, that their people are happy, too. While a competitor can focus more on their own wins, the director should have a more holistic and long-term view of what good outcomes look like. For example, churches have long offered an opportunity to strengthen communities. Activities not only brings people together, but can improve mood and combat depression, singing helps people recover their voice and articulation skills after a stroke. Vicars cannot force people to come and are not paying people to be there. They are paid for by congregations to bring out the best in everyone. That's what all good directors should do. This idea of service in leadership is articulated in our political system, with public servants and members of parliament.

The artist/creator

The artist/creator is someone who enjoys making and mending things. The first group would include painters, sculptors and bakers. The menders might darn socks, mend radios or redecorate the house. All are creative. Composer Anthony Brandt and neuroscientist David Eagleman define the art of creativity as the combination of bending, blending and breaking.[7] Thinking of creativity like that turns it from a rare quality into a pretty common one. What it requires is the resources to learn the basics, and then the confidence to mix up the steps a bit. Putting an outfit together is creative, so is hosting a dinner party. Covid-19 revealed how good it was to be able to create and to make one's own fun. While some workers were put under pressure, others would find themselves at home for months on end, their lives on hold. People who never usually had the time to bake, weave, paint, knit or film videos of their family (singing about being stuck together), did.

It was a rare opportunity to go back to making things, or to have a go for the first time, posting the results on Facebook – for better or worse. There was an element of showing off but a considerable amount of dialogue was about less flashy projects. The making and creating was intrinsically pleasurable and, when the system breaks down a little, useful. Artists and creators show other ways of living are possible.

Mixing it up

What about the problem-solvers, the hunters, the cultivators and carers? You may have a play personality that incorporates other joys entirely, or it may be a mix-up of any of the above. The good news is that there are so many different ways to play. Considering how one can 'play the city' can reshape the way we think about the city, how we move around it and how we use it, and encourages us to suck the marrow out of it. This focus on pleasure is not frivolous. It can also be considered an act of survival. It is through play that we have found our way through tricky situations, and it is through game structures that we can work together to make an impact. The more we think about play the easier it is to understand how our cities have come to be where they are right now. It will also make it easier for us to shape our cities into places where we don't just survive, but thrive.

Part Two:

Play and the City

6

Play and Pleasure

From the very beginning the city has facilitated play, and the playful project. And play and pleasure are intertwined. The city is full of sensations. Our eyes, nose, ears, taste buds and nerve endings are forever negotiating our surroundings. In cities, as in all aspects of life, we are rewarded with good feelings about actions and behaviours that are good for the survival of the species, and punished with bad feelings about things that are likely to lead to our destruction. Noise, stink and hazards act as repellents, while beauty, art, good food and drink and the opportunity for romantic adventures draw us in. It has always been thus. I will argue indeed that the city evolved out of play. As cultures change, the way people play evolves. This is very possibly linked to innovations and events that shift what strategies and skills are required to survive and thrive.

Food matters. The establishment of agriculture is a key link to the settling of people. While cities are synonymous with hard structures and shelters, they exist in synergy with nature and it was the ability to cultivate and control nature both inside and beyond the city limits that made the city possible. The second thing that the city must provide is access to other people to play with. For centuries, if not millennia, a great indicator of success has been the creation and maintenance of gardens, where food, socialising and nature were brought together in spectacular fashion. The Hanging Gardens of Babylon were a wonder of the ancient world – just as the biostructures in Singapore are a wonder of ours. Nature, nipped, tucked but thriving, ever-changing but safe, beautiful, magical, magnificent: a feast for the eyes, the nose, the taste buds and a relief for the ears and the body.

Pleasure and the city: Gardens and girls

The Vauxhall New Spring Gardens, as they were originally called, were laid out on an eight-acre plot on the south bank of London's River Thames in 1661, one year after the Restoration of the British monarchy that had signalled a return to pleasure. It wasn't the first pleasure garden, and there would be many others, but this one is deservedly famous, and its history seems to encapsulate the story of play.

The gardens were open to all – well, at least anyone who could pay a boatman sixpence to row them over the Thames. The journey over the water seemed to mark out where duties ended and fun began. In those days, 'Vauxhall' meant the area around Faulks Hall manor, and was made up of market gardens, orchards and pasture. People went down there to enjoy the sweet air, to listen to nightingales and to have supper outdoors. Samuel Pepys visited twenty-three times. Dining areas were prepared in old coaches and boats dangled from the trees, identified by old inn signs. There was music every night, to accompany the banter and flirtations of guests. It was a popular place for liaisons. For those lacking a willing partner, amorous adventures could be purchased in the gardens' dark corners. Mask wearing was *de rigueur*, and servants couldn't wear livery in the park as it denoted lower rank. You could say it was designed, like the pub, to create a level playing field.

Seventy years after the gardens opened the new owner Jonathan Tyers added a music room, a Chinese Pavilion, and numerous supper boxes near an alfresco amphitheatre and a room for servants. Artists were commissioned to provide pictures, statues, decorations and music. The Prince of Wales attended the opening of 'Ridotto al Fresco' – a night of outdoor amusements – in 1732. Cartoonist Hogarth planned the event, produced humorous pictures for the supper boxes and immortalised the occasion in sketch.[1] A fifty-man orchestra was hired to play six nights a week. Handel often provided music. His *Music for the Royal Fireworks* was rehearsed in the gardens to a crowd of twelve thousand people. The shilling entrance targeted the middle classes to come, eat out, entertain friends and be entertained. Fancy-dress parties were popular with royalty who came in attendance.

Masks, music, art and amorous adventures in the shrubbery proved a winning formula.

As time went on, more Royal parks were opened up for use by members of the public for free: tangible evidence of increasing participation in public life, both political and practical. These parks also contained exotic birds, boating lakes and sporting grounds (as well as further opportunities for romantic dalliance). Paid pleasure gardens now had to offer something novel, like lighting and dramatic displays. By 1820, more than twenty thousand oil lamps (fuelled by seal and whale blubber) lit the Vauxhall Gardens. In 1827, there was a re-enactment of the Battle of Waterloo, with huge amounts of gunfire. As the park was open every night except Saturday, the noise for the neighbours must have become increasingly relentless. Some likened the situation to being on the edge of a battlefield. (When the gardens became a launching site during the hot-air-balloon craze the neighbours might have found it a bit of a relief.)

As urban London sprawled around the park and as new entertainments evolved, Vauxhall Gardens declined. It may be no coincidence that this came about as universities expanded. Balls in the university towns next to rivers and fields may have been more appealing. The Victorian desire for progress and new entertainments put Vauxhall out of tune with the times. The opening of the Great Exhibition at Crystal Palace in 1851 was the beginning of the end, and the gardens closed forever in 1859. The spirit of Vauxhall Gardens lives on in music festivals, in the grounds of grand old houses, in beautiful nature spots by lakes or beaches, with lit fairy trails through the trees, and in university balls, with music and beats pumping through the night. Cities like Madrid and New Orleans, Venice and Paris also put the pleasure of the senses first in their restaurants and night clubs. If they didn't, they would no longer be Madrid or New Orleans or Venice or Paris.

Proximity to orchards, market gardens and nature makes people feel happier. Green belts around cities satisfy urban residents' need for green and a desire for food security. Some countries import the vast majority of their food. Around 6000 tonnes of food are needed each day to feed a city with a population of 10 million. On average, in 2012, food travelled 15,000 miles to get to the Western dinner plate.[2]

There is a growing uneasiness about this and a desire to eat food that is local, pesticide-free and that they can see being grown.

Urban gardening is trending across the world. Rattled by Covid-19, Singapore has determined to produce at least 10 per cent of its greens locally. With a population of five million and 250 acres of farmland, the country has invested in vertical farms and roof gardens and is trying to boost biodiversity to bring nature back into the city. Although they are about 10 per cent more expensive than imported goods the lettuces are flying off the supermarket shelves.[3] In Japan, microfarms have long been dotted around the suburbs of cities. Back in London, The Orchard Project was set up in 2009 to develop inhabitants' skills at planting, managing and harvesting fruit trees. Farmers' markets that sell local veggies and honey are going strong around the world. Even supermarkets and food bags are advertising their commitment to 'local'. Local food offerings are not just about sustainability but help connect us to the place where live. How and what we eat says a lot about the identity of the city. Even sprawling Los Angeles can be made meaningful and pleasurable in the mapping of its food restaurants by reviewer Jonathan Gold. Food gives us a chance to pause and connect with other people. Relationships are often taken to a more intimate level by a meal, whether romantic, sacred or for business purposes. Dancing, eating, the beautiful mixture of structures and the pastoral and the opportunity to find friends and romantic partners make pleasure a visceral imperative for life in the city.

Cities can be marked as sinful for being more tolerant of minority cultures and practices, and for those who have grown up in more conservative realms, this tolerance might come as a shock. Cities are large enough for one to find like-minded people with whom to enjoy one's particular tastes. There are lots of activities going on that are not for everyone, and these activities are to some degree visible, through posters, dress or specialist buildings, from Freemasons' Halls to temples to the red-light areas – which often seem to have the greatest music venues and restaurants right next to the adult entertainment. In the city, different ways of being are visible. To come to live in a city can be quite traumatic in that it forces people to rethink their assumptions. A bit of rupture is not awful: it opens the mind.

Play and the Proto-city

Visceral play and pleasure were at the heart of proto-cities – the gatherings of Neolithic people around temples for festivals. Archaeologist Klaus Schmidt has spent decades of his life investigating the remains of Gobekli Tepe in Turkey. This temple is located on top of a hill, overlooking what would have been fertile plains of wild wheat and trees through which ran rivers, herds of gazelle, aurochs (giant cattle) and other ungulates. The Neolithic people were nomads, hunter-gatherers who took what they could and moved on. The temple, however, was solid and static. It was built around twelve thousand years ago, six thousand years before Stonehenge, and was made up of giant T-shaped stone columns ranged in circles. Each column, some plain, some carved, weighed somewhere between 10 and 20 tonnes. Like Stonehenge, no one knows for sure how they were put in place; it would seem that five hundred people would be required to move one large column. And all this work was to be part of a project bigger than each individual. Perhaps to reach the gods, partly perhaps to create something amazing on Earth, perhaps simply as something special to do with other people. The great stone heads on Easter Island fulfilled the same purpose: an awesome bring-the-community-together project.[4]

The Neolithic religions were strongly connected to nature and the circle of life – fertility, birth and death – the contemplation of which (and particularly death) seems to make us happier.[5] The priests were set above the common man for their understanding of the balance of nature and of their people's place in the world, where they came from and who they were. They would tell the stories and lead rituals, very possibly enhanced by the consumption of alcohol and hallucinogenic drugs. Religious leaders in this world needed to be able to throw a good party. The gatherings seem to be prehistoric equivalents of conferences/ music festivals, rooted in ritual, play, rhythmic drumming, dancing, music and narcotics. Jonathan Rose in *The Well-Tempered City*[6] wonders at the meaning and use of several windowless rooms in Gobekli Tepe, with polished floors and benches, and carvings on columns with animals, abstract humans, phallic symbols and sacred rituals to the goddess of the moon. Sex perhaps? The temple was an enormous piece of work that would have required large numbers of people working together, like in a city, with all of the hedonistic benefits too.

There is no evidence of anyone having lived in the temple, but there are lots of bones of gazelles and aurochs that may have been ritually sacrificed within the circles of columns that defined the holy space. Schmidt believes the temple was a focal site for a hunting cult. Would nomads gather, at certain times of year, to pray to the gods, to feast, to find partners outside their own hunting groups? Was it a place to honour their dead? It is possible. The nomadic tribes that exist today do meet up to share knowledge, to find partners, to shift groups. What does seem to be the case is that despite these people coming together, they went away again. It doesn't seem at this stage that a permanent settlement was needed or desirable. Perhaps these meetings could only last so long before disease from the accumulated waste, or hunger, intervened.

The ancient Olympics seem to have had this problem: huge amounts of food and human waste accumulating behind the arena (and possibly also the corpses of less-successful combatants). Similar issues are front of mind at large-scale modern festival gatherings that create ephemeral cities. The largest is the Kumbh Mela in India. The highest daily attendance – 30 million people in 2013 – had risen to 50 million by 2019. Kumbh Mela is situated at the confluence of the Ganges, the Yamuna and the Saraswati rivers and has been celebrated for over a millennium. The event takes place over a number of weeks and models a more generous way to live, with music, celebrations and free food on offer. This ephemeral city of wood and cloth is created on a grid system, easy to put up, easy to take down. The Burning Man festival in Nevada also involves living a Utopian vision of self-sufficiency for a short time. All materials must be brought in, and then removed afterwards. In theory at least.

At Kumbh Mela they have learned to manage the waste to a degree, but as the festival grows, more technological solutions must be found. It is an ongoing challenge. This might be what happened in Gobleki Tepe: over time they learned to manage the challenges of settlement by designing water and waste solutions that mitigated the pains and pestilence of high-intensity living so as to make a safe space for the fun aspects. Festivals offer the opportunity to talk, share knowledge and connect over the feast, and the imperatives of the occasion perhaps triggered solutions to live close together that usually no one would bother to try and solve. Could these playful, social experiences have been the catalyst that led people over time to engage in more and more complex shared projects, to develop religious and societal frameworks, to build and extend the temple, to develop engineering knowledge, create art, to philosophise and preach on the nature of things, to start to understand and ultimately control nature itself?

The earliest domesticated wheat was planted five hundred years later in a prehistoric village 20 miles away from Gobekli Tepe. This fits the idea that settlements came with the advent of farming, and what is intriguing is that the settlement was not that far from the temple. A coincidence? Rose argues that settlements grew around spiritual sites, translating the skills developed to build structures for sacred rituals into housebuilding, irrigation systems, wall building and so on. The first settlements were close to where food could be grown or caught and water could be found and used for drinking, cooking and to wash stuff away. The ancient city of Jericho had walls not to keep out raiders, but primarily to act as a flood barrier from rising river flows.

Many of the great cities are situated at natural intersections, where the river meets the sea and where traders were able to come with essential products from overseas, at first exotic, like spices, and then increasingly staple, like wheat, sugar and fruit. They were places of exchange, not just of goods but of ideas, where people mixed, talked, ate, drank and partied together. Wherever the heart of power was, there would also be play, pleasure and innovation – Ancient Egypt, Athens and Rome, Baghdad a millennium ago, Italy of the Renaissance and later Amsterdam, Paris and London.

As time went on the skills required to manage every aspect of urban life would become more and more specialised and demand that everyone play their part so that the city could function. Hurrah for collaboration? Well, not quite. Some skills would be more valued than others and decisions over who got to play what role continue to be problematic to this day. The city brings pleasure but also problems.

7

Play in the city over time

The city will promise (to a greater or lesser degree) security and diversity, survival and pleasure, food and sex, but also hierarchy and subjugation. It has been argued that agriculture and settlement were the downfall of the human race.[1] Adam and Eve, by acquiring knowledge, had to leave the Garden of Eden. Settlement allowed hierarchies to emerge, in which priests and kings gave the orders and enjoyed the fruits of the labours of those less powerful or well off. Handwriting was invented not to pen verse but to mark down debts. Settlement seems to have been particularly bad for women's rights. As soon as the temple was established, the prostitute found a role within it, and the dancers, musicians and cooks weren't far away.[2] Being a wife meant more respect and respectability but little more freedom to participate equally in public life. Even today some people have more access to play than others, but through history some groups have had limited access to or time for any recreational activities at all, while others – usually men of the elite – have had sufficient disposable income to hold costume balls, build follies, fund expeditions, patronise artists and scientists, or drink or gamble much of it away.

Wilfred Thesiger, the great twentieth-century anthropologist, noted that the Marsh Arabs, who were nomads, felt contempt and distrust for the corrupt city Arabs. There has long been a distrust of city folk by those in the country, and resistance against the developed world by people who still live an isolated way of life. The cartoons of Hogarth presented a vision of London that was full of vice, drunkenness and disease. Pinocchio, in the original Italian text, is brought into being in a Tuscan village but is lured to Toy Town, where children can play all they like until they turn into donkeys. Colonisation is criticised for ruining indigenous people by luring them into city hell-holes, where alcohol or opium robs of them of their health, morals and self-respect. Cities, in this vision, are unequal places, in which a few grow wealthy and the masses self-medicate.

Returning to live in the wild aka *Avatar* or *Survivor* is presented as an ideal. It has been argued by historian Rutger Bregman[3] that the urbanisation of populations is not because people want to live in cities but through displacement from the countryside by policies in first Europe, and more recently in China and Africa. A documentary on Chinese ghost cities focused on elderly farmers relocated to a seemingly empty city near the border of Mongolia, spending the days in exercise classes, or sitting in their new apartments with every modern convenience and nothing to do. Is it true, though, that people are trapped in cities, or is it that the city offers something we can't find anywhere else?

It may be that it is a bit of both. In practice, if people feel the city is their best option it is remarkable how they will adapt to it and make the most of their situation. This is called synthesising happiness, which feels just as good as the happiness you feel when you get what you want.[4] People have adapted the way they live, play and find joy in their urban environments as these places have evolved.

Ancient Greece

In its heyday ancient Athens sat at the heart of an empire and attracted the brightest minds, artists and traders. It was a democracy, albeit one that did not include the great majority of female, foreign or slave residents. The Athenians ruled together, played together and competed together, and the way they played seemed to echo their politics (and ultimately ours). The root of the word 'agony', which means pain but also trial, is the Greek noun *agon*, which means a struggle, battle or contest. *Agon* was at the heart of the ancient Olympic Games. The Games were violent: combatants competed at chariot racing, sword fighting or wrestling until their competitor gave in or died. Small states jostled with each other for supremacy in the arena. The modern Olympic Games, a display of physical prowess and pageantry that brings nations together and celebrates peace, is a far softer version. Nevertheless, they are still used as an opportunity to show off the calibre of one nation's citizens over another and demonstrate winners by a show of strength.

Agon was also the term used for the debate scene in an Athenian comedy that would have been performed at the Festival of Dionysus. Not unlike a modern music festival, this combined a spiritual element with music, dancing, ritual and theatrical competition. The prize for best tragedy or comedy went to the performance that best captured what it was to live. So the agon was essentially an absurd argument about some aspect of life, played for laughs by two comedians. There were layers of contest in here: the comedians outdoing each other on stage; the prizes awarded to the best show; and the ideas at the heart of the comedy being tested, in theory, by the gods, but in reality by people, not as individuals but as an audience, a public. They might like the performance, or not. Individuals would become aware of what other people thought too, in the way that an audience watching an observational comic like Michael McIntyre may realise through their shared laughter how many everyday life challenges they have in common.

This public response to edgy ideas, put out there in play (but half-serious), might then shift assumptions and influence the public debate back in the forum. Athens was a democracy. Having a sense of purpose was all part of the concept of *eudaimonia*, or having a good life. It was the responsibility of every single citizen to contribute to the good of Athens. This could take the form of participation in politics, in the arts, in philosophy or scientific enquiry, in building projects or in war. Ideas would be debated and tested in the *agora* – the city square – so the old ways of doing things could always be improved and action taken. The projects that were chosen – a war, an enormous monument to glorify a civic leader, drainage schemes that benefit all or building libraries or temples – depended on the power of public opinion. And what was chosen changed the physical character of the city and the social networks inside it.

Ancient Rome

Rome was also full of pleasures and a great variety of goods and games. As in Athens, games were a way to encourage exceptional perform-ance, but the circuses pitting Christians against lions may also have served the secondary purpose of reminding people of the power of the state, and what happened to people who tried to rebel against it. To succeed it was necessary to keep your head down and play the game.

Rome was managed differently from Athens. It was less demo-cratic and messy and more organised and professional. Its ongoing viability depended on hard work, astute management and military might. There was a greater division of power, partly because the empire was so large that this was necessary, but partly to divide and conquer. It was strategic to deploy the fighting men of one subjugated region to fight in another. It was prudent to allow people their own cultural preferences as long as they didn't cause trouble to anyone else. The Roman Empire was liberal. Unlike in Athens, women were allowed to go to the games, own property and businesses.

While Roman competence, ingenuity and legal codes were main-tained the empire opened up a safe space for productive work and enjoyable play. By the end of the empire wealth was concentrated in a handful of families who used slaves to farm their land, and had displaced the great majority of free farmers who were forced to head to the city: landless plebeians to be managed with bread and circuses. Over time a dislocation between principles and reality weakened the structures of government, lessening people's faith in, or fear of, those structures. Decadence has been blamed for the downfall of Rome, but this may not be fair. Displacement activities, like shopping for luxury goods and the drinking of wine, may have been a symptom of the break-up of the empire rather than the cause. Playing at empires takes a lot of effort and resources. At some point, the centre can – or will – no longer hold.

The Dark Ages and the Arab world

With the fall of the Roman Empire, the Arab Empire became domin-ant, spreading as far west as southern Spain. Like the Romans they were relatively tolerant, allowing people to keep up their cultural practices (including following different religions) as long as they played their roles collaboratively and peacefully. Baghdad became the centre of play, learning and innovation with talent heading there to produce music machines and automated water fountains, and develop mathematics and medicine. Much of the ancient knowledge that was forgotten in the West was preserved in the Arab world.

Chess seems to have emerged from a war game called Chattaranga that developed in Central Asia in or around the seventh century AD. By the tenth century it was played in Iraq in the form that we know it, and it was introduced to Europe not long after. The game would have had multiple resonances for daily life. While there were power hierarchies, the game demonstrated the need for people from different classes with different roles and powers. Chess is also meritocratic – to succeed at it requires ability, not high birth. As with the Athenians there was a cultural aspiration to personal growth, to develop knowledge, to reflect, to be moderate and competent. Cities were designed so that homes were inward looking around a garden. They were private, discreet.

Northern Europe was more fragmented, with power separated into numerous smaller kingdoms and city states. Many of these cities were walled and contained defensive structures like castles and garrisons. The marauding tendencies of Vikings (and Goths, Vandals and so on) meant that life outside the walls was chaotic and dangerous, and there would have been a good deal of survival value in holding together for security. Some of the towns and cities had been Roman settlements; many contained churches. A new Roman Empire would rise, and this time it was Catholic; unlike the original live-and-let-live version of Rome, this empire was all about principles and people's hearts and minds. Instead of gathering outside in a square to debate the great questions like the Athenians had done, congregations would gather inside, in a structure designed and built to last a thousand years, to hear the word of an eternal, omniscient, omnipotent God. The Catholic Church informed a good deal of academic medieval thought, and it highly valued obedience and people knowing their place in the great scheme of things. Once again play was part of the picture – and play was compulsory.

The Medieval Christian City

As Christianity spread across Europe various existing beautiful buildings, pagan rituals and festivals were incorporated into the church. The
festivals were rooted in nature's rhythms, connected to fertility and
farming, and may have emerged out of the older festivals of nomadic
hunter-gatherers. Advent, Christmas and Candlemas were built on the
old winter festivals, when little work could be done and temperatures
were low. It made sense, and was a lot more fun, for people to come
together to share physical and figurative warmth, to celebrate one year
complete and a new one coming, and to help the winter days and nights
go by with plays, sports and entertainments. These festivals changed
character over time. St Valentine's at first celebrated the return of the
first calling birds, but by the fifteenth century had evolved into an
opportunity for those romantically inclined to declare themselves. The
winter solstice became incorporated into Christmas, and winter rituals
ran from December through till February. The three-day Shrovetide
festival (from Sunday till Shrove Tuesday) was an opportunity to confess all sins and eat all the fat before Lent. The Venice Carnival, the
Rio Carnival, and Mardi Gras in New Orleans are all rooted in the
same cultural tradition, but look and feel very different.

All around the world families share the old stories and eat up
the remaining perishable food stores in midwinter.[5] The Japanese
traditionally returned home to celebrate the winter solstice, which
has vaguely incorporated the Western ideas of Christmas and New
Year. New Year in China comes in February (around the same time
as Candlemas and St Valentine's Day) and families gather together at
home. There is also a traditional family festival six weeks before. In
New Zealand, the winter festival, the Māori New Year, is around July
time and is called Matariki. People go back to their ancestral lands to
tell stories and feast. It is a time to say goodbye to those who died in
the year. The dates of Matariki vary slightly throughout the country,
partly down to the times the Matariki stars appear in the night sky,
but also connected to how warm the temperatures are (and therefore
how quickly the stores of food will go off). Warmer places celebrate
earlier, and colder places later.

Easter and the story of Christ's rebirth echoed the old stories of the rebirth of the land in spring. Summer festivals in May and June – dancing around the maypole and so on – are all about fertility and sex, while Harvest Festival does exactly what its name suggests. In between there were other festivals – All Hallows' Eve, the day of the dead, was a night in autumn, when the weather was stormy, for ghosts to revisit the living. April Fool's Day was a day (like Twelfth Night) when the Lords of Misrule had their way, a day for pranks and jokes (and may have offered some light relief in the middle of the planting period). On St Crispin's Day in October, there was a bonfire. There were a lot of parties in the Middle Ages.

The church offered a whole system of society that transposed across geographies and borders and became an empire in itself. As well as play, the church was practically involved in survival – in the growing and storing of food, care of the sick and infirm, in the education of children and as a keeper of records. There were clerical courts, and churches were places of sanctuary away from the King's justice. Both King and Church made the rules, and both used Latin to convey them. The job of interpreting the law was done using strange words and concepts; was it like playing a game that you don't fully understand but to which you must commit entirely? The community were obliged to be active in the building of cathedrals, the singing of songs and the production of art and events. The priest, like his Neolithic forebears, became the master of ceremonies, marking up the hours, days, weeks, seasons and years with a variety of physical, emotional and spiritual experiences that brought meaning, pleasure, interest, comfort and order to people who had to face numerous challenges together, from failing harvests to plague and war. The structures in a city reflect societies' values and strengths. These may originate from the top, from people with their own agenda, and yet, to succeed, they must also communicate some value that is more broadly shared: of beauty, harmony, ethics, wonder, service, community, ritual, of trust in a greater power.

The Middle Ages to Early Modern Period

As time went on, the small kingdoms became absorbed in each other, not always peacefully, while the Crusades offered an opportunity to get rich quick while ostensibly defending Christian Europe against heretics. Much of the play, including chess, was quasi-military. Tournaments, sponsored by the local lord of the manor, were displays of military skill in sword fighting, archery and jousting. One way to rise up the pecking order was to become a squire and then a knight, which could lead, if one acquitted oneself well on the battlefield, to greater rewards and titles. For well-born women, play was equally practical. A good hand at embroidery meant finer clothes, skill at dancing or a quick wit meant a greater chance of a good marriage (and a good seat on a horse would help too). The establishment of the Tudor dynasty brought peace after a hundred years or more of internal strife, not to mention battles abroad. This peace was maintained with a show of strength and status. The term 'bloodsport' is now used for hunting animals, but for a long time it was simply 'sport' and was another way of practising military skills. (Rodeos, hunting, fishing and shooting continue, but are less culturally acceptable than they were. Killing off insects and microbes to maintain cleanliness is still fair game. That killing can be enjoyable is rarely articulated, but there is satisfaction in it.)

If the city was a cage, it was at least gilded. Catholic cities are held together by beauty, pleasure, ritual and play – for survival and to maintain the status quo. The more oppressive a culture, the more intense the need for play.[6] Religious intolerance and rules around social stratification rose in the Middle Ages and in Tudor England. There were regulations over the types of clothes that people of different classes could wear, though these were hard to enforce, perhaps because there were also so many festivals that demanded dressing up. The midwinter Roman festival of Saturnalia lived on in Twelfth Night when, at the end of the Christmas period, the fool became the Lord of Misrule, all the servants dressed up, and the nobility were able to slum it.

The situation in Venice was wild and oppressive. Women had limited freedom; Jewish homes were restricted to the ghetto. Catholics were encouraged to confess their sins but failing that, residents were enabled to dob in their neighbours for infractions. To allow discretion, Lion's Mouth postboxes were dotted around the city as a depository for denunciatory letters to be collected by the authorities at their leisure. Without the oppression, would they have needed masks and carnivals when they could let loose for a month? Perhaps not. Countries like India, with oppressive caste systems, also seem to be extraordinarily playful. It is as though the cultural contract is different: know your place, do as you are told and work hard, and you will be provided with food and treats. This may sound infantilising, but some research suggests 30 per cent of people prefer not to take responsibility for things.[7] There is also some sense in just making the best of things and taking the world as you find it. No one will ever be able to entirely shape the world to their desires and rocking the boat may be simply too dangerous.

The medieval cities, in the Ancient, Arab and European world, all had something in common. They not only contained cathedrals or churches but also communities of people living in walking distance from one another, who all had different degrees of power and wealth and played various roles. Food was grown or traded within walking distance; farmers could make it to town for the market and return home by the end of the day. Most places were holistic and produced most of what they needed. People knew each other. These old cities with town squares at their heart are beautiful and functioned pretty well. The Catholic Church did and does provide extraordinary architecture, art, places of learning and cultural festivities. At its best it provides a place for everyone, values ordinary people and provides social support. The have-nots were very well aware of what their wealthier neighbours had and could do, but when culturally everyone had to submit to God and know their place there was limited wiggle room. Venting one's grievances in the pub or the confessional was perhaps the best one could do.

As kingdoms and cities grew, societal structures became more complex and more roles and classes of roles emerged. The publication of a book called *The Book of the Manners of Men and the Offices of the Nobility*, otherwise known as *The Game of Chess,* by a thirteenth-century monk, was quite subversive. It recognised – as the Arabs had – the value of an alternative social structure that did not rely on all-encompassing command and control from the top. This interpretation supported the division of powers and the establishment of guilds, legal chambers and universities, with suitably grand buildings.[8] Cities became increasingly unfair as some grew wealthy and common land started to be enclosed and privatised.

The Protestant movement went further in promoting a vision of freedom, in which ordinary people were more than capable and desirous of taking responsibility for their lives into their own hands. Luther published his critique on the efficacy of indulgences in 1517. They had funded a social safety net however. When the church was reformed, and much of its wealth taken by the state under Henry VIII, there would be left a gap that would have to be filled by the state (the Poor Laws) and charity. Meanwhile, a new liberal order allowed trade, private investment (and borrowing) and education to expand. All this swelled the ranks of the aspirational Elizabethan middle classes, who bought up etiquette books (as did the growing Italian middle class who were lending the money). *Galateo: The Rules of Polite Behavior* (*Il Galateo, overo de' costumi*), written by Giovanni della Casa in the sixteenth century, aimed to aid the common man with his manners and is full of helpful hints about not spitting at dinner and not boring people with descriptions of one's dreams. In the seventeenth century James I had the Bible translated and printed in English. When Charles I drew on his claim of divine right to raise taxes to fight a foreign war the well-educated governing middle classes felt sufficiently empowered to resist. There was Civil War and the Parliamentarians won. It was the end of one game, and the endorsement of another, in which anyone who applied themselves could play.

The enlightened City

The British don't learn much about Oliver Cromwell, anti-monarchist republican that he was, but one of the goals of the Puritans was to expand education and to encourage people of all classes to learn. The percentage of students who went on to tertiary education in the 1640s during the English Civil War would not be reached again until after the First World War. Boys were the main beneficiaries, but girls were also accepted at four boarding schools run by Quakers.[9] Cromwell also decreed that British law be written and argued in English rather than in Latin: a signal that the legal system be more transparent. Echoing the Athenian and Arab world, the idea of a good life was in the hands of the individual. Anyone could make something of themselves, could commune with God without a priest as intermediary, engage in reflection and lead a good, productive and prosperous life. New rules were put in place to encourage respect for the sabbath (without smells, bells and church organs), and the leading of more moderate, and modest, lives. Play evolved accordingly.

Many pubs and theatres – traditional places for conversation and debate – were shut down, though opera and music outside of church were encouraged. Cromwell enjoyed dancing but restricted it because it encouraged other forms of vice. However, a new stimulating public space opened up in London in 1652: the coffee house. It was for a male clientele only and presented as a place of morality (later on some of them doubled as brothels). Coffee was advertised as a way to curb lust and improve health, but of course it is also stimulating for the brain, as well as being addictive (in a good way). By 1663 there were eighty-two coffee houses in the heart of London, popular with the (literally) chattering classes. While the tavern was another good place to talk and share ideas, the coffee house had the advantage that conversations would be more likely to be remembered later. And those conversations were about anything, from politics to religion to natural science. Men enjoyed the opportunity to talk with not just their peers, but also with men across society who had ideas to share in a space where rank didn't matter as much as wit and knowledge. The coffee house held the space for the Enlightenment to unfold: a playful project in itself that involved enquiry, banter, the sharing of information and the display of mastery.

A petition against coffee, ostensibly from women, but probably led by Charles II, [10] was published in 1674. The criticism was that coffee made men talk too much, and become useless in bed. It is possible the king disseminated this questionable feedback to give him an excuse to shut down the coffee houses, perhaps because of the threat that the middle-class intelligentsia would gain influence, or to prevent the spread of information, true or slanderous, that might destabilise the crown. The outcry was enormous, and Charles backed down. The British were favourable to Charles II's return in 1660, but only to a point. It would have been hard to argue for the divine right of kings when your father had been beaten by a commoner who, if not entirely popular, was demonstrably capable.

By the early 1700s, there were more than a thousand coffee houses, and they specialised: some for theatre lovers, others for scientists, and so on. From this playful sphere, new ways of making money emerged. The insurance specialist Lloyds of London was founded in a coffee house. The first public museums were based in them, as were the first stock exchanges, and the Royal Societies of Arts and Sciences. The coffee houses even spawned journals like *Tatler* to spread gossip and jokes. But most of all, coffee houses spawned more coffee houses where people could share, give feedback on and develop new ideas. One could say that all this innovation came about because it was pleasurable and fun, but it was also an empowering space, a space of exploration, where one could see and be seen, talk and be heard, be competitive (the agonistic instinct again), and win a debate or lose it. It was a place where you could get feedback straight away, whether that be laughter or serious input. Social norms shifted as the world was put to rights, and the rights to debate, to challenge the *status quo*, and to laugh at power openly became ingrained in British culture. Even arguments can feel good in a bracing sort of way!

If indeed it was women who railed against coffee, men (or at least those in the cloth trade) railed at women. Restoration London saw fashionable clothing shops opening in Ludgate Hill, and for the first time there were displays where customers could browse at leisure and test soft cottons against their skins. Enabling people to enjoy experiencing calico in a shop boosted imports, from a quarter of a million pieces in 1664 to 1.76 million twenty years later. The trade in cotton would change the world and Britain's place in it.[11] (When the British Navy made it to New Zealand in 1769, some Māori were keen to trade their historical treasures for cotton bloomers.[12]) Clearly there was an emerging class of men and women with time on their hands and some disposable income and there were enough people in the city to make it worth opening shops. It had been a long time since people were encouraged to please themselves, and trade, and economies of scale, made it cheaper to buy fine imports than embroider cloth oneself.

Restoration of the monarchy saw an explosion in comic plays at the theatre, along with dancing, music, games, romance and more gardens. In London Oliver Cromwell had opened up Henry VIII's hunting ground Hyde Park for everybody to use (on Sunday though playing games like early versions of football was not allowed). A pragmatic Charles II would open up St James's Park to the masses (and their mistresses and livestock) of his own accord. The Mall and Pall Mall were both designed for the game of Pelle Melle, with hoops to knock balls through. Vauxhall Gardens were opened.

Gardening was competitive and fashionable, too. The collecting of seeds and plants from abroad was originally to satisfy a desire for the exotic in clothes, foods and fancies, for their inherent qualities and to demonstrate status, but they also stimulated a scientific fascination. Enlightenment scientists and their patrons invested huge quantities of cash in the designing of gardens and the acquisition of rare plants. Many varieties were cultivated to be grown commercially (or the attempt was made), and others collected, stored and kept alive in expensive glasshouses, or dried out in cabinets. To have grown oranges in Kensington Gardens would have been quite a feat, and required hefting the trees into the glasshouse every autumn so they would survive the winter. Central heating was developed not for people's comfort but to keep expensive plants alive.[13] For anyone who remembers *Blackadder*'s Baldrick spending a fortune on a turnip, this wasn't so far off normal behaviour in the seventeenth and eighteenth centuries. Fashions in plants came and went, as with everything else. The tulip mania of Holland had peaked in 1637, with prices for a single bulb reaching multiple times the yearly wage of a common labourer: the first example of a speculative bubble. This didn't stop the rich putting huge amounts of money into growing tropical pineapples a few decades later.

Tending or visiting the botanical gardens and display gardens was and is a fascinating pleasure. The fruits of all this labour did ultimately benefit ordinary mortals, and mightily improved people's gardens and cooking. For those with money, one could eat a greater variety of food in a city than in the country. Some of the restaurants founded in eighteenth-century London – Wiltons, Simpson's chophouse and Rules – survive to this day. Access to these treats though was for the few. For those without money, mortality rates were appallingly high, in the increasingly disease-ridden and inequitable cities.

The industrial City

Pagan culture had been adapted to fit around nature, and church culture fitted around that. When the limitations provided by weather, the seasons and shorter daylight hours were overcome with new technologies like gas lamps and steam engines, a lot of these festivals fell away, while the most important ones evolved. If you had electric light spectaculars, why would you need a bonfire? More importantly, why fill the time with play when there was work to be done? As more people moved into the city, Christmas was a way to bring nature back inside homes temporarily, with holly and ivy stems and decorated yew trees, a German idea originally brought over by Princess Caroline in the eighteenth century and popularised over the decades. The 1840s saw the further evolution of Christmas, with the invention of the stamp, crackers, pantomime, Christmas cards and the mass-manufacturing of toys. Easter, too, remained an important holiday with a connection to nature, with chicks and rabbits (albeit perhaps increasingly defined by the chocolate more than the eggs . . .).

As the symbols of nature come into the city, real nature, however, would be pushed out. It used to be common for kids to run and play on the local commons, and swim or fish in the ponds and streams, but with the coming of the Industrial Revolution this access to nature play was limited. The hunting grounds became parks that could be maintained (at great expense) but the water quality was a bigger challenge. Some rivers had been covered in concrete; others, like the Thames, were simply too polluted to play in. Water play had to be designed back in to the city. By the end of the Victorian era most towns would have a swimming bath and wash house, gymnasium, playground and sports fields for youthful recreation. Curiously, though, these were not really described as play spaces, but would be encouraged on the grounds of health, to improve morals and to keep young men off the streets (and to ensure there would be a fighting-fit population to serve in military conflicts). It was very rare for discussions about these facilities to consider their value in creating happiness, but maybe this was considered a frivolous point or a statement of the obvious. It is clear, looking at the black-and-white photographs of small boys grinning in the Tooting Bec lido, that there was a good deal of fun and pleasure to be had.

Progress in preventing diseases (such as the smallpox vaccination) improved mortality rates, but increased populations further. All these people in the city enabled other forms of play to emerge. The introduction of mass manufacturing in the mid-nineteenth century brought down the cost of clothes, toys, books and novelties, allowing shopping to become a viable leisure opportunity for the middle classes. Le Bon Marché department store opened in Paris, such stores offering the irresistible opportunity for the middle classes to try (and buy) new things. Barriers to purchase like haggling were removed. The department store offered fixed, reasonable prices every day. Macy's in New York and Selfridges in London opened up their displays so that customers could touch things and try them on without negotiating with a sales assistant. Harrods promised to sell you anything you wanted, even elephants. All of the buildings were beautiful cathedrals of commerce.

Customers would wander independently through the glittering mirrored halls, designed to get lost in, to consider and acquire the various treasures of the world. The only thing the stores lacked were clocks to show the hours passing by. To maintain interest stores would hold exhibitions and events, supply waiting rooms for husbands, tea rooms and bathrooms. There were few public toilets and restaurants available to women at that time, these enabled their female customers to stay all day. Given time, a customer would move from wondering 'What is it?' and 'How does it work?' to 'How does it work for me?' and 'How could I possibly leave it behind?' Women, even middle-class ones, had varying access to money to acquire items. Some stole what they wanted, leading to a number of court cases in which it was argued that kleptomania was a mental disorder suffered by otherwise respectable women, rather than a crime.

Unsurprisingly, this led to a good deal of comic satire at the music hall. Victorian society seems to have been both repressive and very playful, with the rise of the sporting codes, pantomimes, music hall, card sending, leisure travel, collecting, parties, self-help, concert and lecture attendance and museums. There was exploitation, but the cultural mantra was 'Work hard, play hard'. Those who did well in industry paid their workers little, but gave back to the community in the end. In the mid-nineteenth century the terrible conditions of the poor stimulated a huge surge in spending at local level to make people's lives better. The pools, town halls, libraries, museums, galleries and playing fields that we take for granted today are a legacy of this.

There was a downside to the industrial city, and not just the inequity. Smells and pollution can make life intolerable. The overwhelming impression British cities made in the nineteenth century was that they were disease-ridden, filthy and overcrowded, and something needed to be done. Infant mortality rates were lower than in the late eighteenth century, but still high, and many adults were physically stunted because of sickness and poor nutrition. [14] People had known since the early eighteenth century that things were wrong with the River Thames, because it stank. It had long been used as an open sewer, and sanitation systems and sewers could not cope with the rise in population. Cartoons were drawn linking Old Father Thames with death and disease, but sorting out the drainage (most pipes led to the Thames) was put off for more than a century because of the cost.

It was the Great Stink of 1858, when hot weather exacerbated the smell of raw sewage and industrial effluent, that stimulated action. During a cholera outbreak in 1854, the doctor John Snow had used a map to show how the disease was linked to the taking of water from a contaminated water pump in Soho. Most of the medical profession did not believe cholera was waterborne until years after Pasteur published his germ theory of disease in 1861. If Snow's work was enlightening it was not viscerally persuasive. The nausea-inducing stink was. The curtains of the Houses of Parliament were soaked in quicklime to try and hold back the smell, while a law was passed in a breakneck eighteen days to create a more permanent solution. Engineer Joseph Bazalgette was hired to create a network of sewers. To make space for these vast pipes, the River Thames was narrowed and the Embankment created with walkways by the river for Londoners to enjoy, which of course at last they could. It did signal the end of the frost fairs that had been held twenty-three times between 1309 and 1814. By making the Thames narrower, it became deeper, reducing the chance that the river would freeze over.

Air pollution from factories, horse poo in the streets and lack of drainage in parts of the city, such as the East End, would all continue to impact on health. A desire to leave the stink and disease of the inner city would encourage the middle and upper classes to remove themselves to the leafy suburbs, close to large parks and heaths, where it was healthier – and, it was generally agreed, a better place to raise children. The steam engines that caused much of the pollution also allowed those who could afford it to escape to the suburbs by train. The nineteenth-century industrial city, then, was a time of geographical separation between the haves and the have-nots, those with mobility and those without, those in factories or sweatshops or literally at the coalface, and those enjoying (relatively) affordable luxuries and central heating. The poor were not the only casualties of suburban growth. For many women, exile to the suburbs could lead to isolation and depression. The price of health and safety, it emerged, was to have less access to play.

There were some opportunities, however. The novelist Charles Dickens shone a light on the inequities of Victorian life, but statistics suggest that for the well-off things were actually better for more people than before. The lower middle-class and working-class people with skills, spirit and a bit of luck had some options: to stay in the UK and start their own businesses, or to emigrate to the New World where they could lead a better life.

The colonial City – creating Utopia (ish)

The promise of emigration to would-be settlers was opportunity. Travel journals, novels and stage versions of *Robinson Crusoe* cultivated this desire for adventure, to create the life for themselves that they wanted, for sexual freedom. (Native maidens seemed to play a key role in the stage versions.) For entrepreneurs, this was a chance to create wealth (often at the cost of indigenous populations). Nascent cities in the New World competed with each other for immigrants to boost populations and return a profit on the investment of infrastructure that either the crown or a private company had spent on establishing them. Advertisements appeared in British magazines illustrating the health and happiness of emigrants in contrast to their sick, starving and suffering peers at home. The New World incorporated remarkable places with, it was touted, copious food, glorious weather and no diseases. Letters to editors on what to take abroad were answered with advice to take pianos so as to enjoy the evening with music. Emigrants en route set up private lending libraries and botanic societies in order to share resources and provide some structure for learning. People took packs of cards and board games like chess and backgammon and on arrival might teach the local people how to play. In New Zealand, one Māori lady enjoyed cards so much she had a dress made entirely decorated with them.[15] The early arrivals would trade with locals for food and would be fascinated by their canoes and costumes. Foreign lands meant freedom from old rules. This meant different things to different people.

One of the great lures of the colonies was the opportunity to make one's fortune, as a farmer, a gold-digger, a trader, a whaler or feather-hunter, even as tourist operators (in 1842 one settler, Robert Graham, was on the lookout for opportunities to create spa resorts). For those playing a longer game, buying up land in the cities of the New World proved a better bet to riches and a step up in life. Being a landowner meant financial security. It also meant the vote. This provided an opportunity for the crown and city-building companies, like the New Zealand Company, to make a good deal of wealth while at the same time ensuring citizens' commitment to a city. Homeowners had skin in the game.

The way it worked was that only a certain amount of land was made available for sale in large lots, which went for reasonably high sums. After a few years campaigning for immigrants the land value would go up significantly, and parcels of land would be subdivided and sold off individually at a profit. Land sale posters in New Zealand in the nineteenth century offered mortgages as a way to enable more people to buy at a level they could not immediately afford. The Bank of New Zealand would send stooges to real estate auctions to drive up the prices. (Making money from land is still one of the main ways to increase wealth in New Zealand but high prices are now making it increasingly hard for young people to buy in.) This increased house prices, but it also meant that by the time of the First World War half the country lived in homes they owned. In the UK at that time the proportion was 10 per cent. New Zealand was known in the 1890s as a paradise for the working man because there were no strikes – industrial conflicts were resolved through an independent arbitration board. There were half-day holidays. All men got the vote in 1879 and women in 1893. Many people having the vote made a difference.

People adapted to their new lands to a degree, but it was remarkable that on the whole they seemed to re-create the city and society that they had grown up with, just with themselves a few rungs higher up the ladder. In the last few centuries colonial cities carved out areas of less-well-used space in mighty empires like China and India to create bastions of European culture. The British mansions of Shanghai would not look out of place in Surrey. In the New World where cities were imported, their names recall where immigrants came from: New Amsterdam then New York, Christchurch, Cambridge. Dunedin streets were laid out by its Scottish settlers as close as possible to its almost namesake Edin-burgh. British Empire expatriates were encouraged by the powers-that-be to 'do' empire.[16] There was a good deal of buy-in to this – perhaps because it allowed people to assert their own cultural identity, to feel they belonged in a strange place where they were a minority, or because they believed in the empire as a tool of progress. It didn't matter if the heat was intense or if they were living in tents, British governors, the military and the middle class dressed for dinner and held garden parties. Middle-class wives of civic leaders felt obliged to hold dances and tea parties where the young could meet. The military were particularly good at throwing parties, perhaps because they were compulsory for officers to attend. Redcoats caused as much excitement in Auckland as in any Jane Austen novel, and when they left New Zealand's shores society, the ladies thought, became very dull. It could be perceived as patriotic or as a refusal to attune to a new culture, but to do things differently may simply not have occurred to anyone.

People made their own fun. This included picnics, parties and horse-racing, but there was huge demand for the amenities of Europe, like libraries, art galleries, theatres, concert halls, department stores, solid-looking schools and universities, and parks planted with oaks and other specimen trees sourced from the empire. Within a few decades they got them. Flora and fauna were imported for recreational purposes, gardening and hunting. These would prove invasive and decimate native plants and animals. Very few people actually came to New Zealand to live like Māori, but in the early days some did live in *raupo* huts, as Māori did. The *raupo* were made of reeds and thatch, which were quite cosy but flammable. In the 1840s the second most likely cause of death for settler women was cooking fires. A major fire in Wellington in 1842 led to *raupo* being regulated out of most cities in favour of colonial housing, wooden kitsets inspired by British houses, but unlike anything you would see at home.

Pioneer society seemed to be split, mainly between two groups. One group had come to lead a good life, and the others had come for a good time. This meant there were lots of churches and also lots of hotels/brothels. Just as Cambodia became a site for underage prostitution in the 1970s, so was New Zealand in the early nineteenth century, though travellers may also have gone to France, or even to the East End of London, to slum it sexually. If this sounds like the Wild West, it probably was. Cities on the frontier are cities on the edge. Their appeal – adventure, excitement, great rewards – has a flipside of danger, uncertainty and loss. The booze, drugs, gambling and women are both a draw and a consolation. A century prior the Caribbean had been a centre of lawlessness. In the twentieth century, war-torn South East Asia took the mantle. Twelve seemed to be considered a reasonable age at which a girl could be sexually active in much of the colonies. This was raised to fifteen, then sixteen only in the last years of the nineteenth century. It was argued by the opposition that girls in New Zealand grew up faster than their cousins back 'home' and that a man would not ruin a girl's reputation had she not wanted it.

Women were recognised as competent because they simply had to step up to get all the work that needed doing in the colonies done. It was a perennial joke in the local edition of satirical magazine *Punch* that it was difficult to find any staff. It is perhaps not surprising that in colonial cultures, where everyone was expected to get on with things, that women got the vote earlier (America in some states, then New Zealand in 1893) than back home. Campaigning to create a fairer society is a serious business but also incredibly sociable – at a time when there were few outlets for respectable women to participate in public life.

One of the difficulties that a number of respectable married women had to endure was that they were stuck in the suburban home with numerous children, while their husbands were spending their wages on booze and girls in the city hotels. Some men went away to pan for gold or harvest native forests, leaving their wives to raise families, doing laundry or cooking to make ends meet. When the husbands came home they had the right to take their savings and head off again to the pub. Respectable women did not drink or go to pubs and, rather than agitate to join the fun, the Women's Christian Temperance Union campaigned to remove women and girls from pubs altogether. Some pamphlets advocated that men be saved from young women, and others that young women be saved from men. In 1885, 18,357 women signed a petition to 'forbid women to serve in any capacity in public houses'. By 1887, a new series of petitions added another eight thousand names to the cause. These petitions, the largest to date, were ignored, which only encouraged the franchise movement to double their efforts. In 1893, women got the vote in New Zealand, and later that year there was a referendum on banning alcohol. The majority of many districts voted for prohibition, but the bar had been set so high (two thirds had to support the abolition, and 50 per cent had to turn out to vote) by the prime minister Richard Seddon (whose political campaign funds were bolstered by a number of breweries) that nothing happened. Reducing the sale of liquor would be a slow process.

Women were at last banned from serving in public houses in 1911 in New Zealand, but there were plenty of exceptions to the rule: current employees could stay, as could the publican's wife, daughters, sisters ... There was little appetite for strict enforcement – just a few nudges to make going out less enjoyable. In 1916, women were barred from drinking in pubs, and men were banned from buying each other drinks. In 1917, as a wartime measure, the men had to be out by 6 p.m. – ostensibly to improve military production. Tables and chairs were removed, perhaps to allow more men inside, or perhaps because sitting down simply took up valuable drinking time. Troughs were installed under the bar, so that men could spit or spill their drinks at leisure without risking losing their prime spot. The fronts of the pubs were tiled, some say, so it was easier to clean up if anyone was compelled to relieve themselves after downing multiple pints in sixty minutes. The idea was that men would then go home, but not all did.

Despite all the restrictions it was easy enough to find work-arounds if you wanted to get high. Some bars were openly defiant, serving drinks illegally or allowing patrons to hide their liquor under the tablecloths. There was a rise in members' clubs that had looser drinking laws. Informal party houses established themselves in residential homes, offering home brew and drugs: heroin could be obtained in pharmacies as cold cures. The problem was it made people quite relaxed about breaking the law and divided people into tribes. Former soldiers congregated in the Returned Services Association, or the bowling club or tennis clubs. Māori and Pacific people went to their own clubs, connected to rugby or the church, to listen to music or dance. All this separation perpetuated a wariness of each other which is ongoing, particularly between those of an older generation. Younger people who have grown up learning *Te Reo* (the Māori language) and Māori values may find it easier to live together.

Participating in dangerous sports was another way of living life to the full. Horse racing, or car racing on beaches, was popular, as was gambling on both activities. Mountain climbing was popular. Learning to fly in New Zealand was so fashionable in the 1930s that you could get coupons on cereal packets. People continued to improvise their own fun over the ensuing decades. Returning soldiers with handy skills would build basic huts in the mountains or by the beach for family holidays or meld together various spare parts to make rudimentary speedboats. There were more parties at home, sometimes combined with house renovations. The combination of beer and chainsaws to remodel wooden houses into open-plan living in the 1960s and '70s may not sound promising, but it was definitely a thing. A campaign was run in Australia and New Zealand to entice real men into drinking coffee in salons, and there is still a very strong coffee culture in the Antipodes, with both countries claiming to have invented the flat white. However, it added to rather than replaced the drinking culture.

In the early 1960s, my mother was a university student, living in Lower Hutt, a satellite town to the capital Wellington. It was boring. There weren't many places to go out in the evening. Some cafés turned a blind eye to wine smuggled inside in handbags and then discreetly poured into coloured glasses or coffee cups, but this was a rare treat and girls couldn't go to pubs, and most, like Mum, lived at home. She would drive four hours to the ski hut in the mountains in winter, for the chance of a party, and signed up to be a stage manager with the student drama club, because that was one of the few opportunities for socialising and engaging in projects with people her age! On graduation, she, with lots of other girls, left the country for the glamour of 1960s London, home of short skirts, great music and universal access to the pub. My mother ultimately married an Englishman, but other New Zealand girls went back home and, in a reversal of the century prior, led the campaign to liberalise drinking laws. In 1967, the 'six o'clock swill' was over, which irritated the bar staff, because they had to work longer. Women had been allowed some access to the pub in 1962 but it wasn't until 1976 that women were legally allowed to access all areas of the pub. One wonders whether their grandmothers would have turned in their graves or approved.

Making your own fun (or work) and turning up to other people's houses with a box of beers and a plate of food (from the ladies) is still part of the culture. The separation of genders at play was also until recently common, with the women congregating in kitchens, and the men in the lounge or on the deck. Kiwi baby boomers are still super handy. They mend cars, create their own clothes, cook, garden and invent things. There is even a popular men's magazine called *The Shed*. Will this continue for future generations? They don't need to know how to do all these things, so maybe not. With the free-trade reforms of the 1980s it became much easier and cheaper to buy things and experiences in the way that most of the modern world could. Of course, this did leave more time for bungy jumping. Play evolves. The desire for living on the edge remains.

The modern City

Much of the thinking behind the modern city as a place of progress was in response to the pollution, lack of sanitation, overcrowding and disease that plagued the nineteenth-century industrial city. One solution to pollution and overcrowding was to escape elsewhere; the other was to improve one's own city. The important initial work was in sorting out water and waste, but the other necessary shifts came with progress in engineering and building techniques that allowed cities to go up and out. The modern city is defined both by the high-rise and the suburb.

The invention of lifts allowed taller buildings and sweeping views that could take your breath away. It would become possible for huge numbers of people to live close to each other, but have their own space and privacy, including having their own bathrooms and kitchens. New York is the archetypal modern city with its skyscrapers, its clean lines and heady sense of vertigo. The huge numbers of people on a small footprint would allow a huge variety of restaurants and nightclubs, cultures and subcultures, but also a huge disparity between rich and poor.

New Jersey and Queens are examples of the suburban paradise to which aspirational families were encouraged to aspire. Enfolded in the appeal was the excitement and freedom offered by the car in which a man, or woman, could move at high speed, accessing myriad places, including large home and garden lots where they could create their own domestic Utopias. This wasn't far away from the colonial promise to create a better life in a pristine new space. The city sprawled in all directions. Affordability came with economies of scale and the imperatives of the factory line. Consumer goods, including cars, became within the reach of the majority. Straight lines, practical, honest, uniform, spoke to a sense of progress and power at a societal level. Life would be better for everyone: you got the pastoral and the urban. The best of all worlds.

The need to pay mortgages on the suburban homes, and to fill them with new appliances, and the need to pay petrol for the car to get to work, perhaps as a civil engineer planning new roads, would also stimulate a taxable circular economy based on consumption. Buying the latest thing and keeping up with the Joneses were encouraged by magazines on good housekeeping, and child-rearing. There was no forced bumping up against neighbours, so happiness depended then on how good you were at creating your own networks and entertaining at home. Play in cities would evolve again.

Modern tower-block estates were also designed so that people would not have to bump up against each other as they had in overcrowded tenements, but as a result they had few places for people to meet each other and connect. Designed without ornamentation – unchic, unnecessary, expensive – there was little variation to mark these apartment buildings out. Ornamentation and variety, it appeared, were actually quite useful for creating a sense of place. Modern buildings *can* function well and be comfortable but this is not necessarily the case, and historic buildings with some maintenance and plumbing can *also* function well. In the name of modernism and progress many perfectly serviceable homes for working people were denounced as slums and destroyed. A cynic might argue that 'progress' was simply a phrase used by developers to justify displacing people and making money.

The journalist Jane Jacobs became one of modernism's most strident critics. She became frustrated with the large-scale redevelopment of New York in the 1960s and '70s, because it ripped out so much of the texture and individuality of the city. Many of the old neighbourhoods of Manhattan had been destroyed and others separated – like the Bronx – by the building of expressways through the city centre. She railed against the grand plans of planners who seemed to be tone deaf to what residents wanted, and completely blinkered about how their changes were pushing people away from cities and from each other, rather than drawing them into it and together. She could see, where planners did not, how isolating both the suburbs and highrise projects were. Her book, *The Death and Life of Great American Cities*, described what makes a city function well – a continuous urban fabric of neighbourhoods that are different but connected, with wide pavements where children could play, and stoops (front porches) for old people to sit and watch the world go by. In modern developments, stoops no longer existed, and homes were far from the street and the action, so there was nothing to see. She wrote of the little stores on the corner, with assistants who knew everyone and everything going on, which were having to shut down. To function well, the city needs to work like a giant modular system connecting up all the parts. 'The greater and more plentiful the range of all legitimate interests that city streets and their enterprises can satisfy, the better for the streets and for the safety and civilisation of the city.'[17]

It was a similar situation in post-war Paris. An idealised image of bohemian Paris in Hollywood movies like *Funny Face* or *An American in Paris* hid a darker side. Pressures on housing led to the building of tenements, and subsequently high-rise towers on the edge of the city, to which the poor – including many immigrants – were relocated. Artists and philosophers railed against the modernisation and the increasing brutalist dullness of the city, through paintings, writing, protests and artistic projects. The *Situation Internationale*, a group of artist activists, developed a practice called The Drift (*le dérive*) in the '60s. People would drift, or wander around the city, following a route that was most appealing to them, before coming back together to map where they went. In this way, they developed a sense of which places drew you in and made you feel good, and which ones were depressing or boring. These artists' work would lead to a whole avenue of research in urban planning and in psychogeography, that explored connections between feeling and place. In a bitter twist, the movie *Funny Face* massively takes the piss out of such French artists/philosophers in between jolly scenes of Fred Astaire photographing Audrey Hepburn in haute couture in the very picture-postcard settings that normal Parisians were being displaced from.

Happy cities – the new urban ideal

The assumptions of modernism – that sanitation, standardisation and the facilitation of the flow of people/vehicles/money had an economic and social value (and that anyone who disagreed was ignorant and standing in the way of efficiency and progress) – were first challenged by journalists and artists but soon also by some city builders themselves, particularly in the older cities that had not been made for cars and were facing problems of congestion, traffic pollution and suburban flight. Concerns over the environment through the 1960s also cast some doubt on the industrial consumer model.

The city of Freiburg, Germany, was, in the '60s, at a crossroads. People were no longer wanting to live in the city centre, or travel in to enjoy time with friends or to go shopping. The local economy was tanking, and roads were becoming increasingly unpleasant and unsafe for children. There was pressure to go with the flow, to continue greenfield development, build more roads and shopping malls. However, there was little money to do this. The tax take was going down, because people who lived outside the city did not have to pay the municipal tax. There may also have been a feeling by those who had rebuilt the city after the war that they did not want it to die. Originally a medieval city, the gaps produced by wartime bombing had been filled with buildings that were of a similar scale. The city was therefore coherent and full of character: a mix of old and new.

The city council changed tack. They made the city centre more conducive to encounters. Through-traffic would be reduced and public transport improved, and some areas would become pedestrian only. Shops decorated the footpaths with cobbled signs, and urban streams were opened up for children to splash in. The town squares would be made vibrant with seasonal fairs and events. The city drew its drifting population back into the centre, and more people wanted to live there, too. As a pleasing outcome (though not the main intention), the city became known for being environmentally sustainable and having low air pollution, because most people walked. The city drew a number of hippy squatters and it was to meet their demand for sustainable housing that a low-emissions walkable-suburb, called Vauban, was designed in the 1990s.

Vauban would be mixed use, mid-rise and joined up, creating a consistent urban fabric. Buildings were well insulated and energy-efficient, and incorporated renewable energies so as to keep energy consumption very low. Even human waste was converted to biogas for cooking. No cars could drive through the suburb, though public transport linked to the centre of Freiburg and from there across the region. This allowed children to play on their bikes and roam around safe from traffic. People have private homes and gardens, so they have control over their interactions, which are likely to take place in the public spaces between the shops, schools and public transport. People know their neighbours by design. The built environment locks in low emissions and community ties. It is widely considered both the most child-friendly and the most sustainable city in the world.[18]

There was a similar story in Copenhagen. Jan Gehl was a Danish architect who had been trained in the philosophies, practice and promise of modernism, but when travelling in Italy in the 1960s his wife asked him why architects did not consider people. Observing the convivial social life that flourished in the pedestrian piazzas he asked himself what made a city function well in the sense that it was enjoyable to live in? He shifted his focus from theorists eulogising on the quality of the buildings and on to the gaps between structures, the places where people were. His book, *Life Between Buildings*, was published in the 1970s, first in Danish, and then in fifteen languages around the world.[19] Like Jane Jacobs, he managed to articulate how the design of cities impacted what people did in them.

When Jan Gehl finished his research he was invited to transform Copenhagen, a beautiful historic city with narrow streets choked by cars. Gehl was able to lead a visionary change, to make it easier for people to walk and sit and bicycle in the city, by reallocating much of the space previously allocated for vehicles. There was push-back of course. Copenhagen was in Denmark, not Italy, people said, so the weather was less benign. People wouldn't sit in cold weather or bicycle in the rain. They liked their cars. It would never work. A motorway would be a better option. Or so they thought. To reduce the risk, planners focused on one area at a time, putting up information booths to allow engagement, and learned as they went. There was opposition but also support from environmental and heritage campaigners trying to keep the city's sense of place and identity.

Cycling, people discovered, was possible in all weathers, even snow. Visit Copenhagen now and you will see commuters on bikes, kids on bikes, seniors on bikes, even mothers on bikes pulling children in carts behind them. With blankets and heaters and a hot chocolate in hand, people came to enjoy sitting in cafés outside. And not just watching each other, but interacting, by plan or by chance. Parks and playgrounds and cafés and shops line the city. Five- and six-storey terraced buildings with apartments are common, providing enough of a market to support lots of economic activity within walking distance. And the city is full of beautiful buildings and parks. Copenhagen has everyday living down to a fine art, and the Danes are reported to be some of the happiest people in the world.

Jan Gehl's great insight was that our activities fall into three categories: necessary, optional and social. The more pleasing the urban realm, the greater the amount of optional activities that took place, and thus the more social activities that can take place. As we are social creatures, the more of that, the better. The more people in the street, the better for the economy, and the more shops, cafés, businesses and activity in the streets, the more interesting the city becomes, which brings in more people, which attracts more people looking for social interaction, and so on and so on in a virtuous circle. A city's design can keep people separate, as the modern city did, or it can bring people together and make them feel good.

What we see matters. If our surroundings are beautiful it pleases us; if they are overwhelmingly dull and grey, they bore and even depress us. The design can support a local economy by holding the space for markets, cafés and play – or it can make it easier to push people through without inviting them to linger. This can be helpful at busy bottlenecks of movement, like transport hubs, but not for everyday life. At a basic level, sun and shade, comfortable places to sit with armrests, flat, safe pavements, water fountains and loos all make the body feel more comfortable in the city, but to love a place we want our spaces to share the stories of its present and the past. To enjoy a city, we need a variety of enjoyable and useful activities. There should be an interplay between citizens, and between citizens and the city itself.

Could there be a science for urban happiness? It seemed there was. New York landscape architect Paul M. Friedberg developed a theory of urban happiness based on *Play and Interplay* (1970) focusing on the structures, from well-designed playspaces to pedestrian laneways that facilitated human encounters, highlighting the need for spaces for the very young to the very old.[20] Jane Jacob's friend and editor Walter White in New York set about trying to work out the principles of happy living – work that became the Project for Public Spaces.[21] White had a wry sense of humour when noting that people tended to sit down when there were places to sit. He and his team recognised how cities could be vibrant by ensuring that there were lots of things going on at once to appeal to a broad range of people's needs.

Christopher Alexander and a team of young researchers in the Centre for Environmental Structure at the University of Berkeley, California, wrote *A Pattern Language: Towns, Building, Construction* in 1977, which laid down in incredible detail, for the lay reader as much as for the urban professional, exactly how places worked to facilitate social cohesion and happiness.[22] Vancouver City created strict developer guidelines to ensure that there would be high-quality, mid-density family housing, with shared spaces for children to play that were overlooked by kitchens so that their mothers could keep an eye on them and could holler down when it was time for dinner.[23] In 1979, Allen Jacob and Donald Appleyard wrote *Toward an Urban Design Manifesto*, developed partially from a seminar at the University of California in 1979, which distilled what urban places ought to be to support vibrant and pleasant urban living. Five physical characteristics were essential:

1. Streets and neighbourhoods where people could dwell in reasonable safety, cleanliness and security.
2. Some density: about 15 dwelling units (30–60 people) per acre of land (not including streets).
3. An integration of activities (living, working, shopping, plus public, spiritual and recreational activities) in some reasonable proximity to each other.
4. Places for people, especially buildings that define and even enclose public space.
5. Many different buildings and spaces with complex arrangements and relationships.[24]

There is no mention of money here, but those cities that prioritised quality of life ended up doing well economically anyway. Homes in 'walkable' urban areas enjoy higher house prices.[25] As Richard Florida noticed,[26] people with talent and options wanted to work in the cities that were the most enjoyable to live in. This did not necessarily mean a council had to invest a lot in entertainment. When you attract lots of people into a well-designed space they will bring it to life themselves.

Urban planning journalist Charles Montgomery encourages people to choose to live in urban places that facilitate all kinds of play, to play a part in the building and shaping of cities and to prioritise and make time for their own play.[27] It helps if culturally there is a permissive attitude to play and that public spaces are varied and easily accessible, which makes it easy for people to participate in public life and do the things they like. Quentin Stevens, author of *The Ludic City*, goes further, 'Play is the actualisation of freedom, adventure, creativity and discovery ... This is part of why people are attracted to cities; it is part of what public spaces are for.'[28] This does not mean chaos if people are aware of each other and pick up social cues. It does not mean chaos if homes are designed so they are not intruded upon and if people can choose whether to engage or not in social interactions.[29] It is worth striving for the right balance between order and improvisation. 'The cities that succeed,' says Deyan Sudjic, 'are the ones that are rooted in the kind of cultural climate that is creative enough to fill the museums as well as build them.'[30]

The city: A lovely place to visit, a lovely place to leave

One of the biggest transformations over the last few centuries has been how cities have evolved from being a destination to being a place of substantial movement within their boundaries. In the fourteenth century, a pilgrimage would be the event of a lifetime. Chaucer's *Canterbury Tales* relate a trip that is less about religion and more about a once-in-a-lifetime group walking holiday. Muslims are encouraged to do a pilgrimage to Mecca, at least once. For them too the opportunity is both spiritual and social. Going on trips was expensive, dangerous and time-consuming. In the sixteenth and seventeenth centuries it would only be merchants, soldiers and diplomats who would expect to travel regularly. Noble families might move between cities, or the court and their country estates. Cities were fun when you had money and servants and best avoided when the summer plagues arrived. Most people who lived in cities, though, stayed there.

In the nineteenth century, people who could get out of the polluted centre moved to the edge of the city and travelled in. Now the city centre is clean and attractive, it is the great mass of people who must travel in every day, while visiting tourists and the lucky few who can afford to live in the centre can stay (in between trips jetting around the rest of the world). Cities have always been porous and sitting on the intersections of transport routes, but now it is normal for the majority of residents to travel every day for long distances and the suburban realm can increasingly look like the urban realm with lots of steel and concrete structures and roads and little green. Budgets to maintain these transport routes take up most of councils' revenue. What can happen though, when the pleasure of speed, movement and novelty takes precedence over the sensuous qualities of place, is that we end up always on the move and never getting anywhere. The findings of the new urbanists help us understand why some places are more appealing than others, but undoing and retrofitting the modern sprawling city is a huge undertaking. The answer may be pragmatic: to allow more dense developments to fill the gaps and encourage more working from home. The form of cities and the way people play in them may change again.

8

Winners and losers

Cities are playful, but they are not always fair. The game for many is to make one's fame and fortune, and property wealth is a key part of the picture. Home is the greatest asset that most families have, and for most it is fortune enough. Talk to investment brokers taking home million-dollar salaries, and they will say that the privilege of the middle is nothing compared to the big guys. For the most successful, playing the city is real-life Monopoly, with just a handful of people owning most of the commercial real estate. Wealth swirls and settles around the city, some legally, some laundered through trusts, property purchases and the rest. It powers the economy, even as house prices fly upwards and out of people's reach. Even in well-ordered countries, the inherent flexibility in urban plans, and the huge potential rewards, make city-building a high-stakes game. A cloak of dullness around these activities renders them almost invisible, but the well-scrubbed yachts bobbing at the waterfront offer a hint at the stakes. It would be wrong not to consider how those at the bottom end have had to support those at the top of the pyramid. Who misses out? There are two groups: the oppressed and the excluded, some of whom suffer being both at the same time.

The oppressed: Slaves, immigrants, minorities, and the poor

Slaves, either prisoners of war, or victims of kidnapping who have been displaced and sold to the wealthy of other lands, have in many cases done the majority of the work for the least reward and with the least time off. A lucky few found agency and interest in the work they were set to do, as bureaucrats and artisans. The Roman, Mongol and Chinese Empires all relied on educated slaves. Most, however, worked the farms or mines and did as they were told. Immigrants and minorities who have arrived voluntarily, or whose parents did, might have to limit their movements and participation to ensure their own safety in a land dominated by another race. Jews, Irish, Chinese and gypsies are just a few of the peoples who have had to (and still must) cope with the ignominy of overt or casual racism, even violence. The lesser 'other' may be different depending on the country, culture and moment in history, but the poorer treatment of some people continues to this day. Hiring someone from one country (or state) to go work in another where they have few legal protections and receive little pay, and who may even be forced to do this work, is a form of modern slavery.

Rules to protect one group's cultural ideals can be racist. The establishment of the US Federal Housing Administration in the 1930s to insure mortgages assessed the risk level (and premium) based on the number of coloured people who lived in an area. An 'A' neighbour-hood was totally white and considered low risk, so insurance was easy to get and premiums were cheaper, while Black neighbourhoods were rated 'D', and home owners would struggle to get house insurance. This meant that it was hard to get mortgages, which in turn dragged down the price of housing. While it was difficult for Black people, regardless of their personal reputation or achievements, to purchase a house, it was relatively easy for a wealthy developer to buy up a 'D' neighbourhood in a good location, evict the tenants, drag down the houses and build anew to sell to a more well-heeled and fairer-skinned clientele. At a national level, the message to one group in the commu-nity was that they were valued less, and that the white community was valued more. White communities are privileged in this scenario, but it is not ideal for them either. For them, the cultural feedback was that they are not safe, that they must be fearful of the 'other'.

Racial policies in predominantly white cities led to the establish-ment of Black cities in the US. This creates ghettos but at least within them people could run their own affairs. Desegregation brought people together but threatened the viability of these enclaves. However, there are still whitopias[1] – and a new blacktopia in Georgia is currently being planned by nineteen Black families looking for a place to be safe doing things their way.[2] As they say, they are integrated racially, so it won't ban white people, but it *will* be pro-Black. Indigenous people have found themselves in a similar position, subservient in the dominant society or marginalised, living together in neighbourhoods further from the centre, or on what is left of their lands. While cultural homogeneity might work for a town, or small community, great cities don't function this way. In great cities, people and activities mix. 'Cities have the capability of providing something for everybody, only because, and only when, they are created by everybody,' said Jane Jacobs. 'There is no logic that can be superimposed on the city; people make it, and it is to them, not buildings, that we must fit our plans.' Leaders, however, have often sought control.[3]

Throughout history, for many of those marginalised, transgression was the only way to play, and discretion was absolutely necessary. Homosexuality has sometimes been *de rigueur* and has sometimes carried the death penalty. Going to church has been compulsory, and illegal. To explore one's identity and enjoy what makes life meaningful for you is the great joy of play – and to not be allowed to practise homosexuality, religion or to be able to speak or joke freely was a cruel thing. For the Jewish community, which had been at the heart of the entertainment industry in Germany in the 1920s and '30s, one of the first losses was the right to play, to joke, to protest and to reinvent themselves.

Many oppressive regimes have found art, play and humour threatening. The cartoonist Erich Ohser had, in the early 1930s, published smart, witty cartoons that criticised the Nazi regime, but he burned his collection in 1933 to avoid being prosecuted. He turned to non-contentious subjects, like the relationship between father and sons, to make a living. In the end, though, he was overheard by neighbours laughing with another cartoonist about the failings of the Nazi regime. He was arrested and committed suicide the night before his execution.[4] Comedy can draw attention to the discrepancy between the 'ideal' and the reality, to a situation that is perhaps not what it should be. If people at the top are holding absolute power, and try and suppress laughter, it is unlikely that the feedback they get is as honest and diverse as it might otherwise be.

In Moscow, there have been times when new ideas and debate have flourished, as in the early 1920s. At other times, this has been brutally suppressed, along with comedy and freedom of speech. During the 1970s, Irina Ratushinskaya and her friends would gather secretly to share their poetry, a dangerously subversive activity in the USSR. She was also a practising Christian. Her engagement in small-scale activism, including signing a petition and joining a demonstration, was the excuse to jail her for seven years. A great number of those who disappeared during the dictatorships in South America were artists and writers. In North America and South Africa, racial separation restricted both how you could play and who you could play with. When so much is restricted, minor transgressions are not a matter of testing the system, but a dangerous bid to join in the practice of life itself when opportunities are slim.

These examples are of oppression but chaos can be equally brutal. War is often described in playful terms – war games; theatre of war – perhaps because in war time normal rules are turned on their head. In a war-torn city, where there are few resources or opportunities, and many recruitable foot soldiers, the only way to survive and to hold a community together is to work around the rules. There will be some criminal element. Even then, city residents become attuned to avoiding trouble spots and to managing their way out of dangerous situations. The greater dangers come from urban infrastructure, or lack thereof. The great losers in war are not soldiers but children. Even in the Congo deaths through violence are greatly outnumbered by those of children, who die of disease.

Crime is also couched in playful terms. There is some evidence, though, that a criminal life, like migration, is more likely to result from a lack of other opportunities than from a desire for adventure. Research on the history of New York's criminal fraternities demonstrated how cultural groups dominated crime and then moved out if it. The worse their prospects in the formal economy, the more appealing a life of crime seemed. In the nineteenth century, it was the Irish who were doing it hard, then the Italians in the early twentieth century, and later on the Black and Hispanic communities. Mobsters might have gathered the family wealth, but raised their children to be respectable. Managing a successful and profitable criminal operation in the long term takes effort and is highly risky. One is never safe from the law or one's rivals.[5] Being a mobster seems to be quite oppressive. It is hard to escape from a career in crime.

Even in the darkest of places some play emerges. When people are oppressed they play more intensely. This was so in the medieval period, which was full of religious festivals. It was true in the cotton fields of the Deep South and the rich musical tradition that was enriched, if anything, by the suffering of those who sang, and it was true in the First and Second World Wars. When men managed to get away from the front then it was all wine, women and song. During the Depression and Second World War dancing was to swing music with fast beats and screaming trumpets. Swing and jazz music themselves draw on the oppressed cultures of Black slavery and forced Jewish migration and ghettoisation. (The music in speakeasies may have also been a bit of light relief to those mobsters.) Music and dance are a means of release. When you watch a film like *Titanic* you can't help thinking it is more fun dancing below decks with the Irish than making polite conversation over a cup of tea with the aristocrats. People who have difficult lives may need music in a way that those who are happy and comfortable do not.

Oppressive situations stimulate a lot of laughter where it is safe to do so. Girls' boarding schools, particularly when they are more strictly run, have long been home to huge amounts of giggling (when teachers' backs are turned). For working-class Victorians, the music hall was an opportunity to laugh at oppressive landlords, mothers-in-law, bosses and policemen. In the First World War, comic newspapers like the *Wipers Times*, named for Ypres, were created to take the focus away from the prospect of imminent death. When Russians get the chance to take off their public neutral 'elevator face' in private with people they trust, they laugh a lot.[6] In oppressive situations, you need to know who your friends are. On the positive side, this can lead to very strong bonds.

Oppression means being forced to do things. Liberal, relatively well-off countries may avoid this on the whole; however, Augusto Boal observed that in Catholic dictatorships there were cops in the street, while in liberal democracies people had cops in their head. We hold ourselves back perhaps because of the opposite horror, of being left out and left alone, not able to participate at all.

The excluded

For a parent, a highly effective punishment for children is the naughty step, time out, away from the family. Being sent to Coventry by peers feels even worse. At a state level, traitors are banished or go into exile. To be excluded is a punishment, and yet, being excluded can be unintended, a consequence of urban design that addresses one issue without considering the whole picture. The pains of the city are disproportionately borne by anyone who is poor: they are both oppressed by their environment and excluded from what makes city living worthwhile.

The greater the proportion of less well-off people there are in a neighbourhood, the fewer the shared resources there generally are. They are often less well connected and have fewer amenities like public transport links, seats, street trees. They may have to walk long distances to reach a supermarket, or a park, or the school. There may be insufficient resources to get to places like the museum or swimming pool, even if the place itself is free. Those who have less cash have fewer options. Those forced into overcrowded housing and housing in less desirable areas often have to endure more crime, more pollution, more noise. Some are so overwhelmed by noise that they become depressed and lonely. Exhausted from trying to endure the unwanted intrusions, they have no energy for anything else. The World Health Organisation reported that 'at least one million healthy life years are lost every year in the western part of Europe' because of noise.

If there is an adjacent highway, there will be toxic air pollution to grapple with as well and fewer walkable routes. It will be harder to find fresh food, and far too easy to find alcohol and drug dealers, drunks and junkies. It will be more dangerous to walk to school unattended. For the newcomer and for the young adult, the city can be a dangerous place, full of temptations and pitfalls. Research with rats suggests that whether or not a drug-taker becomes addicted depends a lot on the opportunities available. Given an as-much-as-you-can-eat supply of morphine, rats would give the drug a go, but were moderate in their intake provided they had a variety of activities to engage in and other rats to play with. Isolated rats with nothing to do, however, kept coming back for another hit.[7] In small towns and neighbourhoods on the edge of the city with poor transport links and limited opportunities, underage sex, drug taking and violence may be less visible but a greater threat than in the city's bustling heart.

Those better off can suffer too. As Anna Minton discovered in the UK, the paradox for people in gated communities is that the more security they have, the more fearful they are and, if part of the security system goes wrong, they are much more frightened than people who have barely any security at all.[8] Similarly in Singapore, one of the safest countries in the world, it is quite common for people to have at least three locks on the front door. All this security reinforces a sense of threat. The worst thing about this separation between people is that it can raise distrust and dislike between groups that contact, and a bit of sharing resources, would mostly resolve. It is easy to slip into thinking that other people's experiences, challenges and hopes are the same as one's own, but this is not true. Being able to see the full picture makes it easier to make good decisions.

Women in the city

Arguably, most oppressed and most left out over the years have been women, who have been more likely to be playthings than players. They have often been excluded from the fun stuff. The punishment for any woman caught venturing into the stadium of the ancient Olympic Games was to be thrown off the side of a cliff. Greek women did enjoy access to the odd religious festival, but they didn't have much access to politics or learning. The women who did play, as dancers, musicians, actresses or wits were transgressive. Being good meant staying separate, faithful and modest. Rights to participation were greater at some times than others. Early medieval nuns seem to have had higher status than those in the fourteenth century. Running a business as a woman was easier at certain times than others, depending perhaps on how needed they were. There have long been horrendous double standards around sexual behaviour. In a walkable pre-industrial city women would be close to the action but would have to be mindful of safety. In the industrial city a woman may be allowed more freedom but lack the means of getting anywhere. In modern Saudi Arabia it seems that it is more important for women to be able to drive themselves around than whether or not they are obliged to wear a headscarf. Women want both safety and freedom. And yet they are often only offered one or the other, and when decisions are made on their behalf the desire to keep women safe has often justified a loss of their freedom.

The suburbs promised a suitable safe domain for women and children but they lacked interest or excitement. In America in the late nineteenth century, the 'new feminists' railed at the increase in both housework and isolation.[9] Their sisters in London were also frustrated but at least had the music hall, department stores and Underground and rail network. Things got worse after the Second World War. In New Zealand new suburbs were built that were only accessible by car, and much of the public transport network serving other areas was ripped out. Women suffered, particularly those living in suburbs without shops or amenities. To make things worse television programmes would offer another way of living that they could not enjoy. These feelings of isolation through suburbanisation seem to correlate with the rise of protest movements demanding more equal participation, first for women's suffrage, then equal rights in the 1960s.

There is a tendency to make victims responsible for the bad things that happen to them. If only, the argument goes, they had stayed home! There was a series of attacks on women in Australia in the 1980s and it was suggested that there be a curfew for women to keep them safe. This was met by suggestions that as the attacker was a man perhaps men should have a curfew. The policy was shelved. There is a desire to keep violence out of the public realm. It is bad for business. Ironically the more women, and people in general, out and about in the public realm the safer it is for them. The eyes on the street make it less likely for attacks to happen. Women are far more vulnerable to attack at home than anywhere else, and when the violence is unseen it is more politically palatable to cut council spending on couple counselling. It is very hard for women to succeed in public life if they are dealing with violent partners. They stay isolated.

Environmental legislation in the mid-twentieth century reduced air pollution and substantially improved the quality of life in the inner city, as did increasingly cleaner vehicle engines. But it has meant that the haves are more likely to be back in the centre while the have-nots are still stuck on the edges, isolated, unless they have a car. Cars – and labour-saving devices – have both isolated women and seniors and empowered them, giving them access to a greater variety of activities than ever before. When women earn more, and when seniors retire with decent equity and pensions, more opportunities for play open up. And with greater participation and happiness comes dignity.

Kids in the city: Angels

Children and youth can also suffer play inequity and lack of freedom. Up until a few decades ago children were able to learn about city life because they were there, watching, copying, getting amongst it. In countries where children join the workforce earlier this independence is still the norm and children are afforded a greater degree of trust and independence than in many places in the West. Rarely a priority for decision-makers, they seem particularly out of place in the city streets of the English-speaking world. When I moved to live in Central Auckland, I wondered if *Chitty Chitty Bang Bang*'s childcatcher had been through.

A report for the RSPB by William Bird[10] demonstrated how British children's sphere of movement has radically reduced in the last century.[11] One family's generational experience demonstrates the point. George was aged eight in 1919, and was allowed to walk six miles to go fishing; his son-in-law could go a mile to visit the woods; his grand-daughter could walk around her estate and go to the local pool (half a mile), while her son can only stay in the cul-de-sac (300 metres). As one parent in the study put it: 'I don't think that they are allowed to. I don't think that a lot of children are allowed to go and explore and be back at a certain time. I mean I used to roam the fields and woodlands and nobody ever thought anything about it, whereas today a lot of parents would say "Well you can't go down there because you might be attacked".'[12]

Instead of people being encouraged to look out for little ones, children have been taught to be wary of all strangers, while adults, particularly men, who are interested in strangers' children are marked out as weird. Evidence of predatory behaviour in some youth organisations underlines that even child-focused activities can entail risk. But there is a danger in removing children from society altogether. The advice of post-war psychologists was that it was more important for a kid over three years old to spend time playing with their friends than it was for them to spend time with their mother.[13] One millennial journalist in Australia wrote an impassioned article about how the words 'stranger danger' had ruined his life, stalling opportunities for him as a kid to go out, do things and meet people.

Statistically more dangerous than strangers are cars, but efforts by parenting groups to improve road safety in the 1970s and '80s (a time when car use massively increased) resulted in hard-hitting advertising campaigns[14] that discouraged parents from letting their kids out at all. Once again, the authorities ultimately put responsibility on the child or parent to prevent injuries, rather than putting any more duties on drivers. Bicycle helmets became compulsory in a number of American states and in New Zealand in the late 1980s and early 1990s, discouraging a huge proportion of cyclists in the process. In Britain, the dangers of cycling were also well disseminated. A nationwide survey of nearly fifty thousand children found that 31 per cent would prefer to cycle to school but only 3 per cent were able to do so.[15]

A century ago, there were excellent public transport systems in many cities around the world, and a very strong feeling that cars were dangerous and driven by obnoxious playboys. The prevailing view was that streets were for people, and anyone who hit a street vendor, child or senior should be charged with manslaughter. As cars became cheaper and offered the thrill of speed and opportunity to their drivers, their numbers on the road kept going up, as did road deaths. Half of the victims were children or youth, and a disproportionate number of adult victims were elderly.

While communities advocated for low speed limits, a sustained campaign in the 1920s by the Automobile Association and the oil industry in America, with the sympathy of Herbert Hoover, then Secretary of Commerce, tried to shift opinion. Tellingly Robert Moses in the 1960s observed that there would be no economy without the automobile. With the dual catch-cry of freedom and safety (and the message of progress), they managed to persuade people that cars were a tool for freedom, and that safety on the roads was the responsibility of pedestrians rather than drivers. Jaywalking became a crime first in Los Angeles in 1925, and the rules set down were turned into the Model Municipal Traffic Ordnance of 1928, an off-the-peg by-law for American cities to adopt if they so choose.

They incentivised reporters to blame pedestrians for getting themselves hurt. To this day, the language of road deaths privilege drivers over any other killers. A person *was killed* by a car, write journalists, as if the pesky car had a life of its own and the innocent driver had nothing to do with it. The AA funded safety workshops in schools, which involved humiliating children who broke the road safety rules. Anyone who crossed the road anywhere but on a pedestrian crossing, it was implied, was clearly not all there.

Attitudes around children's competence have changed with more recent safety-focused legislation that requires parents to provide more supervision. It is no longer possible legally to leave one's children at home or roaming about without making suitable provision for their care. In the 1980s a mother at home in hollering distance might have sufficed on the rare occasions that help was required, but these days most mums work. In America, 'world's worst mother' Lenore Skenazy[16] has campaigned for the right of kids to be 'free-range'. She has come up against the barriers of traffic and regulation, as well as a final pernicious obstacle – neighbours appalled at her apparent fecklessness. Sadly, when something goes wrong in the streets and a child is hurt, it is not uncommon for the parents to be blamed, even when their decision-making is reasonable. If a child does make it to the street or park to play, they may find no one to play with and nothing going on. On the screen, however, is a whole world of opportunity. They can build a city on Minecraft or Sim City! Being online is not risk-free, but these problems are not considered the direct responsibility of governments but of parents.

There seems to be a view that there is no one, except parents, who is responsible for a child when they are not at school or in paid-for care. In contrast, in many traditional societies in Europe, Africa and Asia, it is expected that everyone looks out for the children, and children spend much more time in the real world. In China, festivals offer opportunities for the young and old to produce the event together. In Japan, programmes bring the elderly and children together to enjoy and support each other.[17] Children know they can ask anyone for help, and so enjoy a good deal of independence from before they start school.[18] There is a popular reality show called *My First Errand* in which pre-schoolers head off to the local shop to get something for the household. Send a pre-schooler off shopping in the West, and you can anticipate a visit from social services. This is a shame. Gil Peñalosa, formerly head of parks in Bogotá, Colombia, argues that kids are an indicator species. If a city works for eight-year-olds and eighty-year-olds it will work for everyone.

Youth in the city: Devils

In addition to the prevailing view in the West that young children need to be protected from the world, there is the idea that the world needs to be protected from teenagers. Many people in England seem nervous of kids loitering in hoodies. Why? Perhaps because there are so few opportunities to have any interactions with them. It seems young people are expected to engage in suitable pursuits in their own area, at home, or school, anywhere outside the public urban realm. However, if young people are not considered in planning cities then it is unlikely their needs will be met, and then there might be problems when young people behave like young people. Playing ball near windows will mean at some point glass gets broken.

Contrast the antipathy that seems to exist between generations in some parts of the UK with the multi-generational links in France, Spain and Italy. The young people sit in the town squares, hanging out with their friends until after sundown, sharing spaces with adults. No one seems nervous about each other. Are the kids that different, or is it just the way that they are framed? It may be because continental Europeans are much more family focused and there are more multi-generational events. Children seem more welcome in public spaces, so perhaps by the time they are becoming independent they know people around. University students are likely to live at home. This creates more harmony, but perhaps tends to encourage a more conservative, traditional society that is less innovative? In the Anglophonic world, the transition from teen to adulthood seems to be almost instant. One day you are out in the cold, next you are inside the pub, a fully formed adult (or not).

If children's lives became increasingly managed in the twentieth century, the teenage years had to be substantially reinvented. The minimum school leaving age was raised to twelve in 1899, and it was quite common for many kids to leave school at that age and go to work. After the First World War, the age was raised to fourteen, then fifteen in 1947 and sixteen in 1972. Each time a higher school leaving age was suggested, there was opposition on the grounds that young people without the structure of work would cause mayhem in the streets. There seemed to be a worry that young people would not be able to attune to a life of work if they lived a life of play. What was necessary was to channel their youthful playfulness into some productive activity.

In the Edwardian period, Scouts expanded to keep larrikins (cheeky boys) off the streets to enjoy some quasi-military training (finding something for wayward boys to do always feels more pressing), and strict playground attendants were put in charge of parks. Then there was the expansion of the Boys' Brigade, bands, sporting clubs and church groups. After the Second World War the focus was first to channel youthful energy either into the National Service or into peaceful movements like United Nations Youth, and then came rock music and American fashions – and there was another moral panic.

The Albemarle Report, published in 1960, recommended a focus on youth centres to prevent young people from becoming thoroughly selfish.[19] They had indoor and outdoor spaces, with lots of things kids could use to play with, including gardening and carpentry equipment and sports kit. How they played was up to them. The centres were used by little ones during the school day, by the primary school kids when school was out, and then by teenagers after dinner, for dances, sports clubs, band practices and so on. The idea was that under a kindly eye older children and teenagers could develop practical and social skills, teamwork and selflessness, and learn a sense of responsibility that would prepare them for life. The centres would be voluntary, though, and kids had options. Friedberg called for similar spaces in America.

Colin Ward, who seemed to genuinely like children and young people, argued in the 1960s[20] the city should be a playground for kids, by which he meant that they should have the right to go out, enjoy it and learn skills for life within it, not set apart. He argued that teenage girls making their way to pop concerts and boys to football matches would learn to manage their pocket money, read maps and negotiate public transport. Such a system did assume that teenagers could get to somewhere they were allowed to enter.

Where did the youth clubs go? Universities do offer some of the same opportunities to play at life, and university attendance has massively expanded since the 1970s. Every student knows studying is just one part of the tertiary experience – the rest is to meet people, get involved in activities and have a good time – but this does open up the question of whether all kids should have this opportunity from earlier on. So, where did the Pirate Club that used London's canals go, and the Boys' Brigade, Scouts, Guides and youth centres? Mainly budget cuts, partly childcare regulation. Libraries and youth centres are shut, playgrounds closed due to insufficient maintenance and parks sold off. This is particularly tragic, as their loss correlates with a rise in violence and antisocial behaviour.[21] There are not that many youth centres around in the UK with programming that is planned in collaboration with kids (never mind run completely by them). Bearing in mind that teenagers aren't allowed into pubs or music venues by themselves (and in some areas are not welcome until they are over twenty-one or twenty-five), this means there are often very few places where teenagers are welcome. When there are fewer opportunities to work, we actually need play more. Playing keeps up health, skills and leads to working. Otherwise there is less to do and there is less hope, which can lead to a rise in mental health issues: drinking, drug abuse, depression, anxiety, unwanted pregnancies and violence.

Fear of crime, and criminal young people, has allowed the security industry to expand in the UK. Gated communities and defensive architecture are becoming more common – they are cheaper to insure, but more expensive to build. One could ask if all this is worth it. The great majority of burglaries are conducted on impulse by people who are high on drugs and happy to jump over the fence.[22] Counting CCTV cameras reveals London is the third most surveilled city in the world.[23] The aim is to keep the criminal aspects out, but putting gates up everywhere limits access to what could be enjoyed by all – like playgrounds and sports fields on school grounds – and turns kids into criminals. Play is either designed out, with skateboard nobs on walls and benches, or expressly forbidden. Forbidden behaviour might include loitering in smart shopping areas without buying anything, sitting in a playground meant for a different age group or skateboarding in an unpermitted area. It seems unlikely that they are trying to draw attention to themselves, but simply looking for a place to relax and do something they enjoy with their peers. In parts of Australia, kids have a curfew to lower youth crime. It is notable that crime levels are a good deal lower in Europe, where there is a good deal less defensive architecture and a lot more shared space and multi-generational socialising.

For some children in the UK, this leaves few permitted options, and transgressive play may well be the only sort of play at all. In *Ground Control,* Anne Minton[24] relates the story of a kid who ended up with an antisocial behaviour order for being a passenger on a joyride. This meant that any breach of the order became a criminal offence. The boy ended up getting banned from the housing estate where his own mother lived – for playing football. The poorer an area, the less there is for kids to do in the public realm and the more suspicious people are of kids who are doing nothing at all. The less they have to do, the more they want to do something exciting, and when they do transgress, the more likely they are to be treated harshly by the system. Understanding why joyriding may be appealing doesn't make it any less of a bad idea, but we do need to meet kids' need for exciting play.

9

Conceptualising the city as a game (that is good to play)

A city could be described as a strategic game – a very complex, multi-player, strategic, spatial game in which there are numerous projects going on at once, with different goals and rules defining them, various challenges to negotiate, beginning and ending at different times. At its core the overriding goal of the city may simply be the desire to keep going; to attract people to live there and to keep the economic wheels turning. Ongoing monitoring and feedback is essential. To ensure the game attracts players, it should be good to play. This may mean houses above the water line, work opportunities, decent pay. People must be safe and feel safe and get what they need, water, food, transport, homes, places to bring people together for economic and social exchange. To be happy and healthy, with morale high, requires natural spaces, plantings, arts, sports and events. Survival and joy.

If the city is a site of multiple projects and games, then there must be rules of engagement that allow it to function in myriad ways that optimise wellbeing and happiness. All of us have individual goals and rules (some universally shared, some cultural, some personal) that guide (and limit) us as we try and lead a good life, whatever that means to us. Regulation and codes coordinate building, infrastructure, transportation, public health and business, and ensure enforcement to discourage criminal behaviour and rule-breaking. These rules need to be enforced to send clear feedback to people on what is acceptable and what isn't. Restrictions generate ideas and possibilities in a way that a blank slate does not. Knowing that there will be no exceptions to a rule can save everyone time and resources. The strictly enforced planning rules in Germany and Vancouver have led to structures and urban forms that stand the test of time, while looser, more liberal regimes can end up with more ad hoc developments with buildings of varying quality that arguably creates streets and neighbourhoods that don't cohere or function so well.

A desire that urban projects please citizens is not new. The ancient cities buckled under temples, piazzas and monuments designed to impress. It was perhaps only with post-war modernism that an ideology of equality, efficiency, individualism and accessibility held sway. The focus on certain key measurables encouraged a streamlined vision of progress – never before had such dramatic changes taken place so quickly. It came at a cost that was highlighted by the new urbanists, Jan Gehl, Wally White, Christopher Alexander, Jacob and Appleyard. When the city is designed to be good for play, it should offer sensory pleasures, surprises, excitement, challenges, time and space for human encounters and improvisation, as much as movement and progress. This is now being recognised as important by city leaders. Counter-intuitively, perhaps, electronic systems are now helping provide the data to shift the way we do things to make cities more playable. It makes it possible for citizens to feed back to cities what they value, by showing what they actually do in them, through transport data and social media activity.

Of our own projects some make progress, some don't. Progress can be defined as the accumulation of wealth, fame and glory, measurable contributions to the greater good, or counted in friends and memories. A competitive city rewards competence and good offers, and celebrates mastery (in the arts, in business, in cooking). There are huge financial rewards for a few, but a good city also offers everyone opportunities to enjoy it and to contribute to it. When people play in a city's public spaces in innovative ways, they are redefining what the city can be. Whether kids are competing with each other to do skateboard tricks or practising crazy dance moves in a public square, they will find a delighted audience, without a winner ever needing to be defined.[1] The rules are ambiguous and evolving. A good game, and a good city, finds a balance between structures and improvisation, between rules and disruption, between old and new.

Cities are generally tolerant about how people live – or at least more tolerant than rural areas, because they are usually more diverse. And they are often inclusive. Progressive tax systems and/or a culture of philanthropy can ensure that everyone has access to parks, libraries, sports fields, art centres, festivals and places to connect, play and experience new things. Even back in Roman times, there was an understanding that however unfair people's incomes, however meagre their private space, people needed circuses as much as bread. There have been times when this view has been considered frivolous. However, when civil servants asked Winston Churchill to consider reallocating arts funding into the war effort, he refused, because otherwise, 'What are we fighting for?'

Though leaders have tried to quash sport, the arts, comedy, playfulness and freedom of speech over the years in the name of religion or ideology it is hard to find a holy text or manifesto that prescribes such cruelty: restrictions on play, whether it be poetry in Communist Russia, or women's sport in Afghanistan, indicate lack of confidence and competence. The repurposing of a sports stadium as an execution ground is so shocking because it is so entirely against the spirit of the place. Dictatorial regimes acknowledge and fear the power of play and seek to control it. Preventing access to play for any group in society is the canary in the coal mine for the breaching of civil rights, while conversely the opening up of arts and sports to more people can herald greater tolerance and inclusivity.

There is a value in laughter, even though it is sometimes unkind. Comedy opens the mind to other perspectives. The quips may be in favour of or resistant to change, and the stakes are real. The comedy can reveal the hopes and fears of those whose lives are in play. Numerous comic songs and cartoons about women wearing the trousers were shared during the New Zealand women's suffrage campaign. In one, a group of middle-aged women sit in a hall with posters demanding 'Husbands for old maids'. The caption reads 'At the suffragette meetings you can hear some plain things – and see them too!' Other cartoons displayed diminutive men in aprons, surrounded by howling children, as their working wife returns home demanding dinner. Would the softness of women be lost? A series of other illustrations

133

presented the alternative view, that to fear women was ridiculous. The first female mayor in the British Empire was elected in Onehunga (a district of Auckland) in 1893, the year that women got the vote. Elizabeth Yates would sort out the drainage and pay down the town's debt. Life went on and the urban realm changed for the better.

Comedy has its limits. Yates was chairing a council meeting when a joker took out the fuse from the electricity box, plunging the town hall into darkness. Hilarious. The adversarial system in the debating chamber of Western politics often resembles talkback radio, where wit is placed higher than wisdom, but policy-makers will stay attuned to the debates on the radio and in the press. Behind the scenes, if the system is working well, the nuggets of gold amongst the rhetoric are incorporated into new legislation and regulation to make it tighter. The arguing in parliament, in the courts, over the boardroom table, in a comedy club or in the media tests ideas to see whether they might meet both the long-term need for survival and the values and mood of the day.

To get the best results when playing, the city needs a balance of order and disruption. As noted elsewhere, the city is not a fair or equal place, but there is mastery, and everyone benefits from that. The fashions are gorgeous, the coffee is delicious, the restaurants are special, the music transports you. Urban life is competitive: everyone is a player, and everyone is a fan (of some aspects of it at least). The majority of new businesses in the city fail. In a liberal society, losing, devastating though it might be at the time, is considered an acceptable cost for allowing everyone to have a go. The only real failure is to give up or, worse, not to try at all. Encouragingly, the experience gained from testing the market at the sharp end is helpful for future employment. The challenge of leading a business can develop the capacity for courage, wisdom, humility, compassion, imagination, hard work and grit. The qualities, as always, of the good player.

If the game isn't working then the rules need to change. The city is a shared project, and everyone has a part to play in financing infrastructure and in managing space, water and the resources to build. We breathe the same air, and we are subjected to the same noise and pollution. If it is Monopoly, it is a special type, where some families have been playing for generations and own all the greens, purples, reds and yellows, most people are happy with a single house on pink, blue or brown and everyone else is fighting to get on the board. It may be worth following a more regulated Viennese model, with rent controls, secure tenure and far more state housing that is affordable, well designed and without the stigma that it has come to have in many parts of the world. In Vienna the state housing is *so* well designed that it is said that there the rich want to live in housing projects;[2] and in fact 60 per cent of Viennese residents do, making it one of the most equitable cities on earth, regularly winning plaudits for being both beautiful and liveable. Is it worth regulating to disincentivise land banking and using compulsory purchase to build on empty sites? Should there be a tax on empty properties to stop waste? Should we be considering developing areas way above sea level so everyone has secure housing that is not at risk from extreme weather events? This may not all seem that playful, but unless people are secure and unstressed, how can they find the bandwidth to do meaningful work, never mind find time for play?

A city, like a game, has rules and limits. They are full of physical structures (manmade and natural), regulations and cultural frameworks, which inspire play in a way that limitless space and horizons do not. Each city will develop, depending on its culture and terrain, but there are some key structures that seem to be necessary for any good city to function well, wherever it is.

Key places for a playful city

A really fun city has a mixture of what I call keystone places, good linking infrastructure and structures that allow infinite opportunities for improvisation. Counter-intuitively most of these places all have a utilitarian purpose – to shop, to eat, to learn. Play requires other people. It is less effort to find people where they *have* to be than where they might fancy going. Once a friend is found, however, a jolly chat might lead to something else. Seeking out play is to behave like a crab; it is best to approach it in a sideways fashion and always leave a path open for retreat.

The church/community hall

Temples and churches have been at the heart of cities from the very beginning of urban settlement. As religions have come and gone, the buildings have often remained constant. A 'city' in Britain for a long time meant a town with a cathedral. Tall, beautiful feats of engineering and works of art, the physical structures inspire us to goodness and give a sense of the eternal: a small piece of heaven where everyone is welcome and where the extraordinary is possible.[3] Even for the secular, they are quiet oases of calm, harmony and continuity in a busy world (albeit oases with a certain worldview).

Culturally, religions also offer a reference point and a shared value system for people to build their lives around. Pioneer churches were often well attended – more so than at home – perhaps because emigrants were more likely to be religious, because life was harder or there were fewer respectable activities to engage in where one could meet other people. If not directly playful, religious people can serve as a kindly parent offering a listening ear, a manageable penance and a bit of encouragement around re-entering the fray.[4] In addition to their philosophical, educational and spiritual work, religious houses continue to be a social safety net, providing food, lodging and care for the sick, the abandoned and the poor. Some churches are returning to this work, offering up land for social housing projects and serving as community partners. In New Zealand, if there is a volcanic eruption in Auckland the plan for those fleeing the city is to be looked after by the Church of Jesus Christ of Latter-day Saints.

Churches and temples also create a temporal structure for life from cradle to grave. Religious rituals can mark the passing of a day, a week or a year with prayers and festivals, and all the important moments of life: births, confirmations, weddings and funerals. In the city they are a place for like-minded people to meet regularly and create a community.

Some church buildings have been transformed successfully into arts centres. This seems appropriate. An arts centre also increases participation in the joyful aspects of life, allows access to beauty (painting, singing, dancing), and reimagines the world better. Churches also often bring with them church halls or crypts that can be used for meetings, band practice or children's parties, bringing people together whatever their beliefs.

Shops

It may not be glamorous, but one of the key requirements for a vibrant area is somewhere to buy fresh food: a grocery store, supermarket or even a farmers' market. People have to buy groceries, so if you have a supermarket on a high street, it draws people who may have a look in the other shops too. I love supermarkets and always wander around them on holiday, looking at fish in tanks in China, and the huge selection of wine and cheese in French ones. (I accept this may be a bit odd. Supermarkets are easy to take for granted until they go.)

When Hurricane Katrina hit New Orleans on 29 August 2005, the levees broke, flooding thousands of homes and leading to a mass evacuation. It seemed that poorer areas took the brunt of the storm surges to protect the historic neighbourhood and the economic centre downtown. Lower Ninth Ward was one of them. It had a couple of grocery stores, but with the loss of all these households (there were 1577 fatalities in Louisiana[5] – and many more people simply chose not to return) there were insufficient people in the neighbourhood to support a grocery store and the nearest supermarkets were a couple of bus rides away. They were in a 'food desert', a place where branded stores don't open because they won't be profitable. Nine years later local resident Burnell Cotlon created his own shop, making good a derelict old building purchased with his savings from working at fast food restaurants and dollar stores.[6] His first customers cried with joy at seeing some life back in their area. He has since opened a laundromat in the back (with machines gifted by Ellen DeGeneres).[7] The shop is a focal point of the community, and he is a local hero.

In the UK, many villages and neighbourhoods have taken over the running of shops because they know they are the heart of the community. Stores are run by volunteers on a roster, and profits often go back into community projects. As Robert Ashton, author of *How to be a Social Entrepreneur,* told the BBC: 'A shop isn't just a shop to a village, it becomes the hub of the place. It's somewhere for young and old people to meet. People actually stop for a chat rather than pass each other as they drive to the supermarket.'[8] Having fresh food easily available a short distance away from home can make a huge difference to health and wellbeing – without which it is very hard to get through the day, never mind feel the joy. Where shops are not viable a weekly market might play the same role.

The town square

Before shops, there was the town square that was multifunctional. It was the place to share news and proclamations, and to gather and protest. It was the place for the weekly market, which attracted minstrels, theatre performers and comedians. Italians still have piazzas, Germans their marketplaces. Edinburgh has its Royal Mile. With the rise of first shops, and then the proliferation of cars in the twentieth century, town squares became increasingly used as ring roads and car parks – but the tide is turning.

London's Trafalgar Square, huge, and awe-inspiring, was first laid out in the 1840s by Charles Barry. By the 1990s it was choked with vehicles, and the decision was made to restore what had become a fancy traffic island back to its former glory. The road in front of the National Gallery became a grand terrace, with steps and slopes down to a café in the square.[9] Events can now take place – from Russian winter festivals and the Chinese New Year, to British food markets and Summer carnivals[10] – that couldn't before (and it is much safer now for kids to run around and play).

Land in the heart of Fort Worth, Texas, had been set aside to improve the downtown, but for decades that meant using it as a car park. Visionaries in City Hall chose to demonstrate an alternative. A series of events on 'Sundance Square' took place on the asphalt: summer movie nights, farmers' markets, a Main Street Arts Festival and boxing matches. Within two years the desire for a permanent plaza was strong, and it became real. Roads were removed, dining tables proliferated. Shade was provided by trees and 10-metre-high umbrellas. More water was absorbed in the ground, and temperatures reduced in the shaded areas by over 10°C. An average of ten free events are offered each month, stimulating the local economy, and 88 per cent of locals thought the existence of the square improved their quality of life.[11]

For a square to work well, it should be given a shape by surrounding buildings but also be visible, accessible and have a sense of identity. Shade, seating, water and public toilets make the space comfortable and usable. Finally, it needs to be activated – this could be a permanent feature like a *petanque* court (which you see often in France) or a series of different installations. A good space with a bit of structure can be like an ever-changing theatre! In a bustling protected space, the performers (or buskers) will just turn up and activate the place themselves, particularly if the edge is busy with shops and cafés.

School

All schools bring families together, but a decent primary school within walking distance of home works particularly well as social glue. The most important ingredient for play is other people, and school playgrounds, netball hoops, pools and sports fields create a place for kids to gather in and outside of school hours. In Copenhagen, many outdoor play areas are sited in public squares and are shared between urban schools and the community at large, which means they are really well used. These areas benefit from 'eyes on the street' surveillance that discourages bad behaviour and vandalism.

Primary schools often have a programme of events, summer fêtes and fun days, school plays and concerts, and charity auctions that may not always be super-slick but are good fun. In New Zealand schools with better-off kids must rely on contributions from parents, with annual financial donations suggested (and expected), and fundraising events from cake stalls and sausage sizzles to auctions, quiz nights and even the odd disco. Though the system isn't perfect, it does mean that parents pull together and get to know each other. As a structure for community it works well.

As kids get older, the quality of performance on the sports field or on the stage can be high. Senior schools can provide a time, place and a focus for the whole community to get together and have a good time.

This is notably the case in small-town America. Popular TV drama *Friday Night Lights* was based on the true story of the Permian High School Panthers of Odessa, Texas. Every Friday the whole town, it seemed, came out for the football game. The message is that high school sports can hold small towns together even when recessions are biting.[12]

Schools also have useful indoor spaces for adult education or community groups to use, whether it be sewing, carpentry, cooking or computer classes, language learning or political meetings. Adults also want to learn new things and make new friends – and the room-hire money feeds back into the school. Schools always need more funding, so even if you don't have kids think about going along to their events, whether they be artistic, sporting or purely for fundraising. Racial and cultural divides can fall away in the practical effort of maintaining a school and supporting students.

The public house/café/bar

Social meeting/eating/drinking places function well because they offer sustenance first, socialising afterwards. It is perfectly acceptable to have a coffee or sit and eat alone. The best cafés provide marvellous fat expensive magazines to peruse as you do so. They are also places where one can pick up gossip, enjoy a chat with the server, or exchange a few words with a stranger. It is an inexpensive third space (a place that is neither work nor home) where interesting things might happen and where one can be in close proximity to others, without sacrificing one's privacy. A café is the perfect place to cultivate those light ties that can have such a positive effect on health, wellbeing and longevity.

The pub – and its equivalents around the world, from the French corner bar to the Greek taverna to the Japanese karaoke room, and the American saloon – is more playful. The tacit rules of etiquette, the games and rituals, all hold a structure for infinite improvisation. The rules of engagement are tacitly understood.[13] In a group one is obliged to buy rounds and entertain each other in the broadest sense. If one is alone and stands by the bar, it is an invitation to engage with others. If, however, one sits at a table in the corner, it means 'give me space'. Booze and a general mood of conviviality give permission to explore brilliant and not-so-brilliant ideas and perspectives that can be explored further in the morning, or relegated to a moment of madness. Booze can allow people to speak the truth without being held to account. Anyone and everyone who isn't disruptive is allowed in a pub, in stark contrast to clubs. In an unequal world the pub is a great leveller, where high-born and low can mix, have a laugh, buy each other drinks, mark events and instigate them.

A report was done on the importance of the English pub by Tom Harrisson, head researcher of the Mass Observation Unit during the Second World War:

> Of the social institutions that mould men's lives between home and work in an industrial town, such as Worktown, the pub has more buildings, holds more people, takes more of their money, than church, cinema, dance hall and political organisations put together ... [it is] the only kind of public building used by large numbers of ordinary people where their thoughts and actions are not being in some way arranged for them; in the other kinds of public building they are the audiences, watchers of political, religious, dramatic, cinematic, instructional or athletic spectacles. But within the four walls of the pub, once a man has bought or been bought his glass of beer, he has entered an environment in which he is a participator rather than a spectator.[14]

Quite.

Parks and gardens

Gardens and parklands are infinitely restorative and have always been a priority for those who can afford them. In the mid-nineteenth century there was a strong popular movement advocating parks because of their health benefits. Central Park in New York was designed from agricultural land as a pleasure garden. In Christchurch and Auckland in New Zealand, parks were described as the 'lungs of the city' and planted with numerous specimen trees. As the nineteenth century went on, space would also be set aside for football pitches and club houses, tennis courts, playgrounds, bandstands, rose gardens and cricket ovals. There is a temptation to reduce or remove funds for parks when budget cuts need to be made, but parks are essential for a full life, particularly where accommodation is cramped.

It is often the case that newer and less well-off areas have less open space provision than better-off areas, and what there is may be dreary, like the empty lawns around high-rise towers. As Jane Jacobs noted, no one knew who or what they were there for, so they became locations for drug deals and turf warfare. This happened in the Bronx in New York, which by the 1980s was turning into a wasteland. Located between freeways, the neighbourhood was an inaccessible food desert. Junkies stole copper wires that could be sold for cash and property owners were burning down buildings for the insurance. In seven census areas, 97 per cent of the buildings were lost to fire or abandonment.[15]

However, given some time, space and energy (and limited opportunity to escape) people will find a way. Residents in the Bronx (including many Puerto Ricans) set up community centres and gardening collectives so that people could at least hang out together and grow their own food. These led to housing associations, education hubs and political movements. From disadvantage there can be advantages, and working with the physical structures can allow community structures to develop too.

Parks can be designed in the least likely places. In Bogotá, Gil Peñalosa, Head of Parks, cleared land to introduce new parks in the city centre as part of his campaign to raise the dignity and quality of life of those less well-off. Regenerative agriculture projects and community gardens allow the sequestration of carbon and the provision of more nutritious food, but they also result in more colours, flowers and textures, bees and butterflies, and friendships and wellbeing. These can be installed in abandoned brownfield sites, and even empty car parks, as happened in Detroit, or on old railroads, such as The High Line in New York, transforming eyesores into places of delight.

Parks are also sites of play for children who can shape nature to their own ends, creating forts with twigs, hidey-holes in trees, and bowers between hedges and herbaceous borders. Logs and trees encourage climbing. Families might even make their own treehouse or swing, as long as they are sufficiently robust and not attracting anti-social behaviour. When communities get hands-on this can massively increase opportunities for play in any city. The no-mowing movement has captured corners of parks to help produce pollinator corridors, while other community groups have weeded, planted and harvested fruit, herbs and nuts. If people want to plant an orchard on a neglected piece of heath – why not? Are there any food forests in your city? Why not become a guerrilla gardener and get started? If there are, why not go visit them and map them?

The library

The city has always been a place to exchange ideas and stories as well as goods, and while libraries are rarely as popular as pubs they do, for those who use them, open portals to other worlds. In the UK, before unemployment insurance and the National Health Service, came the Public Libraries Act in 1850, with the first free public library being set up in Manchester in 1852.[16] You can tell that this was an empowering development, because a number of MPs were terrified about what it might lead to! To get the bill through, it was watered down. Only large towns (over ten thousand residents) could set up a library, and only if two thirds of the voting population wanted it, and they could only raise rates by 0.5 per cent to pay for it, and that money couldn't go on books ... Enter the philanthropists John Passmore Edwards, Henry Tate and Andrew Carnegie. Carnegie funded libraries not just in America but in the UK and across the world, even in New Zealand. It is interesting to observe that web freedom has also been led by the pioneers of the internet and communities rather than governments.

By 1900 there were 295 public libraries across Britain, plus subscription ones, and there are now many more. What a library is changes over time. Some bookstacks have been replaced with 3D printers, computers, classrooms and citizens' advice desks. The New York library service, in addition to their collections, provides career talks and homework clubs to help people help themselves. Collections are growing online and wifi is being made available as borrowing of tangible books declines. During lockdown libraries brought documentaries, books, podcasts and music to people's homes free of charge – a boon to those unable to afford Sky or Netflix.

The library is also one of the very few indoor places where people can linger for hours without spending anything. As homes get smaller and more people work from home, the library is somewhere to escape to for a change of scene and to be around other people without actually having to entertain them.

The playground

A century ago most kids played in the street: but post-war, with more car-centric suburbs and high-rise buildings, kids were more often steered towards playgrounds. Many playgrounds are insufficiently challenging. As Jan Gehl noted, often the most useful purpose of a regular playground is to denote a gathering space for kids and provide something for them to do till other kids come and a better game can be devised. That being said, for little kids living in apartments playgrounds are needed and some are much better at facilitating play than others. In the mid-twentieth century English landscape architect Lady Allen of Hurtwood noted: 'We give them an asphalt square playground with a few pieces of mechanical equipment and there they are expected to spend their adolescent lives swinging backward and forward on a swing. It just isn't good enough.'[17]

Lady Allen felt she could do better. She had visited Copenhagen in 1945 and seen the first junk playgrounds, inspired by how children were naturally drawn to play on bombsites. She would no doubt have been aware that London children had been up to the same sort of activities during the Blitz. Bits of old structures stimulated the best sort of play. Over the next thirty years she created more than thirty adventure playgrounds (as they were called in the UK) where there were tyres, wood, ropes and all sorts of loose parts that children could play with and turn into houses and structures to play in and on. Some even had access to fire. It wasn't long before every child wanted access to one.[18] She even created an adventure playground for the disabled. They were free to enter and children (including those disabled children) could come and go as they pleased, sometimes using public transport. A few still exist[19] in England, Scotland (Baltic Street playground, Glasgow) and Wales (The Land, Plas Madoc[20]). They are expensive, as play support staff are required, but research shows that no more accidents occur in such places than anywhere else.

Another great playground designer of the same period was Paul Friedberg. He worked in New York in the 1960s and rejected the classic separate swing, slide and seesaw combination. He produced igloos, climbing structures and joined-up elements that could be played with in different ways. He noted that children love opportunities to test, make an impact on and manipulate an ever-changing environment. The successful playground was robust and offered multiple paths and choices of interaction, so that it could continue to offer children meaningful adventures over time. Elements included different scales, changes in perspective, vertigo, balance, sliding, climbing, jumping and sand. He advocated for modular playgrounds that children could build, and rebuild themselves – 'Supervision is essential.'[21]

The play park movement was also big in the 1970s, essentially as outdoor holiday childcare that resisted the confinements of classrooms and playgrounds. All sorts of equipment would go into the park so that kids could play a wide variety of games in nature (for those less hearty there was a tent with books and board games). This idea is now being revived with certain child-focused activities offered for free for a day, and then the equipment is all packed away again. It is a great way of bringing fun to a park without investing in lots of new assets.

Youth clubs

Teenagers sit in an ambiguous place on the sidelines. They may or may not want to join in, but they certainly want to watch what is going on. Young people love elevated positions, sitting on walls or on steps to watch people go by. Perhaps feeling vulnerable or uncertain about how to 'do' adult, they observe from a defensive position. This may unfortunately seem rather aggressive to those walking by. Perhaps they are pretending to be like their elders, either dominating or indifferent and unwilling to engage. Friedberg felt that, 'They need an entirely new place, an enclave of their own where they can find other teenagers – and very often *only* teenagers.' Young teenagers may have different needs from older teenagers, but all of them need a bit of space where they can 'make the rules as well as the sodas'. Friedberg anticipated centres where young people can develop their own programmes of activities that might include sports, theatre, running radio stations or holding dances. 'The checklist of a centre's facilities is less important than the flexibility and freedom built into it. And the building itself is less important than the attitude prevailing in it.'

Around the world all the play experts agree that good places for children and young people to play require some structure and lots of opportunities for improvisation. We are all aware of cities that are in a state of depression in all senses of the term. The ones that get through have some heroes inside that keep up the structures of play, particularly for the young – the towns that retained their brass bands, or the immigrant communities, like in Notting Hill, that set up a carnival, or the youth workers in community centres in the Bronx where street art and street dance (like breakdancing) were fostered. In Auckland the youth club is having a comeback with art hubs for teens who need a place to participate and have a voice. Originally it was intended that young people lead the space, but it turns out they want and need more support. Experiencing good nurturing leadership helps them to go on and become leaders themselves. Shore Junction is a space for youth innovation, creativity and connectedness.[22] Conservative Vienna has opened a space for teen girls where they can explore who they are in a kind, supportive environment. Importantly, none of these spaces is a school. Nor does youth support have to be focused on a centre, as long as needs are met.

Iceland has gone some way in demanding that young people play, and do so in ways that cause them little harm. Parents and schools are asked to sign contracts that demand more attentive parenting and firmer boundaries. Kids must be in at a certain time (10 p.m. in winter,

12 p.m. in summer – so not terribly onerous), and kept away from alcohol. They are asked to consider the wellbeing of other children too. Families are then funded to arrange activities for the kids that they will enjoy. These programmes have reduced drug and alcohol use, teen pregnancy and suicide rates.[23] It has also meant that Iceland has an extremely good football team punching far above its weight for a country of its size. Boarding schools work in a similar way, except that parents are funding others to be attentive, maintain boundaries and offer extracurricular activities, involvement in sport teams, choir, orchestras and so on. There is still time for free play, but not so much that kids get bored. Youth centres may be having a revival in some quarters but they are often led by individuals with a passion for their community.

The home

The home is a place to work, to play and to rest. Balancing all these things can be a challenge, but it is essential if the inhabitants are not to turn mad. There is often one member of the household who is more dominant. The Vancouver Housing Guidelines of the 1970s recommended that everyone have their own room in the house, so they could work (or play) in peace. Kitchens and dining rooms should not overlap with the lounge, otherwise kitchen noise would conflict with the ball game on the television and vice versa. Kids needed their own rooms, or at least places they could do their thing undisturbed. As more people work from home, designs that can separate inhabitants as well as bring people together will be useful. Modular walls that come in and out as required may become a thing.

Homes have long been places of work but they are also one of the most important sites of play. Homes are a place to entertain and hold people together, particularly in the suburbs where other community spaces or cafés are limited. They are cheap venues where people can be themselves. When we are in public, we all put some effort into holding up cultural norms. At home we can improvise and we can fail. We can speak freely, do handstands against the wall and pick our noses. Home is a place to decorate as we like. Homes hold

147

memories. Mass manufacturing made it possible for more and more people to afford things for the home, and making and maintaining lovely homes is an ongoing source of fascination and satisfaction on TV, in magazines and in real life. Resilience and sustainability of homes is an issue. Survival and joy are entwined in the installation of solar panels, water tanks and decent curtains. Homemaking is good for the economy too. Those who do not own their place or have long tenure are at a disadvantage. There is less incentive to make places nice if you might be moved along. Families need decent long-tenure housing. People who are forced to move regularly have fewer opportunities to connect with social networks, and their kids do less well at school.

Private gardens also serve many purposes: a source of food, a bird or pollinator corridor, a leisure space, a privacy buffer, a piece of art. Whether attached to a single home, or a number of apartments facing a shared green space as in Glasgow or London, the garden speaks of survival and joy. In New Zealand gardening is more popular than any other physical activity except walking. Translating the garden so it survives to become a mixed-density compact city is important. It might be done, though, by including shared gardens, walled gardens, roof gardens, green walls, pocket parks, street trees and leafy squares in council urban plans and budgets.

How the home relates to the world outside is essential. A buffer to the street and the public world provides a little distance and privacy, allowing people to control their interactions with others. A porch or a garden path is invaluable. For people in apartment buildings, paths should not go right next to windows, and acoustics need to be excellent so that noise from inside or outside the home does not intrude. The closer people are to each other, the clearer and more solid the buffering needs to be. Cultural norms around not disturbing each other late at night or early in the morning can help. In Switzerland there are rules about flushing the toilet after 10 p.m! Geneva and Zurich are often considered some of the most liveable places to live in the world. Is it connected? Public campaigns against antisocial behaviour like drink driving have been effective in the past. Could a campaign to discourage making a noise late at night be worthwhile?

Linking it all up

The city needs to be linked up, so that people can connect to jobs and each other, but what exactly is a good link? This is a bone of contention. For a certain type of city builder, a good link might be a wide freeway through which multiple people can travel at speed to the centre of a city. They define a successful link in terms of journey times. The language is economic productivity but also the idea that everyone loves their cars, that driving is fun! Where there are low levels of congestion, this can be true, but driving is rarely as exhilarating as the adverts suggest, because of road rules and congestion. As the roads fill up there is pressure to expand the network further. This can mean highways cutting through and ruining buildings and spaces and creating tedious detours for pedestrians.

Another sort of engineer will see a public transport network of trains and subways. They can also see the city in terms of zones, with different sorts of places in designated areas. Home is over here. Work is over there. Shopping is in another place altogether. Trains are great because they are fast, and you can buy coffee and work on them – whoop whoop. Build lots of apartments near stations, they recommend, and it is easy to catch a train.

Both argue for legibility – for those planning and using the system. Consistency in rules, designs, speed limits, road markings and signage all help drivers negotiate the streets wherever they are, and so, in theory, reduce journey times. This is the goal, the great KPI (key performance indicator). Reduce journey times in cars or public transport and the economy will become more productive. Pedestrian journey times don't count for some reason. (It has been mooted that this is down to the power of the automobile and roading lobby.) The cost of this assumption is that this can make all cities look the same, like airports. Also, when roads are widened journey times shorten justifying the building of more houses further out. Traffic grows again, blocking up the road. Public transport can be crowded and delayed. It is unfun.

On a journey, as in any game or play, some pace is desirable. We want to feel we are making progress. A sense of flow can make journeys less painful even when travellers move slowly. Google Maps diverts drivers away from traffic jams, thanks to the data fed back into it by other drivers, which allows people to keep moving. The radio helps. Public transport, meanwhile, has learned from airports that waiting is significantly more bearable if people know when their ride is coming (and this has been shown to boost public transport uptake massively). In Bordeaux, to encourage public and active transport, a journey planner system was set up to inform travellers which travel mode available to them – bus, tram, car, boat or bike – would be fastest at that moment in time.

If people know they have time to do something else, like buy a coffee, or go to the loo, it makes the journey less stressful and more pleasant. Time offers space for glorious encounters to happen. There might be a brilliant saxophonist busking on the underground, a choir singing carols in the railway station or even some great window-shopping opportunities, but they don't break the flow of the journey – they are highlights on the way, not obstacles *in* the way. In this way, these 'non-places' can start to become places,[24] like town squares, where you can eat and buy things, meet people, shop. This can all matter, because a good game structure allows other games to be built on top: repeated meetings lead to conversations, new connections.

Physical linking up can work in parallel to digital/virtual linking up of all the dots. Michael Bloomberg made his fortune developing data systems, and when he became mayor in New York, he set about creating a department of analytics. By monitoring traffic speeds and foot traffic they were able to re-engineer routes through the city to reduce congestion where needed. Transport cards were useful to speed up journeys for commuters. Not only can they be automatically topped up, reducing the need to queue for tickets, they provide transport agencies with huge amounts of data on where people go and when, which enables better decisions on optimising the network.

Still, city commutes can take a couple of hours each way. The ideal journey time for commuters, according to Charles Montgomery, is 16 minutes. Cyclists, some research suggests, are the happiest commuters of all. How do you gather data for people on bikes or other forms of micromobility? That can be done through data collection, too. The playable cities idea emerged in the UK, in Bristol. It was trying to do two things: make cities work better in terms of getting people around, and more fun so that people would want to live there. They wanted to encourage people to share data on what they were doing. In one project some cyclists were asked to put sensors on their bicycles. The bicycles would blink at other bicycles hooked up in the same way – which was fun – but the main point was to allow city planners to plot their routes to work out the desire lines for a potential cycle network.

Another way to link the city effectively is to have different sorts of places close to each other, so that people can get to most of the places they need on foot. If for children the ideal playground is a meshing of play structures and imaginative meanings that can link up in different ways – the mound that is a platform, a throne and a link to access the rope bridge – then for adults the 're-creational' city 'would be,' as Paul Friedberg suggested, 'crossed with networks of pedestrian-oriented experiences':[25] parks and snack bars, shopping areas and ice skating rinks, theatres and laneways, playgrounds and plazas, workplaces and streets, connecting to the home.

Traffic engineer Jeff Speck[26] suggested a very simple metric for urban neighbourhoods. He argued that liveable cities were walkable ones, and that four aspects were required: walking should be safe, comfortable, useful and enjoyable. People will pay more to live in places where it takes less than 15 minutes to get from homes to shops and amenities; where there are street trees, water fountains and public loos to make people comfortable; where there are well-maintained pavements, slow traffic speeds and short pedestrian crossings to make them safe; and where there are shops, flowers and lovely views to enjoy along the way. Hard feedback that backs this up can be seen by correlating walk scores and property prices. He is describing Florence and Venice, the old parts of Paris and London, Edinburgh, Geneva, Vienna, Kyoto, Manhattan and the smaller cities of Porto, Ghent, Freiburg, Leuven, Itoshima, Guilin in China, Lucerne, Bath, Wellington. All those places we like to visit because they are exciting and fun are walkable!

What is useful and what is interesting essentially depends on the primary purpose of the individual at any given moment, so if you put together all the structures mentioned previously, you end up in a neighbourhood that people want to spend time in. Neighbourhoods will vary depending on who these people are. Immigrant communities tend to cluster in similar locations, but they are most vibrant when they are not separate from the city but interwoven in it, just as the showbusiness, high-end shopping, Chinese and rainbow communities collide in London. Leicester Square, Chinatown, Soho and Regent Street all sit side-by-side. As Jane Jacobs noted, 'A great part of the success of these [vibrant] neighbourhoods of the streets depends on their overlapping and interweaving, turning the corners.'[27]

Creating (or leaving alone) lovely, interesting, different places to linger can be a better way of preventing people from getting lost than broadening roads and standardising signs. Many monuments in Rome were put up for that purpose: to mark where the religious places were, to help pilgrims get around. A sense of place gives a city an identity, a story. Richard Sennett, an urban planner, suggests that to make cities memorable they need to be 'punctuated', as you would a piece of writing, because this gives a place 'the holy grail of urban design . . . places which have a particular character.'[28]

Monuments and statues serve as exclamation points. They are highlights and indicators that you have arrived at the main point. The intersections are semicolons that offer surprises – 'The corner functions as a marker because here the urbanite experiences a shift in focus, a little sensory jolt as he or she adjusts to a change of scale like a shifting of gears . . . you can't really anticipate what's around the corner until you make the move.'[29] The quote mark is the use of street furniture that draws attention to a space and makes it worth lingering in. Street furniture could be chairs, trees, plants, an attractive fountain, or paint or art. If you walk around old neighbourhoods in Paris or Buenos Aires or Lisbon, then it is these points of interest, tucked away in side streets, that keep driving you forward out of curiosity and that help you find your way back home again – like Hansel and Gretel's trail of pebbles.

10

Planning the playful city

One of the appeals of the happy city is that positive outcomes for well-being, the economy and the environment flow together. The changes in Freiburg were led by a desire to improve the economy, Vauban by the environment and Copenhagen to push back against motorways, and all of them ended up as vibrant, walkable, sustainable places that are good for people. But where to start?

City councils can look at the data to help make good decisions. Collating poverty, crime and traffic-accident statistics helps measure progress. Sales data reveals how much money is going through the economy. Foot-traffic counts and transport card data reveal where people go, so as to build a better public transport system. International standards for open space provision or street cleanliness may be set up as benchmarks. Google collects pollution data and one can measure the amount of petrol sold through the pumps as a way to justify a fuel charge.

However, this data is going to be incomplete. Not everything is measured or can be measured. How do you measure journeys not taken by children because the streets are unpleasant or dangerous, for example? And other standards are a bit intangible. A number of 'most liveable city contests' have emerged, but what does 'liveable' mean? The measurements used depend very much on who the results are for. The Mercer Quality of Living survey[1] is designed to help multinational companies that are looking to set up a new branch office assess which cities will be business-friendly and appeal to expatriate workers. Low crime levels, ease of business, cleanliness, good healthcare, general attractiveness of the city and recreational opportunities matter more in this situation than whether a worker on the average wage can get on the property ladder. How do you make the city better for those who already live there?

Removing barriers and providing good transport links for all make it easier for regular people to participate in city life positively and may improve safety for everyone, while also improving quality of life. Medellín in Colombia was a city full of crime. People who lived in poverty on the hillside had to negotiate a long, winding track into the valley for employment opportunities. It was hard to access services, libraries, a good education and jobs. The route could sometimes be dangerous, criminal activity was common. The mayor put local tax money into a gondola and escalator system that brought workers down quickly and safely into the city, and invested in magnificent libraries and shared facilities in the poorer areas. In Bogotá, Mayor Enrique Peñalosa installed a rapid bus network and improved pavements, partly to ease and speed up journeys, but most importantly to treat those less well-off with dignity. His brother Gil Peñalosa put in more parks in poorer areas. This shifting of resources from the wealthy to the poor was a way of allowing more people to join in with the pleasure and the opportunities of the city. Crime levels in both cities plunged.[2]

Be warned, though, that even small shifts can have a big impact, and will be controversial to existing residents. This is not surprising; our chemical systems have evolved to go on hyper-alert when there is uncertainty. We pay attention when our streets are threatened by some new development that will take away our views, sunlight and privacy, and our first instinct is to resist whatever is being suggested. The outsiders – to use the analogy of the kindergarten – come in and take over our play without asking how to join in. There is a better way. To invest in change people need to be excited about what is happening, know what's happening and feel a sense of progress.

Earlier chapters have raised how trialling can be a good way to propose something radically different. The 'Placemaking-by-trial' approach has become increasingly popular in cities around the world. This doesn't mean everything is a success. In Switzerland, different regions have a lot of independence including the right to set their own building code. At one point, one of the regional councils decided to encourage flat-roof construction. When a number of roofs failed, it was clear that was a bad idea. There was some criticism that the central government had not intervened before, but the government's view was that it was OK to allow mistakes at regional level. It served as an example for other regions to consider. This may mean that it demonstrates what *not* to do, but sometimes innovative ideas go really well, and then they can be replicated elsewhere.

When central governments have stepped in to derail a community decision the results are not necessarily better. In the aftermath of the Christchurch earthquakes the council brought in Jan Gehl to lead a community vison-making plan to rebuild the city. The central government had other ideas and stepped in, preferring to create some anchor projects to stimulate the economy. A decade later few have been completed and are being blamed for holding the recovery back. 'They're called anchor,' noted property developer Antony Gough, '[because] they're stuck in the ground going nowhere.'

When regional councils can make decisions that have an impact, they get better at decision-making, just as kids will only learn to cook if you let them into the kitchen. Of course they will sometimes make a mess, but it is only by having a go that they will gain experience and learn. There is some evidence that when life is made too easy for people they are unable to cope when things go wrong. This is the paradox of user-friendliness. The more seamless and easier the experience is for users, the less likely those users will be able to understand how the system works.[3]

Ask residents to play a role in the planning and decision-making in their cities and they will understand better how spaces work and become champions of any change project. Make clear what are the non-negotiables and what is in play, provide expert assistance and then give them lots of time to work things through. This sense of agency can help people to feel connected to their city spaces and to their neighbours, which in turn makes them feel happier, and safer. (And if in the future, systems break down with extreme weather events the better able we will be to shift for ourselves and get by.)

In a test it is best to keep the stakes low. Errors, perceived or real, might terminate a project, so it is advisable to focus on a small geographical area. Investing in good communications so that as many people can feed into the process as possible is important too. If people are and feel they are making a positive impact they will be more likely to support the project. There are lots of useful tools to help people consider how to improve urban spaces. The Place Standard Tool is very good. It looks like a colour wheel and it asks you to assess a place according to various criteria, from safety to local employment, and includes categories like feeling welcome. If people can't answer all the questions they can ask other locals to find out. It does not suggest particular solutions but stimulates the imagination in considering how good places can be. When things go well the results can be terrific, and can bring a community together

One great example is in New York. Janette Sadik-Khan oversaw a transport revolution in the six years after being appointed New York's Traffic Commissioner in 2007.[4] She wasn't afraid of stealing good ideas, and trialling new cycleways and plazas cheaply before making them permanent. Her most dramatic transformation was of Times Square. Times Square had long been a magnet for the crowds, and by 2008 traffic had become so congested that speeds had dipped to around 4mph (or less than 6kmph – they knew because they were measuring it). Meanwhile, pedestrians, who outnumbered car passengers four to one (they were counting them too), were jostled on the sidewalks, held back or even pushed out onto the road. There is a version of road rage for pedestrians, and in Times Square most people were feeling it. What would happen if cars were removed from the space and it became a pedestrian plaza? They decided to find out by installing the first iteration in a day. When road cones are up for months they can be dispiriting – a rapid change, on the other hand, is exciting. But you have to prepare!

Over three months they talked to local building owners and businesses, collected data, planned and computer-modelled alternative transport routes, led a PR campaign and then, at 7 p.m. on the day before Memorial Day 2009, the team started closing off the road. There were deckchairs, live music, tapdancing and free hot dogs. People took photographs of themselves just chilling on the asphalt.

The feedback turned, not on the case for returning cars, but on whether the deckchairs were nice enough. Sadik-Khan's team knew, because they asked and they read the papers, that people wanted to keep this as a pedestrian space. The journey times of cars now taking the alternative route, had, as anticipated, reduced. Success. With a few refining tweaks, the changes became permanent. A similar approach would be taken by many other cities, including at Waltham Forest in London: the neighbourhood is no longer being used as a traffic rat run and is a really lovely place to live.

Sometimes not much change is required. London and Paris are two of the most popular tourist cities in the world. Both have superb public transport, lots of parks and are very walkable, particularly near the centre. Simply by introducing a congestion charge London has massively reduced emissions. Adding bicycle lanes has helped people transition to a lower-carbon lifestyle and move faster, and eased pressure on the roads. Barcelona is built on a grid system. They have created superblocks by taking nine regular blocks and turning them into low-traffic neighbourhoods, channelling the majority of traffic outside them. Less traffic means more place for people, and more space for play.

Shutting streets to traffic has now become a thing around the world. In December 2018, Madrid decided to trial pedestrianising the central city. There was a huge outcry. Some suggested that noisy traffic jams were part of Madrid's culture, including motorcyclists who organised a bike parade in opposition. In the end, most people loved the new arrangement. Crowds of people took over the streets in the evenings in the run-up to Christmas as if it was one big party. On Sunday afternoons, dads and their kids could be seen gliding down the middle of the road on their skateboards. Retail spending went up by 9.5 per cent on the previous December in the central street, and up 3.3 per cent in Madrid as a whole, while pollution levels dropped by 38 per cent for nitrogen and 14.2 per cent for carbon dioxide.[4] The next mayor, who had vowed to restore the cars, found the city had changed its mind, and his efforts were foiled by judges, demonstrators and even the European Court in Brussels.[5]

Is your city playful?

It is easy when finding a new home to consider the quality of the building and the distance to public transport but have a wander around the surrounding streets too. You know if you are in a playful city (or neighbourhood) by considering whether kids over eight years old can go out alone. Is the local culture one that values play and participation? Are there things to do and places to go? Courtyard housing with shared gardens that children can congregate in are good. As are wide footpaths, safe crossings and slow traffic speeds. If the streets are walkable kids can access the amenities designed for them – this will maximise the use of neighbourhood playgrounds too. Children in cities who – by luck or parental good judgement – live right on the edge of a park are more likely to be allowed to play in the park without a chaperone, while a fourteen-year-old in a car-centric suburb may still need ferrying about. The more fortunately situated children appreciate the freedom and the chance to make and develop friendships. They have a better sense of geography, of belonging and of their own competence. They get more exercise.[6]

In Ghent, Belgium, a child-friendly action plan was adopted in 2015. It is led by its own department, with a dedicated play officer, and in collaboration with all the others in council. They worked together to create a child-friendly overlay of the streets. This included reducing traffic access and speeds across the city at the end of the school day, encouraging play streets and retrofitting a 'red carpet' to link homes, schools and play facilities. By January 2020, traffic in the centre had dropped to 27 per cent, while cycling levels are up 60 per cent. They have also installed a number of innovative nature playgrounds and invited classes of eleven-year-olds to come and talk to city officials every week.[7] The kids are happier – and the grown-ups are, too. The city made it into the top 25 small city list of *Monocle* magazine in January 2021.

Where it is necessary for parents to chaperone, adult needs should be met. This means somewhere shady to sit in summer, shelter in winter, water to drink, toilets to use, where babies can be changed, perhaps wifi, perhaps a café, perhaps somewhere to hire deckchairs and outdoor toys. A public barbecue and picnic tables facilitate a meal. Public art works and beautiful gardens are more likely to delight than a bare piece of grass or asphalt. Having a number of activity areas in the same vicinity, targeting different age groups adjacent can be key to encouraging a broad range of people, including family groups, to come.

A playful city must be robust. Paul M. Friedberg noticed, as he built playgrounds in New York in the 1960s, that children would always test the structures around them. They would climb walls and pull fences, not because they were trying to destroy them, but to explore them and test them, to see if they held up. 'We expected children to play everywhere at Riis – among the sitting areas, in the great inverted mountain of the amphitheatre, in the fountain – everywhere. The entire plaza has been designed with permissiveness. Nothing is fragile.'[8] Friedberg was an empathetic man. Where others saw kids hellbent on destruction and wanted to remove recreational areas completely he tried to facilitate a recreational area that would give kids pleasure while also withstanding the pressure they would put on it. People stand on bollards, climb on lamp-posts and skateboard down rails. All these structures need to be strong. People don't play the way they are supposed to! This was particularly the case with teens. Friedberg had installed a quiet secluded seating area for the older people, but of course that was where the teens wanted to go to have their own space.

Quentin Stevens, an urban planning theorist, is an expert on what design elements facilitate play for kids of all ages and he thinks about the city as if it were a theatrical show. 'To understand and optimise the richness of the "place ballet" requires attention to the stage details: to props, to entries and exits, and to the immense variety of acts which discover and engage these spatial opportunities'.[9] Some props were designed expressly for play, like water fountains that shoot out of the ground on splash pads. Others, like street furniture, might be meant for sitting on, but also make great skateboard ramps. If you want a city that lends itself to discoverable moments that are fun to explore, he suggests making the most of paths, intersections, boundaries, thresholds and props.

Paths should be wide, so that other activities in addition to walking can take place, for example the more vertigo-inducing skateboarding, rollerblading, scooting and cycling. If they are away from traffic they will be even more pleasant as people can hear each other speak. Trees and water, like a river or a beachfront, bring in pleasure too. Around the world, from Sydney to Cape Town to London's riverside, there has been a trend to improve access to waterfronts and they become a hub of play with restaurants, bars, museums and art galleries, boats and buskers.

The more richly grained the network of lanes and intersections, the more journey permutations there are, and the greater the variety of experiences and characters you may chance upon.[10] There are so many laneways and paths in the Central Activity District of Melbourne that one can cross just this small section of the city in over a hundred ways, and find all sorts of curious places, people and happenings. The more you change direction, the more opportunities for surprises.

Boundaries that mark the edges of piazzas and squares are often humming. A performer may use the middle of the space, but most of the people will be on the outside, watching. Even where the space is empty, like the middle of a piazza (for example, St Mark's in Venice), the café tables stay on the edge. If a street performer wants people to come closer, he will put out a rope to define the edge of his performance space and demand people sit close to it. Spaces where performers can put on a show, and passers-by can watch without getting in the way of people walking past, allow more opportunities for fun. Teenagers like to watch the world go by while elevated on the edge of them – steps and walls are popular. 'Left-over' spaces can come to life in surprising ways as members of a subculture take them over – for example, the skateboarding pit in London's South Bank.

Stevens identifies the power of thresholds: windows, doorways, grand entrances and gateways. In the 1930s Walter Benjamin, a keen wanderer of Paris, wrote a long piece on the arcades of the city with their bright shop windows that hinted at a more magical world. The entrances to restaurants and bars, galleries and museums are also portals, as are big open church doors, with the rows of glowing candles visible within. Wander around a Japanese city at night and you will find ancient-looking gateways to Shinto shrines. There are lamps and paper prayers hanging in the trees. A gateway can be a portal between a hypermodern and an ancient world.

Props include public art and street furniture. Statues that are on street level and are human-sized are particularly fun to engage with, but oversized children or tiny houses also delight. All artworks, site-specific or not, add a layer of meaning to a place. Street furniture is practical but can also be useful for skateboarding tricks and parkour. Sometimes props travel the world, such as painted cows or theatrical light installations in parks. Enjoy them while you can before they move on. Does your local business association invest in such things? Many do.

Variety and texture, different heights and different scales all open up possibilities too. Stevens asks that builders make their structures generous and robust, noting that people do not play the way they are supposed to.[11] Creating more space than is required allows space for different activities to emerge in the future. Using robust materials, modular elements and some programming allows the space to transform in myriad ways.

Activity: Assess your city

In a nutshell As Jane Jacobs says, the only qualification you need to form an opinion on the city is the ability to open your eyes and look around. Nevertheless, a place tool helps.

Method

1. Download the 'place standard tool' from the internet. There is a good one created by NHS Scotland and the Project for Public Spaces (PPS).

2. Select a public space or two (or three or four) local to you and visit them in turn.

3. When you are on site use the tool to assess the different characteristics of a space.

4. Where a low mark is scored, have a think about what the place lacks and make suggestions.

5. Consider how big an impact those changes might make. Is it worth asking someone else along to assess the space and ask the council for improvements?

Tip Do it with a group of people so you can share ideas.

Variation If you have a good idea to improve a space easily, cheaply and temporarily, then why not have a go? People have painted in cycle lanes and pedestrian crossings. They have installed furniture and planter boxes. One could also light a place differently and do something unusual in the space, like set up an alfresco picnic with hurricane lamps.

Playful cities for everyone

City leaders are aware of the importance of keeping their constituents happy. They invest in lots of projects to ensure that people can participate in the city – through public transport, the provision of libraries and swimming pools and community centres. The venues and city improvement projects that the city prioritises say a lot about the culture of the city. The first rule of placemaking is to start where you are. What city are you?

The joker's City

The city might have a culture that embraces the silly and the unexpected. This may emerge organically; for example, an artist in Barnes, in London, occasionally dresses up as a White Rabbit and waves at people in cars. The business slogan for Austin, Texas is 'Keep Austin weird', while in Los Angeles there seems to be a thing for signs – and not just the Hollywood one. Legend has it that some jokers at the racetrack put up an enormous sign saying WELCOME TO CHICAGO to confuse people flying in. Or the council can take the lead. A jester was appointed by the small town of Conwy in Wales (the first in seven hundred years) for a fortnight in August 2015.[12] Perhaps your city needs a slide at the railway station as an alternative to steps? One such slide, or 'transfer accelerator' as it is officially known, was installed in the neighbourhood of Overvecht in Utrecht, Belgium, in 2011. It allows travellers to get more quickly to the platform when they are in a hurry. It is also simply more fun[13] and gives the neighbourhood a boost. Or perhaps the city should surprise their citizens by funding professional jokers who can transform town squares or parks through lighting and technology to create tricks with shadows and projections?

Rafael Lozano-Hemmer is an acclaimed Mexican-Canadian artist who takes over public spaces and completely reinvents them. Members of the public who stray into the space may find themselves projected at enormous size onto a wall, or very tiny into a sandbox. In one show in Trafalgar Square, he created an illusion in which people seemed to be in the ground, dancing, waving and interacting with the passers-by walking over them.[14] Other artists have been involved in this sort of lighting trickery. In a project called 'Shadowing',[15] people were filmed from streetlamps, and their movements were projected back onto the ground to manifest as shadows that, like Peter Pan, had become detached from their bodies.[16] Mature adults walked past the lamps again and again, trying to work it out. This sort of thing was called a 'happening' in the 1960s. Performers would roll up some-where, perform a dance, or play the cello on a traffic island, and then disappear again. Their work delights and inspires because it is so unexpected. It is easy to have one's senses turn off in the city, but a happening switches people back on.

The kinaesthetic City

Of course a city needs some stadiums, sports fields and courts, but there are other ways to ensure that people can get fit without the major construction price tag. It may be better value to reduce traffic speeds, install cycle lanes or pedestrianise plazas and encourage everyone to move around a bit more as part of everyday life. The road network makes up the largest public space by area, and that can be repurposed for special events. The London Marathon is more interesting for spectators and participants than a run around a track umpteen times, the Tour de France more thrilling than an endurance test in a velo-drome. When Enrique Peñalosa became mayor in Bogotá, Colombia, he established an open-streets day for everyone to get moving. Cars were temporarily banned, so people came to work not by public transport but active transport – foot, bike or rollerblade. Kids could race around and not worry about traffic. People who needed a little nudge to get moving felt exhilarated. It was so popular that Bogotans voted to make it an annual event and wanted to remove all private cars from rush hour by 2015.[17]

Similarly, gym equipment can be set up in parks, either in one place or around a track like circuit training, so that people can get a full workout in the open air. In Madrid, they put exercycles next to the children's playground, so that parental supervisors can enjoy a bit of physical exercise alongside their kids. In Auckland, private companies offer adrenalin junkies a bungy jump off the bridge, or an opportunity to climb around or leap off the telecoms tower on a zipline!

But there is an even lighter and faster version – a community hall can be transformed into a gym or a theatre if there is enough height, sufficient storage and foldable chairs. And so can a market square. Yoga alfresco not only requires less building upkeep, but is also nicer. Repurposing existing space for other sports is quite common. The lake used for swimming in summer is used for ice skating in winter. Gymnasiums are covered in different-coloured tape to mark out different courts for badminton, netball, indoor football and kabbadi. Colonial Australians prioritised cricket, but wanted a game for winter that would keep cricketers supple and fit. They adapted a version of football that could be played on a cricket ground – and so Aussie Rules was born.[18] For kids, a playground with reconfigurable elements means that it can be enjoyed in lots of different ways. If play elements were stored onsite, the changes could be put in the hands of the kids!

For the council looking to facilitate play on a low budget, a cheap and easy way is to stop cutting the lower limbs off trees in the park so that kids can climb them, and to be tolerant of the rope swings that are put up by parents when no one is looking. As long as the swing is sufficiently robust and safely tied on to a wide healthy bough, the risk is probably quite low. And they are FUN. This may seem radical, and to blithely ignore health and safety considerations, but some health experts are starting to rethink what is safe long term and are coming to the conclusion that the risk of an odd knock is preferable to a whole life sitting down developing anxiety disorders.[19] Children need to learn to manage risk. As Bernard Spiegel puts it, '[we] need to understand and value risk: life is unutterably dull without it.' He is co-author of the *Managing Risk in Play Provision* implementation guide[20] endorsed by Play England, Play Scotland, Play Wales and Playboard Northern Ireland.

The explorer's City

Explorers value variety. They enjoy special places that bring together many curiosities, like the zoo, the aquarium or the stardome. The best places for the curious are those that have changing collections, like well-run art galleries, museums, libraries, cinemas and even shops. Aquariums, conversely, are very hard to change, and people rarely visit them more than once. We probably don't need any more aquariums. Food can be a way in to a different culture. Rumour has it that back in the 1990s, New Zealand, hoping to slow down the numbers of people emigrating, started offering work visas for immigrants who wanted to set up ethnic restaurants. If people want to see the world, the thinking might have been, let's bring the world to them!

Cities that are good for explorers are in touch with their heritage, where every stone tells a story – like Rome – but they can also embrace the new and high-tech – like Singapore or Dubai. The Paris Louvre combines a stone Baroque palace with a glass pyramid, incorporating opposites within one location, and that makes both structures more interesting (in my view) than each would separately be. Urban spaces are pretty, urban spaces are gritty. New York is the Empire State Building *and* Central Park.

An explorer's city rewards exploration with surprises and delight. They are like advent calendars with all sorts of different scenes behind the doorways. They have lots of streets and lanes and are good to walk about in. Just as we need variety in play to have a whole life, cities need contrasts, between suburbs and between buildings. Interesting streets are those without looming gaps, yet even the odd gap is good because it can be filled in unexpected ways. Playful cities are quiet, pedestrian – you can hear yourself think. Playful cities are also loud, intense and full of machines whizzing around, like a steampunk fantasy or the Los Angeles highway system. Play is about vibrancy and lots of people, but it is also fishing at the waterfront on a quiet Sunday afternoon or sitting in the nave of an empty cathedral.

The collector's City

The great cities are full of extraordinary collections of treasures. Some are public, some private – and some works of art move between public and private view (better perhaps than storing pieces in dark Swiss bank vaults). These cities are naturally the wealthier ones with more than they need. And yet collections have value. Collections of historical relics allow us to learn from people across time and cultures. The more people we can learn from, the more we know and the more competent we become. Libraries, galleries and museums bring together enough objects and ideas to allow people to join the dots regarding what we know, which can help the rebuilding of a culture when it has been lost. The items themselves can also have ongoing value. Zoos have resupplied animals to the wild after disasters in the natural world. Wallabies, collected in the nineteenth century and kept on an island in New Zealand with other exotic creatures, had become pests by the twenty-first century. They were rounded up and returned home after their cousins in Australia succumbed to disease – a win for all.

In the nineteenth century, knowledge was channelled through libraries and museums, shored up in the great cities, but the greatest repository of information now is the internet. That the World Wide Web is free for all to access is one of the greatest democratic gifts of all time. New technologies are allowing new discoveries, and for information on these discoveries to be shared with peers and the public via museum websites. Meanwhile, QR codes in real places make it possible to collect together all sorts of information relevant to that site, from historical events to geographical features to guidance on collecting seeds.

The value of collections for survival is perhaps most clear in the proliferation of seedbanks. In more recent years seedbanks, gene banks and germplasm collections have been held in carefully controlled laboratories around the world. There were more than one thousand known seedbanks in the world in 2013,[21] and Kew Gardens is one of the finest. Kew claims to hold 10 per cent of the world's biodiversity in south-east London, including all (bar the most difficult to store) of the UK's native plants. They have one billion seeds from ninety-five partnering countries. (Seeds are replicated from others that stay in the country of origin.) Visit the Millennium Seed Bank building and you will find raised beds on the parterre outside that replicate eight threatened habitats of the British Isles. Seeds from these habitats are stored inside to preserve them for future generations.[22]

The storyteller's City

A storytelling city values its heritage and offers ways into the past by keeping its valuable historic structures as well as providing information provided in museums and books. To stand in a Victorian train station or an ancient mosque is to learn something about the values of the past. A great old city will have been immortalised in fiction, on screen or in print, and yet these stories will only have scratched the surface of the gamut of experiences of those who have walked these streets. To really understand historical overcrowding, you need to be able to walk through a tiny old cottage and try to imagine how its fourteen inhabitants would have fitted in. Cities have gone through glorious periods and difficult ones. The stakes have always been high; there have been good choices and bad ones. The monuments to various sorts of failure – traitors' keeps, records of cholera outbreaks, polluting chimneys and memorials to the Holocaust – are as valuable as the fountains, opera houses, town halls and libraries. These old structures and stories speak to us, remind us of how we got to where we are and can serve as a guide for decisions made today. Evidence suggests, too, that cities that maintain their heritage benefit from an economic advantage, and not just from tourism.

Sometimes what is needed is greater insight into what is already in front of our eyes. Historic buildings and structures hold secrets. Engraved street tiles, plaques on buildings and history boards can relay information about and tell the stories of the streets, statues and landmarks from different perspectives. Councils can encourage tour guides to lead walks around the city while telling the history or explaining the geography, the flora and fauna, or local art. Local heritage festivals and readers-and-writers festivals are opportunities to tell more stories. There are always more layers to uncover.

Stories need to be continually written. A storytelling city needs its magazines, newspapers, radio stations, TV studios and film makers, as well as a fast broadband network, so that anyone can tell their story, write a blog, record a podcast, upload a video or post a picture. Council magazines are old-school but serve a valuable purpose in communicating what is going on in a way that everyone can understand. I have already talked about how people can share data with councils to help them plan, but information can flow both ways. In Tel Aviv, Israel, residents' cards ask citizens to share some of their personal data, including about their interests. They are then provided with information on services that are likely to be of use to them; even dogs can get their own tailored recommendations for a good day out. There were high hopes that this could happen across many cities, but this work has stalled a little because of nervousness over data collection limiting the cross-referencing that could tailor information to people.

It is less controversial – and very practical and helpful – to feed information about the city's systems and services back to citizens, so that they can make good decisions over what they do. It was suspect smells and nervousness around swimming at city beaches that stimulated the creation of a Safeswim app in Auckland.[23] The pollution modelling identified in real time whether it was safe or not to swim at a beach. The problem was far worse than feared and galvanised the raising of a targeted rate to renew the wastewater infrastructure. The app technology has now been sold all over the world. In 2020, a new data collection system was funded that would measure king (high) tides in order to provide some benchmarks around sea-level rise that everyone can see.

Over five years, Google Street View cars have gathered data on pollution across cities around the world which has been shared with academics. If this could be represented digitally, on the spot, I wonder how much that would shift feelings towards traffic? The Department of Conservation has set up a number of livestream webcams to allow people to follow the progress of baby penguins and albatross. It is easier to care about nature when one can see it.[24]

The competitor's City

Just as you need enough local residents to make it worthwhile putting in a supermarket, you need a sufficient number of successful people if you're going to fund a culture of luxury with rooftop bars, fine dining or shark ponds. The competitor may be in business, the arts or politics, but successful people attract other successful people with whom they can play or do business – on superyachts and at premier events. The lines between play and commerce are blurred. You know you are in a competitive city when the cocktails cost more than a pair of jeans.

The capitalist model is based on the idea that competition makes things better for everyone, and that everyone (with the stomach for risk) has the opportunity to play. A competitive city that works for its residents has a thriving local economy and meets the global market. The competitive city can also be a playground, a battleground and a celebration party. It has everything a city should have and more: drama, novelty, celebrities, excitement, sensation. The flipside to this system is that these are places where many people lose and many struggle to stand still. This is imbalance in the extreme – vertigo writ large. Playful, yes, but like Russian roulette. To look at pictures of welders having a break, sitting on iron girders multiple floors above street level, is to be reminded that New York was built without a safety net.

The desire to win can drive decisions that are irrational. A number of men have wanted to build the tallest building in the world, even if it makes no financial sense. The Chrysler Building's roofline was redesigned during construction to include a 125-foot spire, simply to beat the Bank of Manhattan building next door. Eleven months later, it was surpassed by the Empire State Building. The latter couldn't fill its office space for years, neither could the Twin Towers, nor can the Burj Khalifa in Dubai.[25] In a truly competitive city some people must lose – and even wins might not be entirely satisfactory. You could say that in a liberal city people get to choose their own form of oppression, and in a competitive liberal city, they have the right to lose.

In a world with infinite resources these follies might not matter, but when so much effort and so many materials get directed into big projects over more modest ones which might bring a greater good, one does question whether it is for the best all round. Some decisions seem reminiscent of the potlatch. The potlatch was a competition in some ancient Native American cultures in which participants (male again) competed to give away or destroy their wealth, until much of their resources were gone. First to stop was the loser. There are tales of wives being killed as they attempted to remonstrate.[26] The game seems bizarre. Who would destroy their resources for short-term glory? And yet . . .

Success is put down to skill, but it belies the reality that luck plays a part. Not because people in the city don't work hard or have qualifications, skills and talent, but because there are more people with qualifications, skills and talent who are prepared to work hard than there are desirable jobs. Cities and countries can be lucky, too. Australia's success at avoiding a recession after the Global Financial Crisis of 2008 was in large part due to the amount of minerals it had under the ground. While the minerals may have been close to Perth in Western Australia, the knock-on effects on the rest of the economy also supported Sydney, Melbourne and Canberra. The casino is the most visible marker for gambling, but there has nearly always been gambling of some sort in cities: at the race track, in the pub, in the gaming arcades, in the stock market, in the bank. Picking winners is what all investors are trying to do, after all. It is interesting that the cities where there is a greater cultural appreciation for the value of luck or fate can often be kinder to the poor. Catholic, but briefly Communist, Vienna, has a much stronger, and more expensive, social safety net than neighbouring Germany.

The director's City

Local politicians don't have it easy. Corruption in the past has tainted city hall, as have accusations of inaction. They are criticised for raising rates and for cutting costs and corners. Many, however, have wanted to get something done, whether preventing disease by sorting out the drainage, improving health by putting in gymnasiums and parks, or creating joy with events. Mayors and civic leaders have long wanted to leave behind a grand legacy project. In Ancient Rome, these were often grand new piazzas, columns and statues. The Emperor Diocletian, however, installed a palace with an extraordinary water supply system (while it was anticipated that ten thousand people would live in the palace complex, there was enough water to supply 175,000 – the system would not need to be upgraded for two thousand years[27]).

In more recent times, mayors have pushed stadiums and arts centres, monumental infrastructure projects like subways and desalination plants and, often, waterside regeneration projects. They are nearly always extremely expensive and ambitious, and generate enormous amounts of excitement from those involved in them. This is playing the city at a grand sale. However, these public works do become part of the city's treasures that everyone benefits from. To get buy-in to transformation, a playful event can help. The Olympics has galvanised change in London, and the America's Cup has done it for cities in Australasia.

Fremantle in Australia had been hit hard financially in the 1970s and '80s. The old buildings were decaying and were likely to be demolished. However, when the Australian team won the America's Cup in 1983, a decision was made to restore and enhance the town, regenerate the waterfront and sell itself to the world.[28] The world came in 1987, and with the huge parties on the boats and off them, tills were set ringing that turned the town's fortunes around. It seemed that there was profit in pleasure. When New Zealand won the America's Cup in 1995, Auckland followed the playbook.[29] Gleaming yachts replaced ageing car ferries at the city centre wharf, and new harbourside bars, restaurants and residences were built, most with sea views. Once again, wealthy boaties from around the world came to enjoy the competition, but also to party and network. While the competition was prima-facie elite, the ongoing benefits of a more attractive waterfront were widely enjoyed and there was a terrific return on investment by the council and private developers who had made the vision real. The deadline of a global event incentivised those involved in the project to complete on time.

This idea that you had to spend money to make money was reinforced by Richard Florida and his influential book, *The Rise of the Creative Class*. Cities needed great, welcoming, places with regenerated waterfronts, activated boulevards, terrific restaurants, a vibrant nightlife, low crime, great art and events, and easy access to the great outdoors for fishing, hiking, surfing and so on. City councils invested in reports on creative cities – like Bogotá, Cape Town and Brisbane – that had kickstarted their economies by regenerating their town centres, to see what might be worth copying. There has arisen a plethora of urban journalism, with established publications like *The Guardian*, new magazines like the *Monocle* and multiple online magazines, all sharing a vision of what the city could or should be. Meanwhile, NACTO guides, aimed at the professional market, document street designs that work best. Some city builders have copied existing towns in their entirety. Hallstatt in Guangdong Province is a replica of picturesque Hallstatt in Austria, a UNESCO World Heritage Site. It is not the only example in China,[30] which boasts numerous replicas of both European and Asian sites, from Rome's Colosseum to a second Great Wall of China. It is not just a desire for Western architecture but, it is argued, an assertion of power and capability. Anything you can do, I can do better. It sounds a bit crazy, but the British weren't far off. What is neo-classical architecture in England but a copying of the aesthetic of Ancient Rome? Then, as now, talented architects and planners shared ideas and moved around. Buenos Aires was laid out by the same planner as Haussmann's Paris, and you can tell. The form of the city also hinted at a certain way of life that its residents aspired to enjoy.

The artist/creator's City

Cities are highly creative places in many ways. Art and objects, goods and services, businesses and bold new ideas are created all the time and offered to the world. And cities themselves are constantly being re-created. Structures and infrastructures are built and renewed. City building seems to be one of the most popular game themes ever, from Monopoly to the Sims. Many cities are works of art in themselves – beautiful environments that bring together water and stone, timber and parkland. Philanthropists also love grand projects like stadiums and performance arts centres, even though they cost a fortune. There is something exciting about the idea of making one's mark.

However, destroying cities simply for the sake of change may be a mistake. Robert Moses, the American master builder, conceptualised the city on a grand scale. Moses started his career in the 1930s, opening up the waterfront for more parks and playgrounds for children to play in, and reducing congestion on the narrow streets by building freeways around the edge of Manhattan as well as connecting bridges between there and other parts of New York. After the war the highways were going through the middle. On a map of New York, a freeway joining places up seems simple and effective, but when beautiful Penn Station in New York was destroyed in the name of progress, some travellers felt that whereas before they had felt like gods walking through the fine halls, they now felt like rats. Cities that were built when they had been centres of global trade are so beautifully built and crafted, and use such fine materials, that it is unlikely that they could be replaced with anything half as good.

Many city leaders have seen themselves as artists, but Raivo Puusemp, the mayor of Rosendale, New York in the 1970s, actually was one. A conceptual artist from Estonia, his work centred around the idea of agency. He created participatory works that were designed to lead people into taking the obvious next step that then completed the work. Aware of the manipulation underlying his 'influence pieces', he moved away from the artistic sphere and into politics, where influence and concept came together more naturally. Rosendale was grappling with infrastructure issues and high debt, and Puusemp led the community into disestablishing themselves as a separate entity, and into becoming part of the next town (also, weirdly, called Rosendale). His artistic practice turned out to be ideally suited to bringing people to a place, figuratively, where they could accept the reality of their situation and take that next step to agree what they needed to do. He secretly saw his role as mayor as a public artwork – and, after his resignation, published a booklet called *Dissolution* that documented the process. For those concerned, the evidence suggests that he was a very popular mayor.

Other examples of artists making it into office include Bogotan mayor Antanas Mockus. He wore a Super Citizen cape and replaced traffic police with mimes. Vaudeville star Jimmie Walker was mayor of New York during the Depression. Arguably, the low-status clowns and quirky artists do a better job than the glamorous showmen with an adoring fanbase who are good at selling a line. Jimmie Walker had his own way of playing the city: he would roll in at noon, see if there were any cheques for him and then go off for lunch. He escaped corruption charges by moving to Europe. Experimental artists and clowns may be better at seeing what is in front of their eyes, and presenting an alternative vision and encouraging others to do so too.

The best cities are complex and contradictory

I stand by everything I have said about play and the playful city, but the opposite is true as well. And most cities would be a combination of all of the aspects above and one could pick the same city to demonstrate very different sorts of urban realm. The idea of the mixed-use mid-rise neighbourhood is idealised by many new urbanist planners, but the opposing idea of zones and sprawl is still common. In mid-twentieth-century New York, this view was pushed by acolytes of Corbusier, including Robert Moses, but it was devastating at a local scale, leading to the removal of entire neighbourhoods and marooning poorer communities, like the Bronx, within flows of fast-running traffic. Moses' parks were big and at the edge of the city. Negotiating the changes and leading a full life required a car. Jane Jacobs advocated a variety of amenities, like gardens within walking distance, where she would find her neighbours and develop relationships. The city should be built, in her view, by the people who lived there. She managed to save Greenwich Village, which has more walkable characeristics. The danger with her approach, argues Richard Sennett, is that there are no great leaps forward, no Eiffel Towers and no public transport systems, because of a desire to protect what is already there. The most playful cities are at the edge of what is possible, slightly off balance perhaps, as they step into the future.

Great cities need both balance and imbalance, towards the large scale and the small scale, the old and the new. We like to live in urban villages that are different from but connected to each other, but the city also has to have a regional outlook and ensure that there is enough density to support its life and movements – and the supporting infrastructure. Great cities are sites of rupture, where new ideas are allowed to replace the old, but ideally not all at once. This doesn't necessarily mean that people are going to enjoy larger cities more than smaller ones. There is a good deal of evidence that suggests people are happier in the second tier of cities, where the stakes are a bit lower and people have more time to play – like Ghent, Glasgow or Bristol. The challenge we all have is to find the place that works for us, that is fun, sociable, and at the right level of challenging. Does it excite you to be a big fish in a small pond, or to accept and relish the variety and challenges of an inland sea? Neither is better.

Sometimes the best ideas for cities come from the frontier. Tech writers Cliff Kuang and Robert Fabricant argue that it is no accident that Silicon Valley is in California, where New Age thinking in the 1960s and '70s met shaggy-haired pioneers of computing in and around Stanford University. They imagined other worlds and lived them. They shared information with each other and committed to sharing the information they found for universal benefit. They weren't competing *against* each other but *in collaboration* to solve problems in order to make awesome ideas work in reality. They demonstrated that there are different ways to live happily, different ways to create success and different ways to connect in virtual worlds. Communes and sustainably minded squatters established themselves all over the world in the 1970s (including, as we have seen, on the outskirts of Freiburg in Germany, that led to the building of the Vauban).

The hippies may have slid out of view with the ruptures of the 1980s, but a lot of their ideas have become part of the furniture. We don't have to conform any more. Rather, we have to find our own unique selling point to succeed in the modern world. 'Be yourself' is not easy advice ('but how?!'), unless you construe it as doing the things you enjoy while staying true to the values you espouse. And this might turn out well. Spend your days surfing? You may end up being sponsored. Want to explore the potential of the World Wide Web? You may end up running Microsoft. Want to game all day? You may be picked for the e-Olympics. Want to be a mermaid? There is a job in that, too. For all of us, it may soon be possible to experience the city through virtual reality and live anywhere. What it means to run a city would radically change as road-widening projects could be abandoned and chunks of cash would be invested instead in giant servers to power a video-game-like urban realm. We would be in the realms of Spielberg. Ready, player one? Perhaps not yet.

Ambiguous structures and improvisation

In the city, there are so many new experiences to engage with – escape rooms, linear parks, giant ferris wheels and augmented reality – and a lot of old experiences taken to the next level – with epic architecture, galleries of modern art, larger stadiums with retractable roofs, and elevated monorails. They have to take space from somewhere, and new permanent structures are expensive. What to do? One approach is to facilitate a large number of activities in the same space. Placemakers call it the Power of Ten. The idea is that there are at least ten things on offer in a place that will then attract enough people to generate a broad range of organic activities. Take a park, for example. There will be open space to play on, trees to sit under and a path to make it easier to walk. Add seats, drinking water, toilets and a playground, plus some of the following – exercise equipment, barbecue and picnic table, tree house, sculptures, free wifi, performing area, café, toy cupboard, skateboard half pipe, pump track, flying fox, nature trail, paddling pool, a lake to swim in, boats, perhaps a performance space, maybe a *petanque* court – and suddenly you have a place that works for a really broad range of people.

Successful recreational places have an ambiguity about them, offering multiple recreational as well as useful activities. These places, like market squares and high streets, bring people together to participate, to watch – as if by chance – and to enjoy companionship through a shared experience that they consciously or subconsciously were looking for. In Central Park, there is a giant fountain where kids can run around and play with toy boats, but which was relatively underused in the 1960s. Then the old nineteenth-century kiosks were reopened as cafés, and the place became popular again. Parents could come for a coffee and to read the papers, but also perhaps, hopefully, to catch up with friends or play a board game. Following the Power-of-Ten rule means diverse groups of people, like a family, can all be catered for in the same place.

There is an even cheaper, lighter way to bring novelty into the city – and that is activation. Think of the city like a vast arena that can put on different shows. Instead of building a rooftop restaurant, why not raise a gondola into the sky with a crane and 'Dine in the Sky'? At New Year, shut the streets to traffic, project a light show onto heritage façades and let the parties begin. If you don't have a giant piazza, why not repurpose the car park for a music festival, or a pump track or a political rally? And the transformation – while less slick than a permanent change – may be all the more magical for being temporary. Activation turns the city into a theatre.

Empty shops can be transformed by performances or installations in the windows. New York department store Bonwit Teller hired Salvador Dalí in 1939 to create the window displays. They were suitably surreal and not universally popular (including three wax hands coming out of a bathtub, a buffalo head eating pigeons and a wax mannequin sitting on coals). When the store installed some mannequins in suits, Dalí, in a rage, jumped into the window space to grab his bath, slipped, and crashed through the glass window, bath and all.[31] Despite (or because of) the controversy the store continued to collaborate with artists until 1979 when the site underwent its most dramatic transformation – the store was demolished and replaced by the Trump Tower. More recently, shop windows have been used to display art during Covid lockdowns. In the UK, in Manchester, '50 windows of creativity' turned the city centre into an art gallery that could be enjoyed safely by residents otherwise trapped at home.

People will not necessarily use spaces the way the designer thought they would, and that can be exciting. On 7 August 1974, Philippe Petit snuck up to the top of the Twin Towers, and with the help of a friend secured a cable between the buildings, 1300 feet above the pavements below. His walk between one high-rise and another was watched in horror and amazement by those standing beneath him. He said in an interview for the documentary *Man on Wire*:[32] 'I started, as a young, self-taught wirewalker, to dream of not so much conquering the universe, but, as a poet, conquering beautiful stages.' His acts were illegal and he was arrested, though he was released without charge. He had made an offer of something so extraordinary and courageous and joyful to everyone who witnessed it that it seemed to open up the possibilities of the world. 'To me . . . it's so simple, that life should be lived on the edge of life. You have to exercise rebellion, to refuse to tape yourself to rules, to refuse your own success, to refuse to repeat yourself, to see every day, every year . . . every idea as a true challenge, and then you are going to live your life on a tightrope.' Why would you punish that?

Cities have always been sites of play. The parks and cathedrals originally raised for the community under the auspices of the Catholic Church are a legacy of another culture that celebrated altruism and play. If there is any kind of trickle-down economics, then it is this public sphere. But the city would not be the city without the full wealth of delights supplied by private enterprise – of department stores with their sights and smells, silks and satchels, of restaurants with seating alfresco or in cosy booths, of cafés, pubs and secret bars, of theatres and concert halls, of parades and protests, of mansions and garrets, of football matches and horse racing, of crowded nightclubs and Christmas markets.

Play evolves. While it is ubiquitous in every culture it looks different depending on where you live. There is some evidence that the more tolerant a culture, the more successful it is; yet the Portuguese and Spanish Empires were also successful, and are often perceived (in the UK at any rate) as violently oppressive. Many Catholic countries seem to have traditional hierarchies (and most of the dictators are now gone), but they also seem to have much more playful societies. There are festivals, feasts, rest on Sunday. The more controlling the country, the more controlled and compulsory the play. Liberal cultures, by contrast, seem to encourage the idea that working long hours and pursuing wealth is the route to freedom and ultimately you can choose the play you want. However, this might mean that play is generally at a smaller scale and many do not play at all. Is the answer somewhere in between? Is it time for a reset of our structures, so there is more time and space for us to improvise the fun stuff, like more pedestrian streets and a four-day week? Is it worth asking whether it is enough for people to be *allowed* to play? Should they be *compelled* to do so?

Cities are challenging places: they are centres of wealth, but they also draw in immigrants, young people and rural workers with few assets to their name, because they offer support networks and the opportunity to make a living. Or because there is nowhere else to go. If we know more now about the formula for happiness in cities than ever before, what can we do to make it easier for everyone to get a chance to share in the fun stuff and have a fair go?

Part Three:
Playing the City

11

How you can bring more play into the city

The best cities are created by everyone. While city councils and businesses will always be keeping an eye on ensuring that the city works as a whole, and will maintain facilities, programme activities and try to create a habitat that encourages play, what is also needed is that *you* get involved. It is people who bring the city to life and make a place. In this chapter, we will demonstrate how you can make a difference.

There are four steps to playing the city. First, becoming aware of the physical, natural, built, historic, geographical, social, regulatory and cultural structures of the city. Secondly, finding friends and other players of the city – getting to know them and becoming aware of their work, hobbies, contributions and interests. Thirdly, having the courage to join in and make offers oneself in a way that you enjoy. Fourthly, to find the wins in what you and others are doing as a way to mark progress.

Progress can be specific – to make an intersection safer, or to develop a walking tour. Progress can be small, like getting a smile from the waitress. For the advanced player of the city, progress might mean making life better for those with less power or wealth (including children and seniors) while not making it too much harder for those in the middle (who often feel squeezed).

These four steps are not sequential, they all flow together: but being aware is key. The first step is to show up and appreciate what your city has to offer.

Enjoy the city

It is really easy to stay at home or to follow the same old routes in your city, noting everything that you value closing down or being destroyed, and not noticing everything that *is* working or perhaps has changed for the better. It is hard to keep up and cities are exhausting, but this is the nature of cities. These ruptures can lead to all sorts of exciting new opportunities. It is worth finding and enjoying what's new sooner rather than later. Play takes effort and time and resource but it's worth it. *Carpe diem*. Seize the day. Life is short.

The first rule of making your city a better place is to appreciate what is already there. Supporting the good things in the city means supporting the local economy too. There has been a big shift in recent years to put our money into experiences rather than more stuff. This is generally a good thing. In cities homes are small but experiences infinite and memorable. If there is a great new theatre production, book a ticket. If the papers are talking about a terrific restaurant, book a table. You may be able to afford this every week, once a month, or for a special treat once or twice a year – but don't miss out entirely! It is often more fun to go out with friends, but when one is venturing into unknown territory to check it out, it can be quite nice to go solo. You won't need to impress anyone with your choice of wine. You can just sit back and enjoy the experience. Cities are very good places to be by yourself, but not alone.

Activity: Dine out solo

In a nutshell A really good restaurant, café or public house delivers not just food but an opportunity to inhabit the world differently. Perhaps the meal takes you to another country or culture, perhaps the philosophical approach is different, perhaps the service is so friendly that it restores your hope in society. Eating at home seems sensible when you have no date or friend to meet but going out brings an element of surprise, of rubbing shoulders with strangers as well as friends and being jollied out of one's normal rut or comfort zone. The very best places treat a singleton as well as a group. Eminent food critic Jonathan Gold started his career in appreciating food, and Los Angeles itself, by eating at every restaurant on Pico Boulevard. As he puts it, 'Food is a pretty good prism through which to view humanity', and it is an excellent way to get a handle on the diversity of the city.

What you need Some cash and a little time.

Method Your city will contain some wonderful restaurants at all budgets. Talk around and establish where the best place to go is within your budget range. This could be a place close by or in a neighbourhood you don't know. Travel if necessary. Go there. Alone. Savour it. Afterwards you could write a kind but fair review about the place on its website. This could be the beginning of a relationship.

Tip Go midweek, rather than on a Friday or Saturday night and bring a book or notebook along. Try not to look at your phone. However beautiful the design of the room, delicious the nibbles or interesting the interplay between other diners, a gadget will distract, while a book or journal fills the gaps without taking over.

Variation You can also visit alone museums, markets, shops, old arcades and department stores, art exhibitions, even the cinema, or a theatrical or musical performance. Be curious.

Attunement or finding your place in the city

To embrace what your city has to offer you have to attune yourself to it, and this means activating your senses. We know how we are rewarded with good feelings when we do things that are good for the survival of the species, and punished with bad feelings when we are in danger. The city, as we have found, has always offered a lot of sensation. Noise and stink and hazards, but also beauty, art and the opportunity to fulfil your desires. Venice, Paris, London, New York. Multi-cultural incarnations of Eve – courtesans, geisha and cabaret dancers – smile out at us from liquor labels, tourist posters and advertising of nightclubs. The promise of physical pleasure is echoed in luxury fashion stores, 'real leather' bags touted on street corners and the feel of other bodies in a crowd at a festival. Particularly fine buildings and views are listed in city guides for tourists, but there are always more things to see. We know that eating well is part of the tapestry of daily life in France, Italy, Vietnam, while drinking is part of the appeal of Scotland, Belgium and South Australia. Music is a huge part of the appeal of cities: London, Vienna, Cuba and New Orleans. We might not go looking for smells in the same way but we find them in department store perfumeries, when walking by restaurant ducting, or relishing the smell of the coffee roaster and fresh strawberries at farmers' markets.

Our sixth sense, balance, is at heightened alert in the city: stepping onto and off pavements, rising in glass lifts up skyscrapers, taking in great heights from above and below. We love whizzing through the streets on bikes and scooters – or back in the day, holding onto the pole at the open back of the bus as it swung around corners. Don't fall, our stomachs remind us, as our hands grip tighter and our senses go on hyper-alert. As it is for the physical world around us, so it is for understanding where we stand in socio-cultural contexts. Our feelings are helpful. We pick up cues from our environment about what we can do and how far we can go. To be street-smart is to be alert enough to our senses that we can negotiate the bad stuff to find the good stuff – including opportunities to play. If you arrive in a new place, you wander around the streets, your senses on hyper-alert, taking in everything. Humans can be territorial, so we are attuned to shifts in our status and safety depending on our location. Some places invite us in – but walk into a dark alley in a dangerous part of the city, and your gut feeling will tell you to go no further. There is excitement, but also a grain of fear in the exploring, which makes the experience piquant.

Copying others is part of attunement. As a tourist we want to do what the locals do. You want to be somewhere buzzing with other people. In New Orleans, for example, you want to experience the music. Wherever you are in the city you are never far from a corner bar with live performers, but travellers will follow each other around the French quarter to find the most popular venues. It is easy enough to just wander in, sit at the counter and copy the other patrons. They all seem to be eating? You order something. They put money in the bucket as a tip? You do too. When in Italy in summer, travellers get to join in with the locals eating and drinking alfresco. When in the Middle East, they will abstain alcohol and cover up. It is normal to ask, when travelling, what it is that people do in a place, and then join in. You'll find secular types visiting New York will attend a service at a Baptist Church, copying the regular congregation as best they can. We become aware of what other people do and where they go to find the good stuff.

How often do we actively attune ourselves to what is going on in our own city? What is the point when we already are local? The reason is that while we know some routes and places in the city extremely well, there are often myriad other routes and places that we completely ignore – and to be honest we miss things even in the routes we do know well. Fortunately there are tricks to becoming more aware of what is all around us. We just need to engage our senses by creating a challenge.

Activity: Go on a sensory walk

What you need Nothing.

Method Explore an area that you think you know quite well but focus on the senses, the smell, touch or sounds in a place. Observe the effect on all your senses.

Variations

- Ask a friend to blindfold you and lead you around an area. You will find your other senses working harder, including your sense of balance. You will become much more aware of smells, sounds and slopes, steps and escalators.

- Look up to the first and second floor, and down into basements for hidden shops, workshops. Try and find clues to different times in history.

The city as a place to test new experiences

In the city, we are constantly being offered new experiences, in music, in art, in theatre. Have you tried eating in the dark, or on long trestle tables laid out in the laneways? Or sought out DJs in what were once municipal toilets? Or tried rollerblading along the waterfront? There are not enough years in a life to do everything. When there are so many options, testing increases consumer confidence. We may take shortcuts, by following the recommendations of a good reviewer or a magazine like *Time Out*, but when the opportunity is presented to us to test things for free, we'll do that too. We know a food that is for sale is unlikely to be poisonous, but we will try it anyway if we can. It is hard to resist enormous food markets, with produce heaped up on display and often a little plate with samples. A sun-dried tomato may appeal to some people, but will you like it? Better test to make sure. We don't stop at food. We like to sit on couches, go on test drives, try on clothes before we buy.

Tests are inter-relational. They are not absolute, but are about the interplay between people and between people and things. In science, a test is acknowledged to impact on what is being tested. When you are trying things out be aware what the test is doing to you! Take shopping for example. When we try on a new outfit we are not just assessing the clothes but considering what it will do for us. We may imagine it will improve our chances to find an attractive lover. It may, but perhaps not. If we already look good we might be better off simply asking our intended out and spending the money on a well-thought-out first date.

Department stores and shopping centres, like casinos and arcades, are delicious challenges. They offer all sorts of new things and entertainments for us to try, in the hope that we come in numbers, create a buzz, stay and purchase things. These stores make it possible for the majority to acquire lovely things and be assured that they reach a certain standard. They are fun. On the other hand, with easy access to credit, payWave and laybuy, they do make it harder to end the month with sufficient money in the bank. To separate commerce and the city would be to rip out much of what it means to be a city, but living in one does require self-discipline. Fortunately, in a city there are lots of ways to challenge oneself that don't involve holding back.

Observing mastery in the city

When I was a teenager, I literally had no idea of what I was missing in the local area of my city because I went to boarding school and was away for much of the time. I have noted that cities can be like advent calendars, with lots of surprising scenes hidden away, where the fun stuff happens. The internet and the evolution of libraries, community centres and arts spaces means that it is much easier to find out what is going on these days. It feels like there is more to do as well, though this may or may not be true. Once one finds one's way onto the grapevine, the world opens up. Of course there may not be the perfect activity on offer, nor the ideal people to do it with, but one should take a chance and see. I am sure that in those small American towns there are a good number of people who are not intensely passionate about football, but they go to the game anyway. The main point of an event is to hold a lot of people in the same space where it is possible to connect, chat and feel part of a crowd. You may find you enjoy roller derbies, music gigs, art installations or the local basketball matches more than you initially thought. Even if you don't, one can't help but be impressed by the skill involved. The opportunity to witness mastery is a great appeal of the city.

The highly skilled artists and performers may not come cheap, but mastery can also be observed in everyday life. Watching fishmongers fillet a freshly caught tuna can be mesmerising as can be viewing chefs working in an open kitchen at a restaurant, or carpenters making furniture. Transparency in local democracy and the justice system is not just about being able to hold people to account, but to observe people tackling highly complex problems with proficiency. It is reassuring to see people being more competent and decent than in media representations. Go and visit the law courts, the government or the local council and see what they are up to. Visit the cathedrals or churches and stay for a service. Then there are people who are in the streets because they want to get out of the house, someone perhaps doing skateboarding tricks. If you allow more time for journeys then you have time for diversion. Or better still, mark out some time to explore your city's treasures.

Activity: Be a cash-strapped tourist in your own town

In a nutshell Your city is full of treasures. Seek them out.

What you need Nothing but an internet search or a tourist guide (both accessible from the library if money is tight).

Method Do your research on the best free activities in your city. This may involve cross-referencing between tourist guides and the websites of local organisations and institutions. Many museums, art galleries and historic houses are free for locals, at least at some time in the week or year. Different cities have different points of interest. It could be a famous hill or volcano, a historic building or a spectacular clock. Find out what is there, and go and have a look. Many radio and TV programmes offer free tickets for their studio audiences. Is there a studio near you?

Variaton Book yourself a room in a backpackers' hostel in a different neighbourhood. If there is a walking tour or pub crawl, join in. Ask for advice on things to do and places to see. Pick the brains of anyone and everyone. Leave armed with knowledge. If you feel weird about this pretend you are from out of town. Or say nothing. Why not have a staycation where you don't have to tidy up after yourself or do the washing up?

Tip Invite someone along. This is an adventure.

Joining in

Wandering the city may make you feel like an invisible observer, but simply by being present you are a part of city life. Just as being in an audience makes a difference to a theatrical performance, so does being in the street make a difference to the buzz, sense of safety and level of congestion. If you want a great city you need to go out and support the good stuff in it. We give feedback on the city in the ways that we use it. If the city has lots of nice bars, restaurants and shops open in the evening, and there are lots of people filling the streets in the evening chatting and laughing as is the case in Madrid, then you could take it that Madrid is a good place for nightlife. If people come into the city to work, but leave in the evening, and the streets are quiet – as in Auckland in the 1970s – then you could say that the city is a bit dead. The crowds in old Times Square in New York indicated that it was a place where people wanted to be, despite its failings, and their continued delight in the space confirms that the changes were a good idea. Henri Lefebvre, a post-war French philosopher, had the idea that the city and culture were constantly impacting and 'producing' each other.

Still, we want, sometimes, to be consciously sharing an enjoyable experience with our fellow citizens, to make our mark, to be seen. This could mean going to a church service and singing loudly from the same hymn sheet or heading to the pub on Saturday to watch the game and shout at the screen along with everyone else. The Danish urban designer and architect Jan Gehl spoke of what he called 'triangulation', which was when a street performance or strange event could unite passers-by in their interest. Suddenly it became appropriate to meet eyes, share a laugh. Joining in with more visceral experiences with strangers makes us feel good. Occasionally that connection develops into friendship.

Just one close friend makes a huge difference to one's life. The ability to have someone who will help you out, no questions asked, who will listen and give honest feedback, and who enjoys your company is hugely important. These friends need your time, as you need theirs. We play to meet people, and then to maintain these friendships we engage in activities together and projects that please us. Many people do not have those close best friends seen in romantic comedies but this doesn't matter because acquaintances and regular social interactions can also be sufficient for a rich life. The city can be a place for solitude – and this can suit some people – but in the city one can at least enjoy the proximity of people and have numerous social interactions every day with strangers. A bit of banter makes a day go by more pleasurably. Time chatting at the school gates, on the phone or online is not wasted. To retire and realise everyone you knew is still at the office would be a shame. If this has happened it may be good to invite old office friends out to lunch occasionally, and start getting busy somewhere else. Young people and seniors will engage in the most in playful activities, probably because they offer the chance to spend time with other congenial people.

One should not have an ulterior motive to making friends, but friendship will always be about give and take. You give, you receive. To the chagrin of the workhorses in law firms, socialising with people and developing a client base may be a more reliable route to promotion than slogging; knowing who people are and becoming acquainted with people who share your values means you know who to call on when engaging in big projects. Seeing how your work aligns with others makes you far more likely to succeed, as does knowing what your friends' goals are. Rome wasn't built in a day, nor by one person. Celebrate the wins along the way. These wins will look different depending on the project, but if you see a win for your allies as a win for you, then you will be winning every day. Where to start? What sort of projects do you really care about? Find out where the like-minded people hang out. Get yourself there.

Activity: Join in

In a nutshell Find out what is going on and join in.

What you need The internet and some cash. Some time. A friend (optional).

Method How did we live before search engines? Cities have always offered inclusion in communities of interest where one can create one's own stories. In the past people might have needed the serendipity of meeting someone in the know to get involved, but now you can help yourself a bit more. Search for an activity you want to do in your local area, and answers come up.

Alternatively, have a look at the local newspaper and find out what is going on and where people are doing things that might interest you. This could be a permanent place or a series of events, a great gig venue or the local branch of the University of the Third Age, or even a conservation group at the local park.

Turn up and join in. Sharing your stories on social media afterwards can also lead to new ideas, opportunities and connections.

Tips

- Develop an escape plan in advance.

- You probably know the buzzing places already, but if you are getting back into the scene ask around to find out where is interesting right now and which are the most reliable or helpful newspaper/magazine listings, event finder websites or social media pages for what you are into, and sign up.

The most important thing to remember is that you are already part of the city, you *are* making an impact, the question is whether you are making the impact that you want. We can be bold – like wearing an extraordinary outfit, hurtling down a busy road on a skateboard or kissing passionately in the middle of the street – or we can be discreet. We can work together and with a little planning change the city even more dramatically. Groups draw attention – like dancers, packs of motorcyclists or choirs – while celebrations, parades, protests and artistic events transform the streets entirely. Gandhi famously advised people to be the change you wish to see in the world. The phrase applies to ethical choices but it can also be applied more broadly. In a city you can demonstrate how to make the city a more playful place by living in it more playfully. In theatre they call this making an offer.

Making an offer

Making an offer is when you do more than go with the flow. It can be an offer of a drink top-up at a party (low stakes) or to take someone out (moderate stakes) or to offer your hand in marriage (high stakes). You make an offer when you start a business, or a band, negotiate a sale of a product or put on a performance in the pub. You make an offer when you propose to do something differently.

When you make an offer you are setting yourself up to win or lose. Making an offer takes courage, because you will be judged. Not only are people tested but also what they produce, whether it be cakes, or musical interpretations, amazing flying machines or other innovative ideas. Making an offer with others, like putting on a play, has greater potential for upside but is riskier and much more effort. There may be pitfalls and rejections and it seems we dwell on our failures more than our successes. So try and succeed! Put in the time you need to achieve what you want and don't let the perfect get in the way of the good. Work out what you are doing (find it), find your people, make an offer, keep the stakes for yourself and others low. If you are happy with your work you won't worry if someone says no – that is their choice – you can make an offer to someone else. In this way you are doing the best you can, you are opening up to collaboration and you will get something out of the experience. Don't be too harsh on yourself if things don't entirely work out the way you hoped (they rarely do). When you make an offer you can change the way other people think. Radical ideas may be rejected at first but ultimately taken on board. Your ideas will evolve too. New ideas are often blends of old ones brought into new contexts. This is what theatre-making is like, often. It's fun, but takes some effort. You can't do it entirely alone.

Making an offer can change the way people think about *you*. For example, offering to get someone home safely communicates to the world that you are decent whether or not the person takes you up on it. Making an offer that is rejected may lead to a counter-offer that is even better. It may not, in which case move on. A good player knows when to fold 'em, as the song goes. Other offers will come your way another day. However, if your offer is accepted and you deliver on your promise, you have had a win and you get to keep that in your pocket forever.

In the city people are making offers, taking offers and developing new offers all the time. The opportunities for stealing ideas and inspirations across cultures and groups is huge, as is the potential for mixing things up. Particularly when it comes to play. Musical genres are always bringing in different influences. 'One song to the tune of another' was a stalwart game on the comedy series *I'm Sorry I Haven't a Clue*. Immersive theatrical productions steal ideas from video games. Sporting rules change to improve the game or adapt it to different audiences. As people's lives in cities changes, so urban entertainments evolve to meet their needs. These are led generally by a handful of people making an offer. As there is always some opposition to change it is best to keep stakes low at first.

Cricket at the turn of the twenty-first century was in decline, with attendance massively dropping. Those less well-off felt it was elitist. Young people thought it was for the oldies. The main point was that the demands of the modern world – and its pace – did not fit with traditional cricket. Three-day tests took up lots of time, which people were no longer able to spare. Even a one-day game took too long. And so Stuart Robertson, the England and Wales Cricket Board marketing executive, suggested trialling a new idea as a bit of fun as a marketing exercise. The game would encourage more hitting and action, by condensing the playing period into twenty overs for each side. What is more, with a running time of about three hours, people could go and watch the game in the evening or in an afternoon, so that it didn't cut into their work or into all the other things they had to do. Other entertainments were laid on like karaoke, speed-dating, guest popstar acts and bouncy castles for the kids. The whole point was to make the outing as fun as possible for people who were time-poor. And soon cricket was selling out stadiums again. Five-day tests still have their place but they are not the only option.

The old rules had been tested by the market and were found lacking. The new rules were tested and they were a big success. 'We had a lot of opposition but there was a lot of support too and it wouldn't have got through otherwise,' said Robertson.[1] Now Twenty20 cricket has become a staple of the sporting circuit because people enjoy it. It is easy to say that there is always room for improvement, and that there is no innovation without trial and no trial without error, but no one likes to be the architect of an expensive mistake. The worst thing is if someone, backed into a corner, feels obliged to double down on their errors of judgement. Failure in a 'marketing exercise' lowers the stakes and makes it easier to talk about what went well so that a better solution can be found.

What do you want to make happen? Can you deliver? Who do you need on your side? How do you gauge progress? Keeping these things in mind can be more scary than just making things up as you go along but, as my sister always tells me, fail to prepare and you prepare to fail. Fear is the fuel for making really good offers and making the lives of those around you better. If you are a bloke who doesn't dance and you are getting married, get some private lessons. Do well, and you won't just pocket that win but be able to win over your wife, daughters and other dance partners for life.

Adopting a (new) identity in the city

So how does the city serve as a place for copying and joining in? Very well. Copying and joining in traditional activities can be a way to strengthen our sense of identity with the people we grow up with, but in cities we can choose to copy other groups that we would like to be part of, so we can be the person that we want to be. We know that when people fancy each other, their body language starts to mirror that of their desired partner, and the same can be said of the way people restyle themselves when they are drawn to particular social groups or industries. Copying other people's clothes, mannerisms, speech and skills can open up opportunities for more substantive role transformation.

This idea that pretending to be someone different can transform you for real is a trope of urban romantic comedy. If you put on a posh voice, dress up and move in different circles you may well start to think and behave differently, and even actually become more capable and wiser, like Eliza Doolittle in *Pygmalion* or Vivian in *Pretty Woman*. Both characters rise up from working the streets by pretending to be respectable, charming and appropriately attired members of society. By looking the part, the women are treated differently and behave differently. As their assignments end, their characters have sufficiently evolved to choose new lives for themselves (well before the men who triggered their transformations have made their minds up about their own romantic feelings).

How you can bring more play into the city

This idea is so strong in the West. Magazines, shops, fiction and marketing all tell this story. Our parents' encouragement to us as children – 'You can be who you want to be . . . if you work hard enough' – is lodged in our psyche, next to memories of dressing up in their clothes. Looking the part is half-way to getting the role. When we go to a job interview, we consciously present an image that fits. Charities exist that lend smart suits to people on limited incomes to help them get the jobs they seek. It is not that we want to become someone else, but the person inside us wants to come out. In Germany they say that city air makes you free; in China there is an understanding that in cities one can wear a different hat. Cities are liberal and offer up opportunities for people to make themselves as much as their fortune.

Like magpies we can gather what we want from the city to suit ourselves. We can take a photograph to our stylist to replicate it; we may be after the shape, or the colour, or the fringe. When we admire the clothes on a mannequin in a shop window, we are not obliged to buy the whole outfit. The shop assistant is making one suggestion on how to put the clothes together. We make another. When we head out into the streets in our creatively created ensemble we are making an offer. We may take a photograph of ourselves and post it on social media and wait for the likes. If Bill Cunningham, *New York Times* fashion photographer, had snapped us on Broadway then we know our offer made an impact! We may well inspire someone else.

These assumptions about the power of transformation rarely take place in the country village – everyone knows each other too well and has known each other too long. It is the city with its opportunities to people-watch on the streets, in nightclubs, at various events, in the shops – both fashionable and second-hand – at the hairdressers, theatres and variety of other businesses that both inspire and make it possible for people to try on other roles. In cities one can start over and make new alliances. It is the density of cities, with the proximity of lots of other people, that means there should be lots of opportunities for us to find our tribe and join in with activities and pleasures that we like.

Activity: How to make an impression

In a nutshell Head out with style.

Method

1. Ask yourself what effect you want to create.

2. Look around at other people who convey this and note what you admire about their choices.

3. Consider what you already have and how it may serve. You probably have most of what you need.

4. Consider the gaps in your wardrobe/make-up accessories/hair.

5. Work out the fewest moves required to create your look.

6. Make those moves.

7. Put it all together and double-check everything looks right. Move with confidence. If people are looking at you then you can be sure it is not because you have caught your skirt in your undies. If you are looking good you are improving the city.

Variation Follow the same principles for a fancy-dress party.

Tip Develop a skill to add substance to your style. You could learn the lyrics of songs to perform, master cocktail making, learn some skateboard tricks or develop your dance skills. When you get really good at something you can wear what you like!

If you want to perform the city offers many stages, but if not this is no problem: the city is an offer in itself. Make an offer to someone to share it with you but do make the effort to plan the day well. Once you start to pocket wins and develop your networks you can raise the stakes a little. Do more, be more. You can re-create my date on rollerblades if you like, or, you can offer something opposite to the daily grind: an opportunity to reconnect to nature in the city.

12

Reconnecting to nature in the city

Cities cannot exist without an ability to manage natural resources. In bygone days, the easiest way to ensure you had everything you needed for staying put was to line up with those natural resources. The issue then would be to retain control over them. Natural fortifications, like mountains and cliffs, can provide security and opportunities to walk, climb, ski and stay fit. Amazing views are both breathtaking and practically useful to spot anyone coming to invade. Water is most useful of all: not only essential for drinking, washing and cooking, but as a site of play. It is stating the obvious but every city is located somewhere because of its geographical attributes. Reconnecting to nature in the city is a way of unlocking why and how the city came to be. Urban dwellers have always needed nature and green spaces for food, and also for wellbeing and peace of mind. Reconnecting to nature is one of the surest ways of raising one's mood and finding some tranquillity in the urban realm. And it nearly always appeals to friends, too.

Water

If one lives by the sea in a place with good weather, the primary play space would be the beach – whether one is into sunbathing, rock-fishing, swimming, yachting, kayaking, windsurfing, surfing, boating, building sand castles, singing around a driftwood campfire or simply walking along it. The idea of a beach is so appealing that a number of inland cities, including Paris and London, have created fake beaches alongside rivers. Other cities, where the beaches are naturally rocky or muddy, dump sand on top to improve them. In the last thirty years, waterfronts of various kinds have been opened up around the world for people to enjoy, from Melbourne to Seoul to Manchester. Some of these stretch for miles, allowing commuters a waterside walk, cycle or roller skate to get to work. With so many harbour and river outlets, it is also possible to kayak around the bays or stand-up paddleboard.[1] The same can happen at harbours. Where harbours are not overpolluted it is possible to fish directly from the waterfront. Some waterfronts, like Auckland's, have fish-gutting stations.

Some cities by the sea, like Bondi Beach in Sydney, have enclosed part of the bay to keep out sharks. In mid-twentieth century New York, when the streets got too hot, it was not uncommon for someone to open the fire hydrant in the street so that kids could run around in the spray, anticipating the first splash pads.[2] Some cities have embraced the Scandinavian sauna on their waterfronts, either permanently or temporarily in winter, so people can enjoy getting hot, then cool off in the ocean before dashing inside the sauna again.[3]

One of the most successful city regeneration projects of recent decades has been the restoration of the Cheonggyecheon River in Seoul, the capital of South Korea. Increasingly polluted in the nineteenth century by sewage, it was concreted over for sanitary reasons, and then in the twentieth century a motorway was built over it. By removing all these concrete structures space was opened up for nature and for people to live, work, hang out and be close to the water. The mayor at the time was so popular he was later voted in as the country's president. The more positive experiences in nature we have when we are young, the more we will do to care for it through our lifetimes. Community groups have led small-scale stream and river restoration projects to improve local biodiversity and mitigate pollution. Litter is pulled out, water quality checked, plants put in and microbiologies charted. It is definitely worth then enjoying the local rivers and ponds with your kids.

Activity: Get wet!

What you need Swimming togs, towel (or clothes you don't mind getting wet).

Method Find somewhere outdoors to get wet. For those living near clean fresh water there may be opportunities for wild swimming, upstream in rivers, or in lakes or ponds.[4] For those living close to the sea, go to the beach.

Be safe:

- Check the current – do not enter if the water is flowing too fast.

- Gauge the depth – there can be rocks and even supermarket trolleys in the water, so get in and check first.

- Don't get too cold – and give yourself a moment to acclimatise to the temperature before setting off.

- Have an escape plan – work out where you can get out before you get tired.

- Know your algae – blue-green algae can cause skin rash, eye irritation and sickness.

- Don't swim alone.

- Watch out for reeds – and if you do get caught, move slowly, don't thrash about.

- Cover open wounds.

- Don't stray too far from the shore.

- Look after the kids – and use buoyancy aids, but not lilos that can be blown off course.

Variation If the water is unsafe for swimming, municipal swimming pools are often historic and can be quite amazing. Some offer saunas and spas; others are architecturally very interesting. Some are indoors, some outside, and they are often very cheap. Russia, Turkey and Japan have some particularly wonderful public baths. Alternatively, there may be splash pads or paddling pools, or fountains (at least for the kids). Failing that: water guns in the park.

Snow

If one lives in a city in cooler climes, then walks, hunting and winter sports, tobogganing, building snowmen and snowball fights provide lots of fun. There may be rivers or lakes to ice skate on, or perhaps an ice rink has been installed. One could take a day trip to the slopes, at least at the right time of year. Skiing holidays became a thing in the late nineteenth century as the tourist industry started to expand, offering new opportunities to play for a wider market.

Ski holidays have turned small alpine villages into burgeoning towns, and hub towns with airports into cities with their own programmes of events. Sapporo in Japan has an annual ice sculpture competition that has featured massive reconstructions of Japanese samurai in battle, St Mark's in Venice and the Sphinx of Cairo. Winter fun is not just limited to places that have a marketing budget, though. One day, when I was living in Blackheath in London, it snowed, so I put on my skis, crossed the heath and skied down Greenwich Park to the Jubilee Line, and commuted up to my work near Regent's Park. In 2018, another cold winter inspired Madelaine Diamond[5] to ski across Soho. And there were innumerable snow fights over lunch break, and toboggans whizzing down Hampstead Heath. Why not?

Activity: Embrace the snow

What you need Warm clothes, gloves and waterproof boots of some kind. Ski kit optional.

Method Take the snow as an opportunity to do any of the following:

- Make a snow angel.
- Make a snowman or other amazing sculpture.
- Have a snowball fight.
- Use an air mattress as a makeshift toboggan and head for the nearest hill.

- Ski to work.

- Put together snowboard ramps on a hill and start practising tricks.

- Play track and chase. The first player sets off across a park. The second must follow ten minutes later and try to follow their friend's footsteps. If they successfully make it to a café before the first player has finished his hot chocolate, another hot chocolate must be purchased for them.

- Tramp across a park to the pub and buy a mulled wine.

Hills, mountains and volcanoes

Elevation matters. Mountains, hills, cliffs and volcanoes have long been valued for providing a defensive advantage. It is hard to attack somewhere uphill, and even harder if it's at the top of a cliff. It is easier to defend a place from which you can use gravity to direct boiling oil and rocks onto one's enemy – and to have the advantage of seeing them in advance so as to get the furnaces heating up that oil, or to lug the rocks to the ramparts.

Heights when combined with rain or snow also provide water security. Streams and rivers follow established paths down the slopes. Glaciers hold water through winter and release it as snowmelt in spring. Water that filters through the soil and rocks and moves quickly is generally fresh and good to drink. Some filters down into aquifers that can be sourced at any time of year. The water helps the crops to grow, while lush meadow grass and coarser mountain grasses are good for cropping livestock. If the cows are on the flatter land, the sheep and goats can negotiate the steeper terrain. The combination of water and hills can allow the creation of reservoirs and dams that not only provide drinking water but also hydro-electric energy.

It is common for volcanoes to leave behind particularly fine soils for horticulture. New Zealand sits on the Pacific Ring of Fire, and is made up of hundreds of old volcanoes. Māori would revere the *maunga* – volcanoes – as the sacred creations of Mataaho (the guardian of the Earth's secrets) and Ruaumoko (the god of earthquakes and volcanoes).[6] Spiritually and culturally Māori connect themselves intrinsically to the land and waterways, and the volcanoes were used for spiritual services, including rituals around marriage, birth and burial. The volcanoes are essential for life. The crater would collect water that would then filter through the soil and rock to be released back into sunlight as springs. The soil was good for growing crops. Steep slopes made it easier to manage human waste. There exist in museums beautiful carved posts that people could cling to while they relieved themselves on steep slopes far away from the living and cooking areas.

The elevation made it easier for communities to defend themselves. The locals would know the ground well, and be able to repel enemies. There is a hill in Auckland called Te Rerenga Ora Iti ('the leap of the few survivors'). It was the location of a Māori fort (or *pā*) and the site of many battles. Many Māori settlements were near maunga, and to this day when Māori introduce themselves they will tell you the name of the maunga on which or near to which they reside. Since Europeans started settling here, the big cities have grown around them too. Auckland is built on more than fifty volcanoes, and views to the volcanoes are protected in planning legislation. Many of the parks are on the peaks of volcanoes, or on valleys floors that are prone to flooding.

Mountains, cliffs and hills are worth exploring. They have caves and crevices, streams and wildlife to find. It is good exercise to reach the top and be rewarded with the view and sense of achievement. Mountains are often the home of spiritual sites, temples and retreats, and there are many stories to discover about them. Since the nineteenth century many of those with leisure time have taken to hill walking and mountain climbing. Some head to the highest peaks but there are often hills closer to home, whether it be Hampstead Heath in London, or Arthur's Seat in Edinburgh, Montmartre in Paris, Table Mountain in Cape Town. Why not spend a day discovering your mountain?

Activity: Climb a mountain

What you need Layers of clothing, including rain gear; water bottle, charged-up telephone, snacks.

Method

1. Find your mountain. This may be obvious or require a look at a map. The hill may be parkland, or it could be built on.

2. Plot your path and perhaps locate a coffee stop near the start, and a pub for the end of your journey. Work out how long you will need including rest stops, and then work back so you know when you need to leave home.

3. Invite friends along (recommended but not compulsory). If you don't bring friends do at least tell someone where you are going. Hill walking can be dangerous if the weather turns.

4. Gather your supplies. Knowing what local refreshments are available, or not, will make it easier to ensure that you bring enough. You may just need snacks or a full picnic for the summit. Bring a bit more than you need.

5. Get going on the appointed day. Use the phone to take pictures and in case of emergency. Enjoy.

6. When you get home enjoy a hot bath. You deserve it.

Variation Join a guided mountain walk or attend an event on a hill or mountain.

Natural rhythms

When you are making more time to play it is worth considering how a place changes at different times of day. The temporal factor matters in life as it does in a game, a piece of music or a play. One wants a change of pace and to experience different things. You may walk through the streets every day at 8.30 a.m. but are you there at lunchtime when the tables are full of diners, or in the evening, or in the early hours of the morning? Different things happen at different times of day. If you can't sleep you could do worse than to go for a wander at night and notice all the activity that is going on that you normally miss. It is not just party-goers out on the street at this time, coming home slightly worse for wear, carrying their shoes.

Animals, too, can find a place for themselves within the structures of the city. The increase in pesticides in the countryside has meant that greener cities have become nature corridors for birds and insects. In some cities, bears, deer, hyena and even hawks, roosting on skyscrapers, have moved in. Visit Texas and you will find tree-loads of bats. Sir David Attenborough suggests that living in the city makes animals more playful and intelligent. Singapore has invited nature in by creating enormous bio-domes and biodiversity towers. Animals can make a home in all sorts of unlikely places. In Canada, bears are known to scavenge around the bins on the edge of towns and cities; in Africa, the hyenas do it. Set up movement-triggered night cameras in your back garden and see what you find.

Cleaner river water has meant that fish have returned to urban rivers. Whether it be urban nature tours, fishing, bird-watching or wildlife photography, or exploring caves underground, there is lots to see of the wilder side of the city. It gives a whole new meaning to 'urban safari'. If you want to support local wildlife, you can plant pollinator corridors in your gardens, parks or berms to attract bees and other insects. If you are more of a hunter type you can start trapping rats that may predate on the birds.

Activity: Add nature to the City

In a nutshell A bit of colour goes a long way. Street trees, hanging baskets, planters or flowerbeds in unlikely places all make the city more lovely.

What you need Seeds or seedlings, and a space to plant, which might mean pots or garden beds.

Method Start with some herbs that flourish indoors, a pot plant, maybe a lemon tree in a large pot outside the door, or a hanging basket on the balcony. Choose plants that are hard to kill and give back in some way – flowers, fruit, fragrance, flavour for cooking or just looking nice.

When you get more handy add more. You could fill the area in front of your home with herbs, flowers and fruit trees, either in pots or bedded in. If you are in an apartment building fill the balcony or brighten up the roof terrace.

The boldest can head into the public realm, turn the green berm on the pavement into a herbaceous border, or convert a traffic island at dead of night.

Tips It is generally considered good practice to avoid planting pests and weeds. In the public realm go for smaller trees and shrubs to avoid hitting water pipes! Try to focus on areas that seem neglected rather than digging up a heritage park. However, unless there are clear rules around planting (for example in rental apartments regarding where you can put pot plants) you can weigh up whether it is better to act first and ask forgiveness later rather than try to go through 'proper processes' as there may not be any. If there is a problem, plants (that are not noxious weeds) are relatively easy to pull out.

A walk at the city's waterfront can allow a view into the port. You might see the stevedores working through the night lifting containers off the ships, or the fishing boats haul in their catch. One can even visit pubs that serve the night workers and enjoy a pint before the sun is up. If you wake up hours before dawn in Auckland you may find yourself at the blessing of a new town square led by the local Māori *iwi* (tribe). The strange sound of the conch being blown at the start of ceremonies has all the eeriness of the 'Last Post' on Armistice Day. As the ceremony continues, the darkness becomes a rosy dawn and ultimately day.

Activity: Play spotlight

In a nutshell Spotlight is tag with torches and is great fun in a park after dark.

What you need At least four people (but the more the merrier). A flashlight.

Method The seeker has a flashlight. He counts to thirty while all the other players go and hide. Then he goes to find them. When the seeker catches someone in the light he calls their name or 'Spotted!', and they are out. When everyone is found the first person to have been caught becomes the seeker.

Variation When people are called out they now help the seeker catch the others. In this variation everyone may carry a torch, but this is not compulsory.

The weather and seasons provided structure to the year and to the day that served us right up until the Industrial Revolution. You couldn't work in the fields in the dark. You made hay when the sun shone. Trees are appreciated for their colours and for their shade, because they provide a structure for birds, but also because they change throughout the year, sometimes bearing flowers, sometimes fruit, sometimes leaves that change colour between spring and autumn. The change of seasons brings different things to see and hear but also to feel. The seasonal variations in temperature, wind, rainfall, sunshine and the humidity change what we can do and how we play. Even the night sky changes, with the shifting constellations and the rising and falling moon.

When things change we notice them more, and this heightened awareness just makes us more engaged with life and happier. But many streets have no trees. Air-conditioned buildings can lock us in exactly the same environment every day of the year and this is terribly dull. Industrialisation did disconnect people from nature, and the increasing secularity of cities in the last centuries might have accelerated a loss of cultural connections too. Reconnecting to natural rhythms is a way of finding variety through the year. At least get out of the building at lunch time and go for a walk and appreciate the blue (or even grey) sky.

The Japanese appreciate the changes in nature. Awareness of the natural order comes through the Shinto religion and Buddhism too. When there is less space one has to prioritise what is required, and so gardens are distilled to the key elements: rocks, water, trees. The Japanese will celebrate the autumn moon with feasting, the arrival of blossom with karaoke parties, and will go on snow viewings. Television news will track the best viewing sites for autumn leaves, and, most importantly of all, cherry blossom. The seasons are ripe for play opportunities brought by nature, whether it be stomping on leaves in autumn, making snow creatures in winter, appreciating flowers and baby animals in spring or enjoying a long summer evening picnic in a park.

Activity: Cherry blossom viewing

What you need Friends, a picnic, some cherry trees in blossom. Alcohol is helpful, a karaoke machine optional.

Method Organise a picnic near some cherry trees in a public park in the early evening. Encourage everyone to bring wine and sort out the food yourself. Raw carrot sticks and dips, crisps, sushi, buns and strawberries will be fine. A traditional Japanese cherry blossom viewing party will involve singing.

Variations

- Let the singing part go.
- Use any tree that is in blossom.

It seems to me that more festivals can be brought back. The Venice Carnival was outlawed in 1797, and the wearing of masks was strictly forbidden. It was only brought back in 1979, but it is going strong. The Sapporo Snow Festival only started in 1950 when a few students built a few snow statues for fun. Sculptures in recent years have been as large as 25 metres wide and 15 metres high.[7] From acorns grow oak trees.

Activity: Embrace Shrove Tuesday/Mardi Gras at a civic level (level: advanced)

What you need An appetite for food and work.

Method Embrace or revive your town's Shrove Tuesday festival. This may mean a pancake race, a festival with particular foods, a giant football match or a carnival with costumes. Manage the football carefully: playing football on public highways was made illegal in 1835.

Variations

- Host a party with lots of good food: you can include pan-cakes or not. The spirit of the festival is to use up and share food before it goes off. One could host a dinner party cheaply with food on special offer from the local supermarket.

- It doesn't have to be season-related. It could be a swivel chair Olympics or competitive hopscotch.

- Create any festival that you like.

Other festivals and 'seasons' have been designed in recent decades to mark the year's high spots and to encourage time off. Some of them are cultural, like the proms or music festivals in summer and the panto season in winter. The Edinburgh Festival marks out August. Fashion has its seasonal collections. The best television series always seem to be screened in the last few months of the year, while great films premiere just in advance of the Oscars. Sports have seasons too. The rugby season goes through winter, and cricket in summer. Then there are events like the Oxford vs Cambridge Boat Race. Every city and every country has its rhythms. There is a calendar of events for the global citizen that picks out the highlights: the Monaco Grand Prix in May, Wimbledon in June, the Melbourne Cup in November, the Olympic Games every four years. These markers are rather valuable for providing space and a structure for enjoyable encounters with each other. We can plan for them. It is far too easy to keep one's head down and delay gratification until it is too late. This year, join in!

One festival that we must engage in is Christmas. Unfortunately, often Christmas ends up being a tremendous burden on one or two people and far too lazy and decadent for everyone else. Like all forms of play and events Christmas takes effort. It is easy to get distracted by the shopping, but there are other aspects that need just as much attention. Fortunately by sharing the load and turning it into a big family project the work becomes manageable and everyone enjoys it even more.

Activity: Christmas

In a nutshell Think about what you want, delegate and ensure everyone prepares in advance – and everyone will have a better time!

Method

1. Ask yourself, and those family and friends gathering at your house, what their expectations and needs of Christmas are. Have one-to-one conversations. Find out how they are feeling. Exhausted or excited? They may have different needs. That is OK. Ask them what those are, and also what their strengths are. Write it all down.

2. Christmas comes with some expectations that are pretty universal. The aim is to 'do Christmas' so that it feels like Christmas, but also to make sure that you and your guests get what you want. If no one likes turkey, don't cook it. However, you will want a good feed.

---

3. The best way to work up an appetite is to have to wait for your food. Can you fill a gap in the morning with an activity? This could be a walk. It could be church. It could be both.

4. Everyone needs a present. Stealing presents can be a great way of mixing up Secret Santa presents and making for a bit of fun. Instead of buying a present for everyone, each person is obliged to bring a present of a certain quality (could be secondhand, cheap or unwanted – could be something around fifty quid) and then everyone takes a number out of a hat. The person with '1' chooses a gift from the heap and unwraps it. The next person in the numerical sequence then unwraps their present and can choose to keep it or swap it with person no.1. The third person may then decide to swap their present with the first or second person, and so it goes on, accompanied by squeals of delight or anguish. (Note, though, that it is generally considered bad form to steal from any children who are delighted with what they have already got.)

5. Decorations and lights are essential.

6. Entertainment is key, yet is often the most neglected element. A meal can only last so long. Church could be part of the entertainment. Carol singing at home is an option if there is someone who can accompany on a musical instrument, or you could head out and sing on other people's doorsteps. Alternatively, you could create a game. This could be a paper chase outside, a scavenger hunt or a family quiz. Ask someone to organise quiz questions in advance based around what the guests have been doing and/or achieved in the past year. The winning team gets an extra present. Other good games to play are: charades, the memory game (where you have to look at a tray of objects before an item is taken away – you win if you remember that item), Articulate and Racing Demons. Look for games that are engaging to play and fun (even if you are losing).

7. Provide contrasts. If you go to church in the morning, pop into the pub before you go home for lunch. If you have eaten too much, go for a walk. If you have been cold, light the fire, or turn on the heating and play a game. If you have raced

around all day, finish up with a suitable movie. If you have spent the day sitting down, and you are surrounded by keen dancers, have a dance. It will take an effort to switch direction but it is worth it to stop the day getting stuck in a rut.

8. Ask people to dress up nicely. Consider even a fancy-dress box. Everyone could bring something extraordinary to put in the box, and take something different out to wear.

9. Divvy up the jobs, the cooking and drinks purchasing according to people's strengths, enthusiasms and levels of wealth. Delegate someone to organise the game, to choose the movie and music as appropriate. Make sure the children have some very important jobs – decorating the house or the cake or handing out nibbles. The person who is doing the cooking cannot also look after everyone and make sure they are happy. Doing drinks is an ideal job for the host as it gives an excuse to have little chats and then move on. You may need to flatter, praise, cajole, remind and encourage everyone else in what they are doing. Holding a party together takes effort but the better you do it, the less effort it feels.

Tip Children particularly love the rituals of Christmas and are deeply disappointed when things are not done properly. Make time for decorating gingerbread houses, going to a carol service, seeing the Christmas lights, going to a show or pantomime or Christmas movie, and shopping in the department stores. You can build up your own rituals over the years depending on what you like. The most important thing to remember is that presents and yummy food are only a small part of the whole thing. There also needs to be play, and people to play with.

13

Your play personality
in the city

It often seems that when we think about play and cities, we think about a certain type of play – like sport, playgrounds and parks – but imagine if the city aimed to appeal to every play type. What would this playful city look like? In this chapter we will have a look at Stuart Brown's eight personalities and imagine.

The joker

A city needs a space for comedians – perhaps a comedy club, perhaps a space in a theatre – but the amateur joker can work anywhere at any time. They are out there putting foam in the fountains, colouring in teeth on posters and planting road cones on the top of Norfolk pines (a recent trend in Auckland, which is impressive because these trees are more than 40 metres high). The rise in the use of mobile telephones has facilitated large-scale pranks – flash mobs in railway stations and games through the streets. Smartphones with great cameras and links to social media can spread funny ideas about the city to networks around the world. In Sweden someone has installed a parallel mouse city on the sidewalks tucked away below the regular shop windows.[1] Around the world we share images of our kids interacting comically with statues.

Activity: Share a joke with the local statuary

In a nutshell Find local statues and create a composition that amuses you.

What you need A friend with a camera.

Method There are many statues in the city, some beautiful, some less so. Some you can sit on, some you can sit *with*, others you can imitate, some you can crush with your fingers. Have a play and take photos of the results. Share them.

Oppression can be for laughter what hunger is for dinner – it makes the good moments all the more piquant. In the modern office, that is collaboratively or oppressively open plan (depending on one's point of view), the out-of-the-way places like the watercooler, corridor or kitchenette can be a place to shake off some tension and laugh for a minute or two. At an urban level it has long been the pub where tensions are released with a bit of comic banter over a beer. If you are a natural comic, why not try an open mic night? If you know someone who is, encourage them to do so.

One great value of comics is to tell it as it is. The group Led by Donkeys used billboards and projections to put up posters that caught the inconsistencies in public statements by politicians in the UK involved in the Brexit campaign.[2] It started as a bit of banter down at the pub, but then a printer offered to assist and up went the first poster. They got a great response so, feeling encouraged, they headed off to Dover (which was 'leave' territory) and high on the side of a building reminded the world of a quote from Dominic Raab: 'I didn't quite understand the full extent of this but . . . we are particularly reliant on the Dover–Calais crossing.' Online supporters provided funding and moral support, and helped to source quotes. Did they change anything? Perhaps not, but it was a laugh and it brought together a community who wanted to be heard.

The kinaesthete

The great value of kinaesthetes is that they are physically strong and able. In times of peace they will become the ballet dancers and athletes that people will flock to watch. In times of war or difficulty, they are the great soldiers. In New Zealand many of the rugby players in times past grew up on farms. In the city there are often lots of facilities: stadiums, pools, sports centres, ice rinks and various courts where people can develop and display their physical skills.

The city, we've seen, can itself be a dance floor, running track, velodrome or skate park. While running on concrete for long distances can put a bit of pressure on the joints, there are large public parks waiting to be used. Skateboarders often prefer to practise their tricks in the wild rather than in the official skateboard park. Rollerblading or scooting are fun ways to get around flat cities. If there are waterways one could row upriver. Being on the coast offers up opportunities for windsurfing, surfing, kitesurfing and boating, not to mention swimming or diving. Why not try and get to work in a different way? My friend Jenny who lives by a sheltered harbour sometimes used to paddleboard up an estuary to work and home again. Now she works on a different job across land she uses a scooter.

Action: Find a new way to get around the city

What you need Active transport – foot, bike, scooter, rollerblades, canoe, stand-up paddleboard.

How to Using your preferred form of public transport, chart a safe path through the city. This may take you to places you don't normally see. Give it a go.

Tips

- Take a friend.
- If your route takes you off the beaten track or onto water do tell someone where you are going.

There is still room for vertigo in the city. Cyclists, research suggests, are the happiest commuters, perhaps because obstacles rarely slow them down. They race past traffic jams and drift slowly across intersections with pedestrians when cars sit at red lights. They have to engage with the journey because they are pedalling, they have moments to breathe *and* get some adrenalin when they freewheel down the hills, *plus* they get all the endorphins from the effort. People on skateboards, scooters, rollerblades and skis enjoy the same sorts of chemical rewards.

It is always more fun to be part of a gang than a solo traveller. This can be safer too, particularly for cyclists. The more there are, the safer they are on the roads. Keen cyclists created a global movement called Critical Mass in the first decade of the twenty-first century. They reclaimed the streets by organising large group bike rides through city centres every Friday evening. Urban bike rides at night continue, with lights on wheels flashing and music systems blasting: it is a crazy and exciting way to play the city. It is not without its dangers, and needs careful organisation, but it is worth it for the feeling of camaraderie, the speed and the joy in taking possession of a realm so long the preserve of cars.

Action: How to create your own bike event[3]

What you need A small, keen team, and a bit of patience and imagination.

Method

1. Craft a creative concept for your bike ride – it could be for kids, it could be a bike ride at night, it could involve costumes, etc.

2. Find a convenient location for your event.

3. Choose a day and time that will appeal to your audience and ensure a good turnout.

4. Check with the council whether you need a permit (and perhaps apply for funding).

5. Promote your event online.

6. Spread the word to your local biking club, as well as any target groups, e.g. schools, outdoor shops, universities, your company, friends, community centres, and so on.

7. Organise a place to meet and a place to end that has refreshments.

8. Ensure that there are volunteer bicycle marshals riding with the group, and people at both the check-in and the end of the event.

9. Take lots of photos and videos, and post them online.

Kids in NZ love the flying foxes that are common in parks. Their older siblings have naturally taken to the proliferation of micro-mobility over the last couple of years: scooters, electric bikes, electric skateboards, segways. Speed is fun but brings risk. It is also easier to miss things. A great way to get around is to walk.

When you walk, your brain can focus on three or four things around you at the same time. Points of focus are in three dimensions: the lane or shop doorway has depth and context. Travel becomes a sensory experience: you can feel the sun, the breeze, the rain or the cold. You can hear and smell better, and you can more easily stop to look a bit closer at something before moving on. You can touch things, you can sit and you can taste the salt in the sea spray. When travelling in a car at 50kph or more, people can only focus their eyes on one thing, and that is the road ahead. For train passengers, objects and structures almost appear flat, a 2D image passing your windows. You have a much greater sense of place at a human scale when you are walking and cycling, compared to when you are driving. There is also the interest factor of being amongst other people – people like to watch each other more than anything else – and there is a chance you may bump into a friend or see something extraordinary.

In the 1990s, the rise of the internet and the opportunity to post homemade videos inspired many ways to play the city, perhaps themselves inspired by Philippe Petit and his high-wire walk between the Twin Towers. Parkour and freerunning began in Paris, pioneered by David Belle and his friends, who jumped and climbed over various obstacles like stairs, barriers, scaffolding, walls, roofs and so on. Competitions and demonstrations have stimulated ever-more dangerous runs, with athletes launching off roofs, landing on slivers of window ledges and scaling cliffs. The Australian Dominic Di Tommaso makes a living improvising off urban structures as a professional freerunner. He can jump off a helicopter's landing skids onto the roof of a domed building sited on the edge of the cliffs. (He is sponsored, naturally, by Red Bull.) In only a marginally less dangerous way skateboarding does the same thing – skating down handrails and over structures. The structures inspire moves that are awesome to watch.

Meanwhile, in New Zealand, A. J. Hackett has commercialised the bungy jump off buildings and structures with elasticated ropes tied round people's ankles and, most recently, the Nevis catapult, which launches passengers at 100kph with 3Gs of force. It combines height, flight and speed, and is described as 'four minutes of sheer terror followed by the adrenalin high of a lifetime'. Alternatively, one can whip down an almost vertical zipline off a telecommunications tower, or clamber around the outside of tall buildings and bridges. It is pure vertigo.

Activity: Make your own hillslide

What you need A cardboard box and a steep hill on a dry day.

Method Check there is a safe landing/slowing down area at the bottom. Flatten the cardboard box. Sit on it. Slide. Climb up the hill again. Repeat.

Variation In wet weather a wet slide can be created. You will need a plastic tray to slide on rather than cardboard. A very muddy, steep, slick slope can be negotiated in just swimming gear.

The explorer

It is important to remember that many of the great explorers we learn about in history rarely went to places that no one else had been; they just went to places that none (or very few) of their countrymen had been to. Explorers were often helped by indigenous people. Even the great Captain James Cook in the South Pacific was assisted by Tupaia, a Tahitian navigator and priest, who had a map. With this in mind it is absolutely worth exploring places that other people already know a lot about. There will be walking tours in your city for tourists, or for locals. They might cover historical events, geography, architecture, local artworks. They are often very cheap and definitely worth a go.

Seeing the city from the perspective of someone else who lives in it can be illuminating. In 2010, a group of former gang members from South Los Angeles started a tour called LA Gang Tours, in which they gave oral histories of their lives. Being able to tell their own stories to predominantly white tourists opened up opportunities to connect people who wouldn't normally cross paths. In London, it is possible to take a tour run by people who have become homeless – an experience that provides answers, but also opens up more questions about how the city is run and for whom. Being shown around an area by a local can shift your feelings about a place. The back of the chippie means far more to you once you know that is where your guide enjoyed their first kiss. Explore the city with different people and you find different places. Even the bits you thought you knew.

Exploration does not need to involve walking; research can be carried out at the museum or in the galleries. Delve into the archives and research papers to find out how the city has come to be the way it is. Find out what was lost along the way. We love playing hide-and-seek as kids, and accessing forbidden places never stops being exciting, whether it be exploring abandoned London Underground stations, catacomb skull stores or secret tunnels in old houses. In the Cappadocia region of Turkey, there are not only tunnels, but entire secret cities built underground with churches, homes and kitchens, complete with air shafts and water tunnels. Their purpose was defensive: when trouble was coming, the thousands of villagers of Derinkuyu went underground. . . now you can follow them. Or you can find the secret places in your own city by looking at council maps[4] or by using light detection and ranging technology.[5] Forty-two of Auckland's volcanoes have produced lava caves, some hundreds of metres long. Some are in people's gardens and have been used as practice air raid shelters. Chirag Jindal, Auckland artist and graduate of the University's School of Architecture and Planning, mapped out the lava caves beneath the city. The spooky images can be seen online. The same LIDAR technology has been used to explore subterranean Rome (useful for preventing engineers from building over sink-holes!). Archaeologists now use this extraordinary tool to explore ancient cities buried below the surface.

Technology can aid exploration – videocams under the sea can capture what is living down there. Microscopes can help you explore what lies under your feet. Citizen Science projects can allow large numbers of people to work together to establish new knowledge. Video technology can share back this information to people so they can get a sense of what is out there, or how things used to be. Architectural research of Auckland's old produce market has given a coder sufficient information to re-create it virtually. Those who log in can then fly around the old cruciform building. Improved mapping of Egypt and old sites like Pompeii might allow visitors to explore ancient civilisations through headsets. Perhaps this will be how we explore our own cities? I find it hard to imagine a world that does not include the physical, embodied experience – partly because I get such pleasure out of moving, dancing and using all my senses – but my children perhaps might.

Explorers can challenge other explorers. The Australian art historian Alice Proctor created a blog and walking tours when she was unable to find a job after graduating. While there have been debates about colonial statuary and imperial appropriation for a number of years in colonised countries, those conversations were few and far between in Europe itself, where so many of the world's treasures have ended up. Alice thinks institutions need to be more honest about how they came to acquire their collections and has developed 'Uncomfortable Art Tours' at six of London's cultural institutions, including the National Gallery, British Museum, Tate Britain and the

Victoria and Albert Museum. It is no coincidence perhaps that these institutions were established during the height of Britain's imperialism. Proctor tells the stories of some of these objects, demanding that museums should 'own it as if you stole it' and be upfront about some of the murkier aspects of provenance.[6]

The British Museum in turn has confronted the criticisms (though they have not at the time of writing returned items like the Rosetta Stone or the Elgin Marbles) by resetting the balance and explaining how a number of things have been acquired not through looting but by more curious means. Dr Sushma Jansari, the curator of the Asian ethnographic and South Asia collections, has set up a series of talks that address the complexities of the past and the value of exchange. 'If you just say East India Company, general, collection of mainly Hindu and Buddhist material, most people would just say: "Must be looted." But this is a guy who converted to Hinduism; he practised ritual bathing, hired two Brahmins to look after the collection, he was absolutely opposed to Europeans proselytising Christianity in India. When you tell a more nuanced story, it doesn't fit other people's agendas but it's still fascinating. That's the difference between what we are doing and what other people are doing.'

Activity: The Drift

In a nutshell This is based on the *dérive* of the Situation Internationale. The idea is to drift around the city considering how it makes you feel.

What you need Transport to an area of the city you do not know; a map; a pencil.

Method

1. Open up a map of a part of the city you know less well. Put on a blindfold and mark where you will start with a pencil dot.

---

2. Find your way there by taxi or public transport (the point is not to return to your starting point).

3. Keep your phone in your bag in case of emergency (you may get lost), but try not to use it.

4. Follow your nose around the city, going down the streets that look most interesting. Jot down the street names. Keep walking for an hour exactly, and then stop at the first café or pub that you find.

5. Find your bearings and fill in your pathway on the map. Mark up anywhere particularly interesting you would like to go back to.

6. Have a nice chat with the pub owner about where you have been and what you particularly liked. Listen to what he says about all the better places you missed. Go and visit them.

Variation Turn it into a group activity. Do the drifting solo but share notes in a pub afterwards and all mark up the same map.

The collector

One value of the collector is to ensure that we have more than we need in preparation for difficult times. Another is that it means some things survive down the generations that help us remember our past. In times of plenty what interests us is curious. Collectors can be greedy, status-driven, fickle. At the turn of the last century, shortly after Japan was forced to trade with the USA, there was an obsession amongst the better-off to collect Netsuke, little Japanese figures that could be displayed in glass cases. The wealthy meanwhile were creating their own zoos or funding archeological digs in the ancient world. In the 1980s, collectable teaspoons were a ubiquitous feature in National Trust gift shops and around the world. Why? Perhaps they combined a memory with a practical usage. Stir your tea and think of Edinburgh Castle . . . it was a thing.

Shoppers can be in thrall to the very old and the very new, with collectable limited-edition shoes, albums or prints collecting a premium at the tills. Like Harrods, great cities offer everything. Publishing reps would hoard first editions of books in the hope that some would be worth a fortune by the time they retired. And if they weren't, at least they would have plenty to read. Collectors are also interested in experiences. Climbers bag mountains and playboys add telephone numbers to their phones. What is a bucket list but a to-do list of experiences to be collected? Photos and blogposts (and teaspoons) serve as proof and reminders of the events. We collect stuff – clothes, CDs, artworks, books, photos. They hold the memories of our lives.

Collecting isn't a terrible thing, as long as the benefits are shared. During Covid lockdown, museums invested in remote digital experiences. This opened up their collections to the world. It also made it possible for people to share their own collections online. There are a number of museums, run by passionate individuals, that have no physical presence at all. The NZ Fashion Museum is one of them and was established by designer Doris de Pont. It has the same purpose as any other museum, to develop social knowledge and stimulate discussion, but it has far fewer overheads and can be enjoyed by anyone, anywhere. As collections are forever available they become an amazing resource for researchers. One of the great merits of such an online collection is that one does not have to own anything or take anything into one's possession. One could gather a collection of images of things one admires and then curate an exhibition that puts them together and makes meaning from them. This could be a collection of photographs taken of the neighbourhood over the years by a variety of people. It could be a series of photographs that you take of things around the area that interest you. Collections can be themed around art, architecture, culture, children's lives or anything.

Sometimes it is the items themselves that matter, and a photograph won't do.

Activity: Start a collection

In a nutshell There is something special about real items. If you are a keen collector then you can turn archivist and gather local seeds, copies of the local newspaper, old books, testimonies from older folk or artwork from up-and-coming students. Focus on things that you believe have value and which the institutions and other people seem to be neglecting.

What do you need Time, patience and, increasingly, a budget.

Method

1. Your collection will start from a personal fascination with an item, and you'll find yourself gathering more. If you realise that you are a collector then do it well. Do some research and find out more about your objects of interest. It is worth cataloguing what you have so you can keep track and ensure that your collection is stored appropriately.

2. Ask yourself why you like these items? It is much better to be guided by what pleases you, rather than by the goal to make a profit out of the collection one day. However, if something pleases you then it probably offers something valuable. If it is a book, it may be because it details animals long extinct. An old machine may demonstrate old technologies that may be useful again. It may be seeds for local plants that are at risk of dying out.

3. Reach out to other collectors to see if you can make useful trades and to share knowledge. You may wish to put together an exhibition or to write an article together on why these objects matter.

4. If the collection has been gathered from the city, it may be worth exhibiting there. This could be in a local museum or library or in a more unusual place like a railway station or café. Consider bequeathing it to the city as a record, or to another collector you trust.

The storyteller

To try to capture the city and to tell its story is also to try to understand it, to solve the question of why a particular city is the way it is.

News and investigative journalism, as well as the commentators – food critics, theatre critics, art critics, writers on urban planning – give focus and shape to a complex, dynamic landscape. Good criticism not only draws attention to mastery, but also gives it context and suggests to the reader why it is worth greater consideration. Then there are the absences – the stories of what cannot, or could not, be said – and the erasures matter too. Kenneth Tynan with British theatre, Jonathan Gold with LA restaurants and Judith Thurman with fashion in New York all focus on the arts, and through that, on how to live. Urban critics like Reyner Banham in Los Angeles and Simon Wilson in Auckland open the door to new ideas and new ways of thinking about the interplay between cities and the lives, aspirations and values of those connected to them.

Local radio stations, newspapers and magazines open up a space for getting messages across. As international media organisations pull out of the local, the gap is being filled by independent owner/editors. Sometimes communities have bought their papers back and run them as non-profits. In late 2018, in Chateauguay Valley in Quebec, Gravite Media offered to give the lossmaking local paper, *The Gleaner*, to the readers it served.[7] At a community meeting, $1 was paid for it, and the next summer saw the paper's re-emergence. It is still publishing, with both an online and a printed presence. In late 2018, a survey in New Zealand found that 29 per cent of people found out what was going on at the local level from their community newspaper or magazine, compared to social media at 23 per cent and the Neighbourly web-site at 12 per cent.[8] In this world of rumour, there is something very valuable about a printed paper that you know will look exactly the same to everyone who reads it. Even a single page of A4 pinned on community notice boards or distributed in cafés can be helpful. These papers are put out with very small teams and they need content. You can write for them.

Activity: Capture the city in words

In a nutshell Sharing well-considered stories about the city can help everyone understand, appreciate and connect to it more; think about the travel writer Jan Morris or the arts/urban planning/food critics.

Method Consider where your great interest lies and start posting reviews on local goings-on online somewhere. Make it a weekly discipline. Go for urban activities but you can be as quirky as you like: walks in different neighbourhoods, interviews with different immigrants on their perspectives of the city. If the subject interests you and you write well, it will probably interest other people too.

You might even find that you can volunteer to work on the paper/local radio/news website. If there is no local media, perhaps start a blog about your city or town. Every city is full of people's stories and is more interesting than it may at first appear.

Variation Create maps that also capture patterns in the city – perhaps of an urban food forest, heritage, or the characteristics of different neighbourhoods.

If the explorer likes to go on a walking tour, the storyteller likes to lead them. It takes some work to set up a walking tour, from sourcing information, planning a route, developing a script and an angle, to then promoting the tour itself. By telling a story about your city, you start to really think through how things actually came to be, which leads to more questions and more answers. When you share one story with other locals, you discover so many more; and the more stories you know of the city, the more interesting it becomes and the more you connect to it. To get started you may need clues – some preservation of heritage, library archives or people to talk to – or you may find that you have lived so long in a place that you are already a repository of knowledge. Jane's Walk is an annual global festival in which local people lead a walk around their local area explaining how and why it matters to them.

Activity: How to lead a local walk

In a nutshell When you teach, you learn twice! Find out more about your local area by leading a walk.

What you need Access to a library or the internet. A piece of paper and pen to plan. A bit of time.

1. On a map, mark out ten locations, not far from each other, that capture what the city is about and that you can incorporate into a walk of no more than two hours long.

2. Choose a theme – historical/natural world/socio-cultural/ underbelly/teen/artistic/criminal/shopping/how the neighbourhood has changed over thirty years. Or something else.

3. Research the places through books and websites to find more detail.

4. Walk the route and check that there are spaces where a large group can loiter.

5. Write the key facts on cue cards, and practise the walk with friends. Top tips for a walk include:

    *   Stories that debunk myths.

    *   Stories that encapsulate the city's history (or your theme).

    *   Unexpected interactions and experiences. People like surprises!

    *   Some simulation – you could dress up, or pretend to be a historical character – or simply help people to imagine what life can be like for other real people.

    *   A duel – have a debate with someone local over what is true (warn them in advance).

    *   Jokes – make 'em laugh!

    *   Some myths – it is OK to bend the truth a tiny bit.

    *   A meta-narrative or theme to hold the walk together.[9]

6. Let people know!

7. Arrive at the meeting point half an hour early and carry an umbrella. Drink a coffee (it builds confidence).

8. Introduce yourself and the tour, and set off.

Tips

- Bring a water bottle and a phone (to take pictures, and in case of emergency).

- Avoid noisy spots. Speak clearly and audibly. Don't go on too long!

- If you don't know the answer to a question, say so.

- Bring a friend to wait with you at the beginning of the tour for the first few times, so it is less scary, and ask someone else to do your marketing – because selling yourself can be hard.

- If bystanders do not like your stories or cause trouble, then move on quickly.

- Be open to your stories changing as you gather more information. Being in place can help you critique the established story. Considering different perspectives is good.

- Enjoy – being animated and passionate about the city helps walkers understand cities better.

The competitor

The city is a great place to come, be challenged and make something of yourself. To succeed in one's career takes commitment and effort. To succeed in play does, too. And yet better to try than not at all. Competitors enjoy testing themselves. This might be against the elements if they go sailing or fishing, or against themselves if they go on long runs. If you are competitive it is also satisfying to see how you fare compared to everyone else. Have a go at a poetry slam, karaoke night, or enter the Ironman or any challenge where you will have an opportunity to win or at least chart your progress.

Activity: Sign up for a challenge

What you need Equipment needs vary. Money for registration fees.

Method There will be some physical challenge in the city, possibly to raise money for a good cause, or simply as a 'fun' event. This might be a marathon, a sky dive, an ocean swim, a winter swim, a dance-off or a sponsored walk. Sign up. Put the pressure on to hone your talent.

Variations

- Sign up for a challenge in another city and enjoy a mini-holiday as well.

- It could also be a non-physical competition, whether coffee-making, musical (there are lots, aimed at everything from choirs to brass bands) or an open mic night.

Tip Sign up a friend up as well, then training can be done together. Alternatively join a club that enters competitions and you can enjoy the experience without doing all the administrative work.

As a competitor you will put in the time and preparation to win as you hate to lose. But you winning doesn't mean that everyone else loses. Less competitive types thoroughly enjoy seeing a master at work, particularly if they are the direct beneficiaries. Are you a great singer? Sing. Are you ready to break a world record? Tell everyone. They will enjoy the show. A friend of mine had a brother, father and husband who were all officers in the army. I have never known another family so up for and adept at organising costume parties. A reaction against spending a good deal of time in uniform and being a small and interchangeable part of something bigger than any one individual? Perhaps. In any case, we all loved the parties and our hosts. Do you organise great parties? Do it. If you are new to it, here are some tips.

Activity: How to throw a good party

In a nutshell When you throw a party you are offering people a space to have a good time at no cost – surely people will want that? And yet we have all been to parties that haven't quite worked out. Some of them have been our own. There are some tricks to making your party a success and it does require a bit of effort.

What you need A fun space to be rowdy; entertainment; food; drink; people.

Method

1. If you are new to party planning, share the job. Event planning is one of the most stressful jobs there is. Besides, if there are two of you, you have more people to invite and to meet.

2. Decide on what sort of party you are going for. What do you and your friends want and need right now that you can realistically provide? Parties can range from a pot luck dinner, to a wild night of dancing. What appeals? Costume parties are like marmite, some love 'em, some hate 'em. If people get in the spirit they can be a great way to start conversations. Or people may not come at all.

3. Organise the entertainment aspect first. If your friends are great DJs, pin them down for a date before booking a venue. If you are throwing a ceilidh, make sure you have a great band and caller. If you want to have lots of party games, ensure that you have someone to lead them. Bring out the toys. Sometimes the entertainment just means the presence of particularly fun and/or popular friends. If this is the case, make sure some can and will come.

4. Organise a place and time. It is a great idea to choose a venue that guests have to come to by a certain time because that traps them for a while. A party on a boat is good, or a trip to an island, or a country house. Work out where the food and drink are going to come from. Have lots. A Saturday is generally better than a Friday. When you are in your twenties this is because by the time your mates turn up to a Friday party they are already drunk. When your friends are older it is because on Friday they are exhausted. On Saturday everyone

is fresh, rested and ready to go. Some people won't be able to come. You can't please everyone.

5. Get the invitations out a few weeks in advance with all the relevant information attached and double-checked for accuracy. Sell the theme and the entertainment. If you have locked in the bucking bronco – tell them – if it is potluck and poker, tell them that too. Yes, you can use Facebook but you should also send personalised invites out by email as calendar invites and ask for RSVPs. Or call.

6. Keep a list of who's coming, who's not coming and who's still undecided. Call everyone up to chase, to acknowledge with pleasure they are coming, or to note that you are disappointed they can't make it. Facebook makes it easy to say yes or no and then not follow through. A phone call makes it real. When you are on the phone it is worth telling people which of their friends or people of interest to them will be there. Other people are the great lure of a party. If you get the right people in the room you are 90 per cent there. Text the guests again a week and/or the day before to remind them.

7. A week in advance, double-check food, drink, space, shelter, decorations, lighting and entertainment (and what you are going to wear) is all arranged.

8. If you are partying at home tidy and clean the house no later than the day before. Make sure you know where everything is going to be. Put the white wine in the fridge. If you are partying elsewhere make sure you have everything you need to take with you by the door. Get a good night's sleep.

9. It is the day. Decorate and sort the lighting so the party space looks great.

10. It is the start. People are often late (unless you are on a boat). Stay chilled. Welcome everyone, make sure they are comfortable and introduce them to someone. Now, you can enjoy your party!

Tips

•   The fewer the people, the more the entertainment is provided by the combination of people you put together. The larger the number of people the better the entertainment has to be because it will be harder to ensure everyone is looked after on the night. Putting the food down one end and the drink the other is one old trick to get people to mingle.

- Don't balk at putting on the pressure when organising a fun event but also make sure you deliver. Make it clear that you expect people to turn up and chase them up. If people repeatedly back out at the last minute then do not rely on them or promise their presence. If they come, it is a bonus.

- If it is culturally appropriate in your circles, consider asking for contributions to the party. BYO is pretty standard but you can also ask people to bring particular foods – be specific. If you are on an island, ask them to book tickets for a certain ferry and put in some money for accommodation.

Variations

- Make someone else's party go well. Get the dancing started, force people who you know usually like dancing (or doing whatever is on offer) to join in. Ask for their participation as a favour, and refuse to take no for an answer.

The director

If you have a vision to make the city better then you have a role to play. Placemaking efforts don't just come from the top. Over the years community leaders have raised funds for public swimming pools, the restoration of churches, the establishment of libraries and the setting up of societies. Streetfilms[10] in the United States reports on cycling organisations, community groups and bold individuals who have transformed streets and public spaces so they function better. Cycle lanes have been put in with traffic cones; pedestrian crossings have been painted in by parents to demonstrate the need for a safer way for their kids to get to school; extra pavement area has been painted out into the parking bays to allow for alfresco dining. Guerilla gardeners have taken wastelands on traffic islands and turned them into gardens.

Directors make things happen, and good directors make other people's lives profoundly better.

One of the oldest forms of play directors is the choir leader. Get a lot of people singing together and the effect is dizzying. Historically, community singing happened in church but increasingly it is being organised in the secular world too. The Really Big Chorus has been going for more than forty years and is made up of thousands of individuals who come together to sing in enormous venues like London's Albert Hall. No audition required. The great majority of singers are not professional and put in a bit of money to cover the costs, including that of the choir leader who goes above and beyond to help bring out the best in the singers in their charge.

Rohan MacMahon, a management consultant in Auckland, started a street choir after joining the board of the homeless charity Lifewise. Open to everyone in the community, but particularly targeting those on the margins, the choir brought people together and boosted morale through the therapeutic power of song. Over four years, the choir grew from just three people to a core group of about thirty, from all ages and backgrounds. Today, the Auckland Street Choir is in demand, performing at gigs and events across the city. It seems that more New Zealanders sing in a choir than play rugby.[11]

The director does not need to be the musical director who leads the choir. They could perhaps be one of the singers. They may well keep a low profile – but without them things don't get done. Melonie Roberts arrived in New Zealand from the UK in 2009 and, unable to find a choir that suited her, set up her own. After a blitz of advertising, she mustered thirty-five people for her first meeting. By 2016 there were eighty regular members.

Activity: How to set up a couch choir

In a nutshell The director is a visionary who can identify what a group of people may need, sows the seeds of ideas and puts together the people required to make it happen.

What you need A lot of contacts, some organisational skills and a winning smile.

Method Talk to people. If it seems that lots of people quite like the idea of singing (perhaps they used to sing but don't have an outlet any more) ask around to see if there is anyone local who might lead it. Consider what the choir is for. Is it to compete? Or is it mainly a social occasion with wine? Choose the choir leader accordingly and set expectations. If the former you may want auditions and down payments. If the latter you may have a revolving door policy. You may want to make an offer to people and see if the demand is really there. Suggest a term's worth of meetings and confirm with all those interested the time, costs and location. Encourage the people there on the first night to ensure that at least a few who come can report back on how fun it is. Be patient while numbers grow. Keep talking to everyone about how it's going so as to steer musical choices in a popular direction. Enjoy.

Tip Share responsibility for the project with other friends and the musical director. Don't force it. Trends rise and fall. People are always busier than you think they are. If it doesn't work out, move on to another project.

Rob Hopkins, the initial leader of the Transition Towns movement, doesn't see himself as a director. 'It's not my movement,' he says, 'we're not a franchise model.' Like the choir leaders, he got some people together in a room and gave them some tools to bring out the best in them. He had been living in Ireland, working as a permaculture teacher and involved in the establishment of an eco-village, when he went to a lecture on Peak Oil and realised that the world was unprepared for a life with no oil. With his students, he started to consider how communities could transition to a sustainable future by looking at energy, food, transport, homes, education, the local economy – all the pieces of the puzzle that make for a functional community. He reckoned that if the government wouldn't make an impact, and an individual couldn't, then perhaps a forward-thinking community might. Totnes in Devon had its fair share of alternative lifestylers, so he moved there in 2005 and found a keen audience. Alongside Naresh

Giangrande, one of the locals, he led a group of residents through a series of workshops and worked out an Energy Descent Plan[12] – how to survive with less and less fossil fuels by any means possible.

The Transition Towns movement provides a structure within which communities can improvise. Because the fossil fuel problem could be tackled from so many different angles, a community could make the changes that they felt were most important and that they were in the best position to deliver. In Totnes, urban farming was led by a woman who had long coveted more garden space and had the skills to teach the new recruits. Other groups have focused on farmers' markets and waste reduction.

Transition Towns started in small towns (where people know each other already), but there are also groups in cities, working on reducing plastic and supporting social entrepreneurs through the provision of space, services and mentoring, as in Lambeth.[13]

Pushing projects at a local level is effective because there are lots of people around to join in, and the projects are usually doable. Church roofs are fixed. Swimming pools are installed by public subscription (Lewes, East Sussex). Beaches and rivers are cleaned up. Parks and playgrounds are created or improved. Some of these projects take longer than others, but they are deeply satisfying when they succeed, because they have a tangible impact on people's lives.

The artist/creator

Covid might have revealed a latent desire for making things, but learning the basics for creative projects is perhaps harder than it sounds. Many people have insufficient space or resources to do these things. Big suburban houses are OK: they have sheds, garages or spare rooms for tinkering in, but homes in the city are smaller. The Covid lockdown was a very different experience for people in overcrowded conditions, with no access to a garden or a park, or an oven, books or tools. It underlined how the home could be a good site of play, and a good site of work, or not.

But there is a way. And that is sharing creative spaces. A number of social enterprises have sprung up to facilitate 'making', despite smaller living spaces. In Auckland, they include the Library of Tools and the Gribblehurst Hub, which combines a community shed, garden and crafts room. In a little back street in one of the grittier inner-city areas is a carpentry workshop, The Warren, where people can hire a bench, learn the basics from an old pro[14] and even sell what they make. The Central Library offers craft classes, from scrapbooking to 3D printing. It is not only fun, but it livens up the library.

The public space can be a space for making art, and the biggest public space is the streets. Sketching the public realm is a great way to see the city better. As Erich Ohser wrote in his book *In Defence of Drawing* in 1943: 'If you draw, the world becomes more beautiful, far more beautiful. Trees that used to be just scrub suddenly reveal their form. Animals that were ugly make you see their beauty. If you then go for a walk, you'll be amazed how different everything can look. Less and less is ugly if every day you recognise beautiful forms in ugliness and learn to love them.' In Huntly, Scotland, Deveron Projects argues that the 'Town is the Venue', and they have literally made the practice of everyday life an artform, and bring aspects of life into art. Growing food, making bread and walking all become forms of art and are critiqued as such.[15]

For a long time it was hard to find indoor community spaces that people could use, but things are changing. Venue brokers offer online search and booking systems to rent out spaces owned by local government, community organisations, churches and schools to community groups, adult education classes, artists and the general public. It is easy to find the right space, at the right time, and at the right price. Some companies specialise in finding spaces for artists to work at reduced rates. You might then see pop-up art exhibitions and music recitals in empty shops on the high street. Or perhaps a science lab. In Seattle, Pop-up Science move between neighbourhoods, activating all sorts of different empty spaces for a week or two with workshops, talks and opportunities to experiment.[16] Artist collectives, like Renew Newcastle in Australia and the Urban Dream Brokerage in Wellington, have organised pop-up foodbanks, art installations and performances in abandoned shops. You could propose an idea.

We like to watch, and we like to participate in the production of art. In New York, Improv Everywhere, led by Charlie Todd, involves tens of thousands of people who are summoned to create happenings in public spaces, from dancing to activating office block windows with performers so people are encouraged to look up. You don't need to be a professional to do art, and you don't need to be a 'creative' to create. Isabel and Alfredo Aquilizan, from the Philippines, masterminded a participatory art project that engaged with family, relocation and homemaking. It involved hundreds of locals creating little houses out of cardboard boxes, which were then assembled together and attached to the mast of a wooden boat. This created a city that was then dangled upside down from the foyer of the Auckland Art Gallery, like a Shaun Tan illustration made real. Artists in the community can make fun things happen for everyone to enjoy.

Action: Create a happening

What you need Friends, portable music system with speakers.

Method

1. Work out a performance. This can be a song or a dance routine of about three minutes.

2. Find a suitable stage in the city.

3. Perform the routine, then move on quickly to another spot.

4. Repeat the routine.

Tips

- Practise until you are as good as you can be, and smile!

- Get a friend to film you or take photographs to share later.

- Try to find unexpected places, like traffic intersections or balconies, or places in the city that need cheering up.

14

Playing on the edge

The line between exploration and trespass is hazy. Get away with breaking into the park at midnight for a secret drink, and you feel a thrill. It is an adventure, a one-off, but you might also take away the idea that, because you *can* access the park, and because no one is enforcing the rule otherwise, you are actually *allowed* to access the park. Getting into the park is taken for granted, and so one pushes further, perhaps into the lido for a midnight swim.

It does feel glorious to feel one's own power, to feel free to do what one likes, and pushing the boundaries never quite stops. In a city, rule-flouting takes place at a lower and a higher level. At the lower level because there may be no other options, and at the top because with power, wealth and charm it becomes easier for some to negotiate their way around the rules or to ignore them altogether. Those in the middle seem more likely to play by the rules. Misdemeanours that get the pulse racing can be exceedingly tame: stealing a packet of crisps or queue jumping at Wimbledon. A little danger can go a long way, because most of us have too much to lose. Given the choice, few would want to take on a life of crime full time, and yet there is undoubtedly a thrill in crossing the line sometimes.

The flipside of the excitement of play is fear, but that also means the flipside of very reasonable fear (of being hurt, of being caught) is excitement. Doing something that you would quite like to do can become super-desirable simply because it is forbidden, and conversely, feeling obliged to do something can put you right off. Getting away with something that is not allowed shouldn't give you a frisson of pleasure, but it does. What a flying suit is for physical vertigo, engaging in criminal or immoral behaviour is for moral vertigo. Sometimes, in the case of joyriding or rioting in the streets, both physical and moral vertigo combine in a heady, highly dangerous rush. In this chapter, I will look at these various aspects of rule-breaking as they intersect with the city, and at the constant challenge of balancing the excitement and vertigo of the city with, well, balance.

Playing at breaking the rules

Geoff Manaugh's *A Burglar's Guide to the City* makes the point that we all fantasise about breaking and entering, whether it be through detective fiction or films like *The Italian Job* or *Ocean's Eleven*. But we also live through crimes vicariously in real life – the most compelling news is about awful deeds. If we enjoy imagining transgressions, we probably shouldn't be surprised to find our children enjoy acting them out. Whether they are taking on the role of cops or robbers, the difference is minor: both have the right to drive too fast, shoot at each other and generally break normal laws. The boys, and some girls, at the local kindergarten all seemed to go through a stage where they would use sticks as guns and pretend to shoot each other. In adulthood, paintball allows us to target friends who we hope will gratifyingly 'die'. For the thinner-skinned, laser tag can offer a similar experience: players with different speeds and skills run happily around a modified warehouse with laser guns, targeting each other. Being able to shoot one's spouse and children in play can do wonders for the family dynamic.

Activity: Translating 'Among Us' in a public space

In a nutshell 'Among Us' is a bit like wink murder with tasks. Originally a computer game, it has been translated into a multiplayer playground game that can be adapted for multiple situations. In it a group of 'good' people try to fulfil some pre-ordained tasks before they are all killed off by the 'imposter'. The 'good' people must therefore keep a wary eye out for this person and identify them before it is too late!

What you need Five to eight people are ideal, plus some playing cards (or use a 'selector' – someone who is not playing).

Method

1. Before the game begins the players establish what tasks might be appropriate for the space they are in.

2. The imposter is either whoever picks the jack from a selection of playing cards, or is chosen by someone who is not playing. If the latter method is used all players shut their eyes and receive a tap on the shoulder. The imposter gets two taps.

3. The players divvy out tasks. The imposter cannot do a task but can 'pretend': for example, if a task is moving rocks from a to b, the imposter can't pick up a rock but can fiddle about with it, find excuses to drift off elsewhere and so on.

4. The imposter kills people by touching them with their fist (using a stabbing motion).

5. When a player thinks they can identify the imposter they call an 'emergency meeting' in which an accusation is made. The players vote to exclude that person from the game, which may or may not succeed. If the vote fails the accuser is out of the game.

6. Everyone left in the game returns to their tasks until someone else dies or the tasks are complete. Note that the imposter can accuse others.

Variation Wink murder is more static. A group of people (the more the merrier) sit in one room, all visible to each other. Everyone draws a card from a selection that contains one jack. The jack is the murderer. They surreptitiously wink at people who can 'die' dramatically. The winner is the person who accuses the murderer correctly. The accused shows their card. If the allegation is correct the accuser wins the game; if they are innocent then the accuser must 'die'.

Another game, the XD Dark Ride experience, takes place in a small curtained-off space dominated by a 3D cinema screen, with moving chairs creating the sensation of falling from a great height onto river rapids, or of moving at high speed through industrial wastelands. In it, a group of friends or family members compete with, but not against, each other to defeat a common enemy, winning points as they shoot down zombies or Mad Max lookalikes. Game developers Triotech target the lucrative family market, they say, for the greater good: a family that plays together, stays together. That parents may take on the role of vigilantes in play allows them to explore working as a team in a state of crisis. The vicarious pursuit of criminal transgressions in games or in one's own imagination is fine: no one gets hurt.

You can play out crime fantasies in the streets, hidden in plain sight. A Ukrainian friend revealed to me that she used to follow strangers' cars to find parts of the city she doesn't know. We once pursued each other on foot through the streets of Auckland. The game was to make it difficult for her to keep up, but not so hard that she lost me entirely. It was a great way of showing her the lesser-known corners of the city, the cut-throughs within buildings and the industrial waterfront wastelands that people generally avoided.

We weren't being original: the artist Vito Acconci turned stalking people into an art decades ago. 'Following Piece', a series of photographs of the backs of the heads of strangers he had followed around New York's public realm, was presented in the Museum of Modern Art in 1969.[1] You might think that this would never be allowed today. Then you read a guide on how to improve urban spaces, and one of the methods is to follow people around (or watch CCTV footage) to see how people use the space.

Around the same time, Augusto Boal in Brazil directed his actors to 'perform' arguments in the street and to pretend to sexually harass their fellow actors on public transport, to attract attention and to see what bystanders might do. Sort of wrong, and yet sort of interesting. (Boal wasn't popular with the dictatorship and eventually had to flee the country.) Punchdrunk's immersive theatre productions, performed in abandoned office buildings, including the old post office sorting station in Paddington, London, allow audience members to break some of the normal rules of engagement with actors, following them down corridors, having intimate moments with them and watching, silently, voyeuristically, in masks, as the characters suffer.

Theatre-maker and academic Emma Willis wrote her doctoral thesis on Dark Tourism, the phenomenon of travelling to historical sites where terrible things have happened: the killing fields in Cambodia, the First World War battlegrounds of Flanders; the concentration camps of the Holocaust. There are urban equivalents: the instruments of torture in the Tower of London and the London Dungeons, Madame Tussaud's Chamber of Horrors. Few of us in the West will be forced to witness a violent crime, or execution, these days (thank goodness), but we may well still be drawn to the sites where these things have happened. In the words of my young friend Jack: 'Great, I like death!' Those who study this morbid fascination believe that doing so makes people more thoughtful about the darker aspects of life, and may lead us to imagine how we would endure similar difficult circumstances and consider what moral choices we would make. Jane McGonigal noted, when creating the game Tombstone Hold'em, that people are cheered up when reminded of death. This is not to suggest for a moment that people are glad that others have suffered; perhaps it is more that it puts one's own problems and failings into perspective. Perhaps it reminds us to be happy in our ongoing existence. Perhaps also we need to be reminded of brutal realities, that choices matter and that fortunes can change. We go to great lengths to reduce small risks in modern society. It may be useful and galvanising to be reminded that the dangers we face are real.

Activity: Go on a dark tour of your city

In a nutshell Join a dark tour of your city and consider how and why those terrible events happened in the past.

What you need A tour to go on.

Method Sign up for a tour and go.

Variations

- Create your own tour by reading local history books and websites and investigating archives. Seek out the sites where these events took place and develop a walk. Were there witch hunts in your city, or plagues? How did your city fare during the Civil War or in the Blitz? How were people in the past punished for transgressing, and what had they done? What modern stories of horror and suffering can be identified?

- Create a story of horrors to come.

Pretending to murder people around the town has long been the focus of the Cambridge University Assassins' Guild. Participants are given the name of their target – another student member – who they must kill, while also evading the imaginary knife of the student hunting them. The last person standing is the winner.[2] For some players, the aim of the game is to win, but for many it is a good opportunity to meet people because 'it provides amusing circumstances . . . that a wide variety of people appreciate'. They are right. The game serves as an ice-breaker and takes the pressure off. Counter-intuitive, perhaps, to befriend the person who is murdering you, but probably more effective than asking someone directly if they would like to hang out with you more. Those students who sign up but then don't play get marked as 'incompetent', and can be killed by anyone – which, the website notes cheerfully, offers up an opportunity for someone to make contact (and possibly make friends). It should go without saying that the killing bit is all pretend – and after one is dispatched, one is free to join the police . . . Costume re-enactments of famous battles, complete with costumes and replica weapons, also provide an opportunity to kill at scale.

Murder mystery dinners in set locations have long been a thing, but there are also games in which players traverse the city. CluedUpp[3] is based in the UK, but the games they create are played in thirty-eight countries around the world and have involved, they estimate, about half a million players. Their stated mission is to turn the city into a playground by creating experiences that allow friends and families to connect in unexpected ways. Players download a GPS-connected app which is tailored to their city, and head out. When they unpack one clue and get to the right spot, another clue is released. These games came out of the informal games that exploded with the arrival of mobile phones with GPS in the early 2000s. Originally perceived as creative art and presented as fringe experiences at the Edinburgh Festival, games have been harnessed as marketing tools – campaigns have staged wild thefts and getaways in city centres for YouTube consumption, to attract attention to their products, and now as commodities in themselves. Play trickles down. None of these activities, one notes, actually involves breaking any rules, just imagining that one is, but there is a frisson to be enjoyed in going a little further.

Breaking the rules to find solutions

Often what we think of as cheating could also be described as copying, collaboration, innovation and thinking outside the box. Nevertheless, for many, even quite mild rule-bending can be unsettling. There are thousands of laws that we are not aware of in everyday life. We don't need to know them, because on the whole we just do what everyone else is doing – until it occurs to us that there may be a better way. One way to lobby for a better urban realm is to publicly demonstrate an idea that you would like others to steal.

In 2017, I signed up for a course on Urban Planning and Society, and one of our assignments was to consider how to repurpose a car park for Parking Day on 3 September. This semi-official global street design festival started in 2005 when, legend has it, two landscape architects at the Rebar Studio in San Francisco put some money in a parking meter and created a tiny park with turf and seats in the parking space.[4] The guys hung out – passers-by took photos of them – and at the end of their allotted time they rolled up their turf, packed up their seats and headed off. The point, of course, is that there are lots of things to do in public space that are better than allocating it for cars. It caused a stir – weren't parking spaces just for parking? When

I decided to do my car park installation, my friend Jacinda's reaction was the same. Was it allowed?

I didn't know if we were allowed, and I was as nervous as she was, but I promised that I would take full responsibility for any breach of regulation. (We had no idea what we might be guilty of or what might happen. Arrest? Someone in a suit telling us to go away?) The two of us, with my four-year-old daughter, laid out a game area in a parking space near the community centre, with a table, chairs, radio, board games, drinks and snacks. As the street was then designed, there was a road between the small square and the centre, making it danger- ous for children to run around. An hour and a few friendly chats went by, and the three of us relaxed and played hopscotch on the pavement as we demonstrated that kids needed a place to play in the city, too.

I don't think we were alone in feeling nervous about making a scene in public. It is common for organisers of protests to inform the police and get permission. Having got away with our venture once, next time round we weren't nervous. We brought in couches and invited a band. Within a year of me putting out my play area (one effort amidst the work of numerous campaigners), the road was redesignated as a pedestrian space where children can, and do, play safely. A year later, and a decision was made for the whole street to be pedestrianised. A year further on, and they are still working on it.

Progress can be very slow, even for small projects. Another amateur placemaker in rural New Zealand has spent years painting a pedestrian crossing on the road near the school. It was painted out a number of times, but finally the school principal noted to the press in 2018 that a pedestrian crossing would be a good idea.[5] A year later, school pupils presented a petition for a crossing to the local council, who then funded a permanent solution. It hadn't been installed by late 2020, though.

Lack of affordable housing in urban centres is another issue, and once again creative solutions have been developed and modelled. It has been worked out (in New Zealand at least) that building consents are not needed if the house can fit on a trailer and thus is officially a caravan rather than a permanent dwelling. Parents with gardens can thus allow their cash-strapped offspring to live independently in a tiny house in the garden. Cheating? Sort of, but perhaps an indicator that there is a market for homes that are small but well-designed, with secure tenure. New developers are taking note that there is a consumer interest in this, just as developers in the 1970s noted the potential of New York lofts that artists had been squatting in. Resource consent applications have started coming in to councils for build-to-rent buildings that combine bedroom suites with bathrooms, kitchenettes and just enough room for a couch, TV and a table for two. These apartment buildings, rather reminiscent of student halls and youth hostels in Europe and Japan, also often have shared spaces at the ground floor and rooftop levels.

Boundary-pushing, looked at this way, doesn't seem that alarming, but a helpful way to present alternatives. Solutions that seem unrealistic can become the new way of doing things. Play trickles down from top to bottom, and it also trickles up. Until it doesn't, and then the pressure for change may build and threaten existing structures entirely.

Protest as play

Protest is a particularly urban phenomenon – sometimes peaceful, sometimes not. The power is in the masses of people that simulate an army, marching through the streets and taking over public space. Protests are deadly serious and yet they can also be extremely playful. They are about poverty and suffering, war, injustice, damage to the environment and the right to work and be free – but a protest will also be exciting, novel, challenging and fun. Protests signify distress, but they also set an alternative vision for a future with hope – hope that their demands will be answered. And sometimes they are. Equal rights legislation in the 1960s and '70s did come off the back of a well-run campaign of petitions and protest. However, it is easier to push a stone downhill than up. More workers mean more economic growth so the changes had broad benefits for productivity and consumer spending. It is easier to get change through if it is in the economy's or the leadership's interests.

The Extinction Rebellion protests in 2019 were a little different. The demands weren't about inclusion in the system but changing it.

The school strike for climate has pushed climate change action higher up the agenda. This mainstreaming of the issue indicates there is progress. While Greenpeace campaigners have long hassled would-be oil drillers and military ships heading off to do nuclear testing, Extinction Rebellion – based in the UK but with pockets of supporters around the world – has made activists out of grandmothers and civil servants. As one former head teacher noted, since British Prime Minister Margaret Thatcher found out about the dangers of climate change forty years prior, emissions had not gone down in the UK, but up 60 per cent.[6] Most of these protestors would have preferred government to have tackled climate change emissions through legislation and enforcement, but there comes a time when enough is enough. Normally law-abiding participants gathered in urban spaces, mentally prepared to be arrested for being obstructive.[7] There was an element of excitement to this which was appealing. They were in a heightened state, mentally stimulated and braced at the prospect of being part of a group of people crossing a line for a cause of such importance.

Making a stand is at the core of protest, literally. You need to be present, taking up urban space, transforming it entirely, in the moment, and if enough people are involved, forever. You might join a public meeting in a park to stop it being severed by a highway (as with Washington Square). You might join a march. People's impact is exponentially increased when they organise themselves and work together to get a clear message across. When huge numbers take over the streets, limiting some of the city's normal functioning, in order to ask for justice and political reform, as with the Arab Spring, the Occupy Wall Street movement and Black Lives Matter, or action on climate change, they unnerve decision-makers. How they respond is uncertain. Street takeovers send a very strong message back to the leaders of the city that all is not well. Protests are exciting and frightening because it is playing at the edge. Sometimes that is necessary. Over a century ago, poverty in a mining community in the South Island of New Zealand led them to organise a night march asking for food relief, otherwise they would starve. Their march was conducted as a funeral cortège with torches. It was very quiet. It was very shocking. Funds were found.

Play as a way to explore possibilities

Whether the freedoms of the city are dangerous or empowering depends on one's culture and point of view – but for many playing against the norm in the city is alluring at least at some point in their lives. This might be manifested by dressing flamboyantly to express one's identity with a counterculture – like punks and goths – or not wearing anything at all – like Living Theatre artists in New York in the 1970s. Gentle subversion manifested itself in illicit bungy jumps off Brooklyn Bridge. Folk would arrive under cover of darkness, get safely attached to the ropes, leap and then retreat with friends, trying to control their laughter no doubt, when they don't get caught.[8] It manifests in the sneaky installation of fairy lights in the shape of a giant cock and balls in Moscow. It manifests in yarn-bombing and unauthorised street art, the organisation of parties in abandoned spaces or the clambering up onto the roofs via fire escapes or scaffolding to enjoy the sunset. It might involve exploring one's sexuality or gender identity. It might mean heading out to the beach at night and skinny dipping. Or it may just mean being entirely true to yourself, whatever anyone else thinks. American singer-songwriter Dolly Parton's advice – to 'find out who you are and do it on purpose' – has great scope in the city, particularly for artists. Along with Vito Acconci and Augusto Boal, there have been a number of other artists, before and since, whose identity has been wrapped around the desire to purposefully explore and demonstrate new ways of living.

The 'avant-garde' describes some of these pioneering art forms, but while minimalism, conceptualism and so on were supposed to challenge the status quo, some artists in Argentina thought their impacts bypassed the intended beneficiaries (aka the people) and amused only the intellectual elite, who had sufficient time and fancy vocabulary to argue about what it all meant. They decided to develop a form of art that was less esoteric and more direct. Artists would model exactly how life could be in the real world, but they would do it in a confined time and space so as to focus the mind. It was the time for a new avant-garde: a purposeful subversion or 'life as form'.[9] The artists of Buenos Aires kicked off in 1968 with the 'First

National Meeting on Avant-Garde Art' – and the main idea was that art would be direct, clear and would allow anyone to participate. On the one hand it was art as activism, designed to change society irreversibly, and therefore subversive, but on the other it was a way of changing the world through positive modelling, rather than complete destruction.

The first work was *Tucumán Arde* or 'Tucumán is Burning'. The artists collaborated with academics, journalists, photographers, film-makers and unions to find out what was actually happening at a sugarcane plantation where restructuring had resulted in widespread unemployment and hunger. They created a multi-media exhibition in union halls and invited a wide audience, using a teaser campaign involving graffiti, playbills, cinema screens and posters – as you would for any fun event. They displayed documentary photographs, government-authorised propaganda, press clippings and academic findings (often at odds), and they projected films and delivered speeches. They turned the lights off every half hour, to underline the problem of reliable access to utilities for those in the provinces versus the cities. The exhibition was a huge success and has become a much-adopted approach for exhibitions in museums and galleries of modern art.

In New York, between 1969 and 1974, the combination of people leaving the city for the suburbs, the Vietnam War and the oil crisis caused huge economic strain. Artists played in abandoned structures. Gordon Matta-Clark roasted pigs by dumpsters and fed passers-by. He cut up a house with a chainsaw as a way of challenging and changing structures physically, conceptually, culturally and politically. His friend the dancer Trisha Brown created pieces on and down the side of buildings. There were drugs, discos and dancing. The city administration however was getting poorer and poorer and there were fewer and fewer jobs. The city ended up in the thrall of the banks and was transformed into a neoliberal financial centre. The Bronx burnt but from the ashes came youth clubs, community centres, street dance, street art and urban agriculture, that pointed to how life could be better.

In 2018, Tania El Khoury performed her work, *The Search for Power*, with her real-life husband in a disused electrical station in Kuopio, Finland, as part of ANTI Festival, the annual festival of play.

Audience members sat around a table laid for a wedding feast with drapery, fruit and wine, but instead of a plate and cutlery, each place was laid with a magnifying glass and a folder. Over the course of an evening, we discovered why the performers' real wedding had been cut short by a power cut. The tale of greed and corruption went back more than a century, and was told through a series of documents the artist/researchers found in the government archives of Beirut, Paris and London. It turned out that electricity had simply been established by colonial landowners to run trams, so as to inflate land values, and the 'need to improve the electricity system' had been used as a way to argue for development loans ever since (that never seemed to do the job they were meant for). No one had ever really intended to create a proper functioning domestic supply. The setting was dramatic, and the art was all the more subversive for being true. We know cheats are not well thought of in society. Presenting the issue well may be necessary to shift the narrative.

Other works are more participatory – opening up an opportunity for participants to share their experiences and knowledge, as a way to cut through propaganda and mainstream news. Jeremy Deller's *It is what it is: Conversations about Iraq* incorporated a military vehicle from the war in Iraq, and it has been used across America to start conversations about what war is really like. Mapping projects in San Francisco have been brilliant at revealing the realities of gentrification and displacement (Urban Displacement Project). Jeanne van Heeswijk has also engaged in a series of projects to counter gentrification. She started by recording and sharing diverse stories of East London residents to amplify voices generally unheard. Most recently, she has established an artisan bakery to provide a focus for resistance in a working-class Liverpool neighbourhood to try to prevent gentrification. Artists may seem unthreatening, but a lot of the work is designed to challenge and change the system.

The opportunities for and dangers of breaking the system

Creative cities are innovative and exciting when artists fill the gap between what is, and what needs to be. Cities are at their most creative in times of uncertainty and flux but this comes with its own dangers of anarchy and chaos.[10] The Creative Cities exhibition at the Tate Modern in London in 2001 looked at ten twentieth-century cities and celebrated their moments in the zeitgeist. All were going through some sort of change of structure – political, cultural or geopolitical. The sense of excitement is tangible. One wishes one could experience these places first-hand, to be in turn-of-the-century Paris and Vienna; Moscow in the early heady days of Communism; or newly independent Rio or Lagos in the 1950s and '60s. In all cases, the innovators were doing things that previously had not been allowed, either illegal or which had been considered inappropriate in conservative cultures. Activities included fly-billing, and experimentation with clothes, music, ideas, living arrangements. One wonders about the human cost of this creative flux. Could it have felt to some more conservative people that what others were doing wasn't allowed, was dangerous?

In all these countries, the huge pendulum that swung away from the status quo swung back with force. A depressing pattern emerges, of playful innovators quashed by the political or military machine. The First World War ended the party in Paris and Vienna, military coups and/or dictatorships clamped down on freedoms in Russia, Nigeria and Brazil. Within a decade or so of new beginnings these countries seemed to become more oppressed than before.

The Creative Cities exhibition hinted that cities on the edge are exciting but traumatic and difficult to sustain. Perhaps stability and a shared sacrifice is a more reliable path to a better world than revolution. Compare the creative cities with London in the Blitz in the Second World War. War was oppressive in the very real sense: people had less freedom of speech, political participation, movement, and life choices. Normal rules didn't apply and co-operation and loyalty were all that counted. Killing – normally forbidden – became part of life. Back at home, there were fewer things to buy, and what there was could be destroyed at any moment, by bombs or perhaps by invasion, and yet there was rationing and a sense of order despite the chaos. At the end of it, all parties (even the Conservatives) determined to make the UK a more equal place, and used this as the basis of their policies the Beveridge Report. And they did. The UK was arguably a duller place in the late 1940s and '50s, but it was a much fairer one, with greater social mobility.

Other ruptures and disasters can precipitate creativity. Cities that need mending offer opportunities to do things better. After the Lisbon earthquake and fire, the city was rebuilt in the modern style (complete with zoning), able to withstand earthquakes. Baron Haussmann recreated Paris in the late nineteenth century, primarily to quell the disorder that was enabled by the narrow streets and multiple laneways, but the process would also reduce disease, improve lighting, infrastructure and transport, and introduce new parks for recreation (themselves a re-creation of the parks of London). In recent years, creative city builders in Africa and Asia have leapfrogged over a whole stage of expense – maintaining electricity infrastructure – and gone straight to solar panels and microgrids.

While it is sensible to turn disadvantage into opportunity, no country, or politician, is likely to precipitate a disaster so as to come out from it well. While councils and countries seem to achieve little in one year, an extraordinary amount can be achieved through due process over a decade if there is a clear vision and political will.

Art needs to speak truth to power – tensions can be useful to improve the system. They can make people wake up – including city leaders – and see things from more perspectives. The *enfant terrible* of public art is street art, which can range from magnificent reproductions of Renaissance artworks to tagging. It is an artform that divides people, though less so than it did in the past. The England-based street artist Banksy feeds back political critique in his art and enlivens the street at the same time. Others stick to slogans that shout out a point of view. Whether the art is political or whimsical, derivative or original, street art can complicate and add interest to the landscape. Street art can also demonstrate how public space could be used differently and better. Whether street art and graffiti stay is very much dependent on the feedback of locals, on whether they like it or not. If people like it and there aren't many complaints, the art may well stay. The same applies to the pop-up gardens and plantings. They can be an attraction for visitors, as Lisbon, Melbourne and Bristol have found. Now street art is equally as likely to be used to market a city to visitors who are looking for an authentic experience as it is to be scrubbed away in the small hours. In New Zealand the Dunedin Street Art project[11] was led by a group of fans who helped artists to connect with building owners and to negotiate the bureaucratic processes. Now their walls are filled with great art. The art is thought-provoking and beautiful and funnily enough instead of hiding the buildings beneath them, you notice their qualities more than ever. You can change a city without losing it.

15

Playing together nicely

We've been talking about good design and how cities can facilitate play and survival. We have looked at grassroots action. Now we're going to look at the why and how of bringing the two together, for a collaborative and positive approach. Revolutions can feel like progress but then focus and resources are diverted to rebuild a system – and is there time for that in the face of climate change? Placemakers say start where you are and work together. The four steps of playing the city are to find the gaps, build a team, make an offer and try to win. There might be value in considering what a climate-surviving city would look like, and then asking how one could achieve it in as few moves as possible?

The team of five million

New Zealand lies far away from the majority of the world's population. This disadvantage became an advantage with the onset of Covid-19. The pandemic came late. Chinese residents asking for the Lantern Festival to be cancelled in February were ahead of the curve. They knew what was coming from conversations with relatives and friends on the mainland. Most of us carried on with our lives. Italy was in lockdown while we carried on going to the theatre. When the government acted, the goal of lockdown was to flatten the curve. Prime Minister Jacinda Ardern called on the team of five million to give up their freedom for a month, to go hard and go early so as not to overwhelm the hospitals. There are high levels of trust in New Zealand in general, including of its government. The degree of trust and collaboration may be linked to the 'two degrees of separation', where everyone seems able to access everyone else. It may also be that while there is a huge disparity in levels of wealth, there is less disparity in dignity between people than in some countries. It is generally culturally unacceptable to show off and there is an aspiration to be kind, and considered kind. Importantly, Ardern was a good role model. Perhaps, like so many working parents, she too relished a bit of time at home with the little one. The oversight of the Covid response was given to the head of the opposition. As in wartime, all parties vowed to work together. The leader of the opposition chaired a committee to oversee decisions made and to suggest improvements to legislation made under urgency.

At local government level too there was unprecedented collaboration and collegiality. Library staff and the independent Citizens' Advice Bureau stepped up to volunteer their time to check up on seniors at home who might need help. Less happily, the huge cut in council resources meant an emergency budget. Auckland Council gets a large part of its revenue from tourism levies and shares in the airport and the port. Finance and Performance Committee chair Desley Simpson brought all council politicians to the table to discuss the options to reach some sort of consensus on the cuts and compromises needed. The most local of local politicians – the local board members – meanwhile engaged with residents and local groups to try to ensure the priorities were right. Following the 2020 election the relationship between council politicians and local MPs (albeit the ones in opposition) seemed to get stronger. To enable local and central government to engage with each other would be a positive step.

The word 'parliament' is rooted in the French verb *parler*, which means to talk, and talking (and listening) is at the heart of political decision-making. The job of councillors is to keep talking to everyone and ensure channels of communication are kept open so people can work together, both inside and outside the organisation. However, silo thinking has long been a problem within large organisations. As the city gets larger, the economy becomes more complex and industries more specialised, there is a danger that those running it spend more and more time with others like them, with similar pools of knowledge and bias. In Auckland, the wastewater team and drinking water team rarely get together, despite being part of the same council-controlled organisation, and the in-house stormwater team doesn't party with either of them.[1] The staff are competent; but making teams bigger adds complexity. Smaller councils, where everyone is in the same building, like Palmerston North, can find themselves able to move much more quickly on new and innovative projects. By being able to get a team of diverse people in the same room they can turn a chore into a meaningful project, transforming 'work' into a form of play. However, progress can be made in larger organisations as well if there is sufficient will.

Every month, town-hall discussions can be a place to share concerns and ideas on particular issues. All are welcome. Many local councils allow public deputations at their meetings and set up community meetings over particular issues. Despite media focus on central government, many of the decisions and funding of services that make the city work well are made at a local level: the enhancement of town centres, urban planning, waste collection, public art, the provision of public transport, water, housing, parks, playgrounds, benches, libraries, toilets and events. If you have a good idea to make the city work better or are facing issues, then let your elected representatives know. These community discussions can lead to a change in direction when endorsed by the powers that be. Some changes can take years, but some small projects can be facilitated in a matter of months.

Activity: Connect to your local council

What you need Nothing but a little time.

Method Contact your local council staff and request time to make a deputation. If you want your proposal to be minuted then ask to be included on the agenda of the formal business meeting. Prepare your speech, with a PowerPoint presentation that can be saved with the minutes.

Tips

- Keep to time and be clear on your core message. You have one chance to impress.

- Ask a friend to film you speaking to the council, which you can then share. You may find you have a lot of supporters.

- If you know others, share your views organise a petition to deliver to the council. The more people sending a message, the more weight it carries.

Variations

- Tell the council you have an interest in a particular sort of project and see if such work is already going on with which you can join in.

- Apply for funding to enable something that needs doing.

People on the ground can see the gaps that need filling and increasingly councils are working with NGOs to support community members to get actively involved in projects, including tree-planting days, restoring wetlands, catching pests and monitoring wildlife. A project my local board supported recently was to put up gauges showing how much the sea level would rise around the city. There is also more partnering with indigenous people. In Auckland, *mana whenua*, the dominant Māori iwis (or tribes) in an area, Auckland Council and Auckland University have co-led projects to explore how mussels may improve water filtration in built-up coastal areas. Another iwi Ngati Paoa, with the support of the local board, has set up a two-year *rahui*, a no-take of mussels, scallops, crayfish and abalone for a nautical mile around their homeland, Waiheke Island near Auckland. Projects work very well when there is grassroots interest. A no-mow programme, advocated by local naturalists, has meant sections of parks have been returned to meadowland to attract pollinators. This could be great for local biodiversity.

Filling the gaps

Yellow brick road

One of the gaps in cities concerns good recreational space for kids. We want them to get into spaces where other kids are, so that they can play together. Hanging around the school at pick-up time is an excellent solution, because the kids can then use the school playground for longer while parents chat happily to other adults. Some schools lock up the playground after school hours. In some communities there are very few facilities at all.

This was the case in the Iron Triangle, a working-class suburb in Richmond, California, so-named because of the railway lines and motorways on its borders. The playground was old and tired, and the residents wanted a new one. Eventually, a terrific new playground was designed and installed, but this led to a second issue. How could the kids get there? A kid at his youth group suggested a yellow brick road be built to link the school and kindergarten to the park. This route would be fun and safe: the community would know the kids were there, and so traffic would slow down. His youth worker thought it was a great idea, and so began a decade-long project that got the whole community working with a walrus-moustached transport engineer, elderly playground attendant Eddie and an artist who wanted to create a totem pole for the new roundabout.

Volunteers knocked on doors, did research, got involved in a co-design process and even trialled the idea, including installing the totem pole to check the fire engine could get around it. And with a couple of tweaks to the design, it could. It took a while to get the funding to make the changes permanent, but eventually it came. When at last the street was closed to traffic, the kids got on their bikes and cycled around the totem pole '50 million times. They couldn't get enough,' said youth leader Toody Maher.[2] While the kid who had the idea is now old enough to work in the youth centre, the project itself has transformed how the community works together, and a new generation of kids gets to play more often.

We can go without the playground if we can reclaim the streets. In Britain, the play street movement encourages the closure of residential streets to traffic for a few hours over the weekends or after school, so that kids can get outside and play with each other.

Action: Set up a play street

What you need A street, friendly neighbours and a bit of patience with paperwork.

Method

1. Talk to your neighbours and garner support.

2. Get permission and support from the council to close the street.

3. The council provides a checklist to ensure that all health and safety measures are looked into and that you have volunteers covering everything. Tick it off.

4. Tell all the neighbours the time and date, and encourage the kids to bring things to play with.

5. Play out![3]

Tip As the Hackney Play Association notes, you don't have to organise things for the kids to do; they will enjoy coming up with their own fun. Encourage the kids to bring along whatever they want – this could be tricycles, it could be anything. As a back-up there is no harm in providing some chalk, skipping ropes, hula hoops and soft balls.[4]

The High Line

The High Line in New York combines the desire for play, nature and a safe pedestrian route in one project. The initial idea came from the owner of the abandoned elevated railroad but it was two locals, Joshua David and Robert Hammond, who made it happen. Neither was an architect, or seasoned campaigner, but they knew how to sell an idea and were great at throwing parties to raise funds for the cause.[5] There was a desire for a park, and they knew it had to look stunning, so they ran a competition which drew in a number of designers, landscape architects and visionaries, and got people thinking about what The High Line could look like. One idea was for a mile-long lap pool, and another a rollercoaster that swooped up and down above a meadow. A more practical design followed, with a meandering path instead of a rollercoaster that went through a variety of plantings, art installations, water features, seating etc. More and more support came from all tiers of society, from Hillary Clinton and Michael Bloomberg to local families, friends and the Rainbow community. It was this enormous team of champions that helped the project clear the regulatory and funding obstacles in its path.

Refuge

In Australia, Art House Gallery has engaged with the existential crisis of climate change through Refuge, a series of participatory artworks that directly address the possibility of disaster and how to act when disaster strikes. Each project brought a broad range of people together, from elders to engineers, to collaborate and think through what they should do if the worst came to pass. They have over the last few years turned the North Melbourne Town Hall into variously a relief centre to deal with an imaginary flood, envisaged the increasing likelihood of five consecutive days at over 40°C, dealt with a pandemic and, in 2019, examined displacement prompted by climate crisis. The final Refuge was set for 2020 and was to 'explore the confluence of multiple climate crises and asks: how can we share resources equally in times of hardship when the worst comes to pass? The fifth Refuge explores displacement as a humanitarian crisis and directs our focus towards culture, spirituality, relationships and ritual.'[6] The final work had to be addressed online. In 2020 there had been devastating bush fires, a drought and a pandemic.

Gapfiller

Facilitating people to fill in the gaps after a disaster would also be the work of Gapfiller, an artist-led placemaking initiative based in Christchurch, New Zealand. It had been generally believed that Christchurch wasn't particularly at risk from earthquakes, but on the night of Saturday 4 September 2010, a 7.1 magnitude shake changed that. Buildings were damaged and the earth liquified, but people got back on their feet. However, the aftershocks kept coming, and five months later another major quake would hit the city, this one at lunch-time, killing 185 people and injuring several thousand. Over a quarter of the buildings in the city centre would fall or be demolished. Adding to the sense that this was a biblical moment, red crosses were marked on the doors of those structures deemed unrepairable.

It was a massive shock. A huge loss of heritage, of livelihoods, of homes and of people. One of the first installations by artists involved white chairs assembled as if for a church service. They all looked a little different: there was one to represent each person who had died. Another intervention was to install a beautifully lit dance floor and coin-operated outdoor jukebox in an empty lot, named the Dance-o-mat. It wasn't known whether Christchurch folk, who had a reputation for being more conservative than most, would want to dance with strangers, but it turned out they did. It was so popular that it lasted for years, and was then re-created in other cities around the country. Another group projected video games onto the sides of buildings and invited people to come and play. It is ironic, perhaps, that a number of the artists who led the project at the beginning had been involved in the Free Theatre, a confronting avant-garde theatre that had long been trying to shake up Christchurch society. When the earthquake did that, they responded by bringing some magic to the streets that helped heal society instead. Like good players, they pivoted and did the opposite.

Transition Towns

We have seen that Transition Towns started at a grassroots level but have often involved local council to fund solar panels and other initiatives. In Bristol, Lewes and Brighton in the UK councils have supported local currencies. In Ungersheim village in Alsace, France, the mayor and local authorities embraced the movement and formally resolved to become a transition town. Since then the Transition Network website reports that they have, amongst many other things: become a Fairtrade town; formed a citizens' forum about renewable energy; launched a local currency, 'Le Radis' (the radish); mapped the biodiversity of the area in an 'Atlas of Biodiversity'; returned a former mining waste heap to nature; installed a 120m² solar thermal installation at the swimming pool and a wood biomass boiler, which heats the pool and several adjoining buildings; built Helio Parc 68, a 5.3MW solar installation and industrial estate; changed all the public lighting in the village to low-energy bulbs; assessed all public buildings for their energy consumption; made land available for a PassivHaus co-housing project, Eco-Hameau Le Champré; completely banned all pesticides and herbicides in public areas; bought a working horse to help with local food cultivation and to pull a carriage to take local kids to school; changed the catering arrangements so that the local primary school now serves 100 per cent organic meals every day, including snacks; and transformed 8ha of land owned by the Commune into an organic market garden, Les Jardins de Cocagne, which produces sixty-four varieties of vegetables, provides 250 baskets of food for local families and runs stalls at five markets every week. And built a canning factory.[7] It makes you wonder what the hell you are doing with your time really.

All these shared projects, including beating Covid-19, bring communities together and make them stronger, more competent, more connected and more resilient. Those involved have people they can call on when the next challenge comes.

For the love of bees

The philosopher Alain de Botton has a theory that the art a society favours fills in a gap in their lives and this may well be true. Since the free-market reforms there has been a massive rise in participatory art projects engaged with both the practice of everyday life and the preparation for an uncertain future. Artist Sarah Smuts-Kennedy, of For the Love of Bees, started a regenerative agriculture project in urban spaces as an art project, on the subject of healing the connections between land and people. She has taken abandoned lots in Auckland and transformed them into sustainable professional market gardens where farmers and volunteers can work, hang out and connect with each other. She has been at the heart of the Urban Farmers' Alliance and Compost Collective. Regenerative agriculture is one of the most promising ways to sequester carbon, while also improving food security and nutrition. Play and survival are tied up together.

Sustaining enthusiasm in big projects

Play can be as low-stakes as Pooh sticks, but if you want to make an impact with your play, you need a bit of commitment, and that is hard work. Patience and persistence are required to build personal capacity and community capacity. A swimming pool isn't organised in a week. The High Line took years. In these examples, there was a fixed goal in a finite game. Other projects, like leading a choir or running a community garden, could in theory go on forever, but often don't. Many projects peter out because people get bored and want to go on to something new. This doesn't mean they failed. A succession plan may be a good idea for a profitable business, but in a passion project it is trickier.

Where someone new does take on a passion project, the project will probably change a lot – and that is also fine. The Transition Towns movement came in waves, with groups of people getting on board, and then after a few years leaving again. It took a while to see that this was not failure, but renewal. Saving the world is an ongoing task. If there is no end in sight it does make getting involved a bit daunting. No one wants to be the person who leaves others in the lurch, so it is a relief to know that you can withdraw with dignity. Play takes effort and sometimes we just need to stop. If you are not allowed to stop, playing becomes first a burden, then torture.

City leaders in Hawaii recognised that city improvements could take years, and it was hard to engage local people for the duration. Their solution was to bring people together for one discrete fun project – like improving the town centre – for just six months. When the changes are made, they have a big celebration and let people go back to their everyday lives. People who want to keep being involved can sign on for another project, perhaps one that is paid. This happened with The High Line. The Friends of the High Line took on the contract for the management of the park: what started as a playful project became a revenue-generating business that they are now really good at, and it has become work. For them, play will now probably mean something else.

There are all sorts of ways people can join in for a short time. Volunteer at an arts festival. Sign up for one term of knitting classes. Restore a stream. If you are an Easter Islander, perhaps carve an enormous stone head. If you are an Ancient Egyptian with nothing to do during the times of flood, why not help build a pyramid? These community projects can bring people together – but then they end. People can rest and, when they are ready, ask themselves – what next?

16

Levelling up

We are not simple beings, or chess pieces. We can be more than one thing at once, and are many, many things over the course of a lifetime. Sometimes we are directors, making things happen; sometimes we are down at the pub telling stories of how it all went wrong. Sometimes we are riding high with a win at the dog track; sometimes we are trying to make a costume for our kid's school play out of scrap fabric and cardboard. Sometimes we are serious and sometimes we are silly. Flipping between activities stops us getting bored and means we achieve more. School students in Finland have little homework and enjoy the shortest school days, and yet they top the charts when it comes to results.

Sometimes we just want to stop, sleep or sunbathe in peace. We need to go home and not be intruded upon too much by the outside world. For those living in busy city centres, noise pollution can make them sick, physically and mentally. Many of us don't get enough sleep, and yet rest is one of the most effective happiness and beauty treatments there is. There was a great picture that went around Facebook, showing a pair of pie charts. The first was 100 per cent work. 'This is what I first thought would make me productive.' The second chart depicted what actually did boost productivity: a day pretty equally divided into work, sleep, and time exercising and having fun. A city that allows us to engage in all these parts of life, by making space, time and resources available, is a playful city.

We are drawn to cities because of the combination of sensations that we can enjoy if we explore a little: touch, taste, sight, sounds and smells. The 'sixth sense' of balance is essential for negotiating the city.

The city itself is dynamic, a place of constant movement and rebalancing. Vertigo, that sense of being on the edge, about to lose one's balance – slipping, sliding, speeding and swinging – is also part of the city's appeal. Managing the round-and-rounds and particularly the ups-and-downs of the city is a quintessential part of urban life. The city is a site of breaking limits, of new achievements. Buildings get taller and taller, with scientific and engineering break-throughs with concrete, steel, glass, electricity, lifts. Just as you get used to a place, it changes again. Just as you get used to a role, the company restructures and you are in a new one. For the playful, and particularly for the young, being in the city where new exciting things are happening is hugely appealing.

We like to win and to be ahead of the curve, but we are also pro-social and attuned to feedback. Most of us don't want to be so far ahead that we are on our own. How we behave and what we are aiming for is defined by the pressures of existing structures – our understanding of physical and social limits. The structures of society provide a network of friends and acquaintances, in which we can find our place, share knowledge and work together. By engaging in the play/work of copying/joining in, making an offer and being attuned to feedback, we learn to live and contribute to the society we are in. We want to make an impact and be valued, but we also want to help others and make the world a better place. It is possible in a big community project to have a win without any losers.

We test the world around us. Before we stand or climb onto a structure, we test its robustness, and similarly we test rules, cultural expectations, each other and ourselves. There is a thrill in creating new stunts on a skateboard or in leaving those road cones on top of trees. We learn to play the game *and* find a way to improvise play (and a life for ourselves) in the gaps within the existing structures. The rules can stimulate creativity, as can old ideas. There is a satisfaction in taking existing knowledge and bending, blending and breaking old ideas to develop new ones. This is sometimes controversial. It is good to be tactful, but a desire to copy and innovate is part of the human condition.

Play takes effort. It is risky and resource-heavy. We gasp at the mastery of dancers, tumblers and high-wire acrobats, who move across space as though defying the laws of gravity. And yet we are also aware of the training, the falls, the number of steps they have taken to achieve what they can do. When we start something new it might energise us, but after a while it also takes effort, and that is why projects that last the length of a school term or semester can be good for making a modest but real impact, without tying people to projects for many years. Or we can engage in easy play, like baking a cake or watching TV, that can be very enjoyable and restful but may not allow us to meet new people or make a huge impact on the world. We should always go to the party, because good things happen.

There are ways of playing that feel intense and bypass mastery. The first is cheating. The second is shutting down the game so no one can play. Civilisation and order depend on everyone within society doing their bit: knowing what the rules are and holding them up. Systems need to be enforced to prevent cheating, but they must also be responsive to prevent outcomes being unfair, to ensure there is a way to win, to provide a safety net and evolve to survive. If the system repeatedly fails at this another system will emerge to take over. No empire lasts forever. In the short term this can be chaotic and in the medium term oppressive. Fortunately, it is possible for systems to change direction and do the opposite. And this can have an energising effect. We can set new goals and rules and measures if we want to and can organise ourselves together. Saving the world will rarely be described as a big playful community project, but it could be like that.

An encouraging final point

Never before have we been as connected as we are today. Young adults have grown up with the internet. They have grown up with the tools to collaborate at their fingertips – literally. Video game structures that were designed for play can be restructured to allow massive teams of people to work on cancer research and to stimulate problem-solving for other real-life issues. The international collaborative work to find a Covid-19 vaccine demonstrates how different countries and agencies can pull together to face global crises. We share information every day and find answers to our questions. Social media can produce silos, but it also can break down barriers.

We have reconceptualised the city, a place of work, as a place of play, and we have reconceptualised play, rather than being a mere frivolity (though it can be that), as an essential way to find out who we are, what we can do and how we can connect with others. Play can be taken very seriously, and can involve a huge amount of commitment. Play is not the opposite of work but its younger self, trying things for fun to explore what is possible, and in the process, sometimes, shining a light on the way ahead. Play is not limited to activities in an ordained place or time, but is interwoven into everyday life, depending on our state of mind.

We have all we need to be happy within our bodies – it is extraordinary that people can be just as happy when they don't get what they want, as when they do.[1] We create our own happiness by releasing the chemicals already inside us. It is within our power a great deal of the time to stimulate their release. We can do this by getting sunlight and exercising; by activating our senses and engaging in the world around us; by behaving in a pro-social way; and by engaging in projects that are meaningful to us. We will always worry about something, but we can keep things in perspective and enjoy what we have. Not being able to control everything is OK. Not knowing what is coming can make life more fun. Living well is to win.

Money, conversely, should be considered as an aspect of the game, rather than the end game itself. Life is less stressful when there is a safety net and the stakes are lower. It is very important to keep society in play and, like helping a child out in Monopoly, quantitative easing means more money can be distributed to keep more people in the game. Financial debt does not necessarily have to burden our children, but ecological debt definitely will. We have really big hairy goals against which we must measure our progress. Increasingly companies will have to play the game differently and report on measures that go beyond the economic.

We are wired to be adaptable. Getting distracted is not necessarily a waste of time. Our magpie-like interest in magazine articles, documentaries and futuristic novels and films that have no relevance to our current activities can be of benefit when situations change – and we realise we have already thought about the issue. As labour-saving devices reduce the number of housework tasks, old-school activities like preserving jam, spinning wool and knitting have been reconceptualised as forms of play. This pleasure in keeping up old cultural knowledge may be helpful if the world around us shifts again and we are forced to live in a simpler way. The highly complex and serious rules that govern cities – building regulations, water standards, transport management and revenue collection – can all be changed if our values and vision change. And if we want a world for our children to play in, then change we must.

Change is frightening and exciting, but when the chips are down and we face a common threat, whether environmental (as in Christchurch), medical (like Covid-19) or military (as in the Second World War), people tend to pull together and cope – and even, at times, dare I say, enjoy it? Evidence suggests that if met with a coordinated and collaborative approach, these challenges are more likely to boost morale than depress us. During the war, people were told to stay cheerful, and they did. War and financial austerity can be oppressive, but there is some evidence to suggest that people play more intensely under difficult circumstances than when times are good. When there is a gap, the most creative people in society try to fill it with something better. Perhaps it is a survival instinct to keep connecting, innovating and exploring alternative, better ways of doing things; perhaps play is most valuable in that it keeps up enthusiasm when life is full of challenges and there is work to be done. Would the Beveridge Report have been as ambitious if it had been written in peacetime, in a time of complacency, I wonder? So, have courage. You only live once. Enjoy it. You can feel in your bones what your next step needs to be.

It's time to make your move.

References

Introduction: The vital importance of play for all ages

1 Pinker, Susan. 2014. *The Village Effect*. New York: Spiegel & Grau.
2 Eames, Tom. 2019. Did Freddie Mercury really take Princess Diana to a London gay pub in the '80s? Smooth Radio. 24 April 2019. https://www.smoothradio.com/artists/queen/freddie-mercury-princess-diana-vauxhall-tavern/
3 Mount, Harry. 2020. The Queen's Big VE-Night Out: what really happened? *The Telegraph*. 8 May 2020. https://www.telegraph.co.uk/films/0/queens-big-ve-day-night-really-happened/

Chapter 1: Play and pleasure

1 Huizinga, J. 2016 [1938]. *Homo Ludens* ('literally' Playful Man'). London: Routledge.
2 A lot of games seem to prepare children for the challenges of Paleolithic life. Tickling forces the juniors to submit (and enjoy it), chasing them makes them physically strong and able to hunt, and hide and seek will help protect them from danger. In all these games, children test themselves with and against each other.
3 ESPN. 2019. 'Clemson's Dabo Swinney tops salary list at $9.3M, passing Alabama's Nick Saban at $8.85M' https://www.espn.com/college-football/story/_/id/27901802/clemson-dabo-swinney-tops-salary-list-93m-passing-alabama-nick-saban-885m/
4 Martin, T. 2017. Another Roll of the Dice. *New Statesman*, 19 January 2017. London.
5 Brown, S. 2009. *Play*. New York: Penguin.
6 Caillois, Roger. 1962. *Man and Games*. London: Thames & Hudson.

Chapter 2: Playing to learn

1   Brown. ibid. p32.
2   Suzman, James. 2020. *Work: A History of How We Spend Our Time*. London: Bloomsbury.
3   Kuang, Cliff & Fabricant, Robert. 2019. *User Friendly*. London: W.H. Allen.
4   Bregman, Rutger. 2020. *Humankind*. London: Bloomsbury.
5   Huizinga. ibid.
6   Walter, Harriet. 2004. *In Other People's Shoes*. London: Nick Hern Books
7   Huizinga. ibid.
8   Kuang & Fabricant. ibid.
9   Friedberg, Paul M. & Berkeley, Ellen Perry. 1970. *Play and Interplay*. New York: Macmillan.
10 Eagleman, David & Brandt, Anthony. 2017. *The Runaway Species*. New York: Catapult.
11 Kuang & Fabricant. ibid.
12 Schechner, R. 2003. *Performance Theory*. New York: Routledge
13 Brown. ibid. p19.
14 Huizinga. ibid. Huizinga felt the creation of beauty through poetry and music was a sublime form of play. He accepted this didn't fit into his 'play is violent' theory.
15 de Bono, Edward. *Six Thinking Hats*. London: Penguin.
16 Harford, Tim. 2016. *Messy*. London: Abacus.

Chapter 3: What is a game?

1   McGonigal, Jane. 2011. *Reality is Broken: why games make us better and how they can change the world*. New York: Penguin.
2   Montgomery, Charles. 2013. *Happy City*. London: Penguin.
3   Bennet, Jane. 2001. *The Enchantment of Modern Life: attachments, crossings and ethics*. Princeton: Princeton University Press.
4   Suzman. ibid.
5   Little, Brian. 2017. *Who are you, really?* London: Simon & Schuster.
6   Johnson, Steven. 2016. *Wonderland: How Play Made the Modern World*. New York: Pan Macmillan.
7   Cassidy, Cody. 2020. Who invented the wheel and how did they do it? *Wired*.

8   Campbell, James D. 2012. *'The Army Isn't All Work': Physical Culture and the Evolution of the British Army, 1860–1920.* Abingdon: Routledge

Chapter 4: Why don't we play (more)?

1   Brown. ibid.
2   Dehaene, Stanislas. 2014. *Consciousness and the Brain.* New York: Viking.
3   Schechner. ibid. p.105
4   Brown. ibid.
5   Gladwell, Michael. 2013. Complexity and the 10-000 Hour Rule. *New Yorker.* 21 August 2013. New York: Conde Nast. https://www.newyorker.com/sports/sporting-scene/complexity-and-the-ten-thousand-hour-rule/
6   Sutton-Smith, Brian. 1997. *The Ambiguity of Play.* Cambridge, Mass: Harvard University Press.
7   Nutt, David. 2018. It's irrational to deny people access to LSD. 25 February 2018. Radio New Zealand National.
8   Campbell, James D. 2012. *'The Army Isn't All Work': Physical Culture and the Evolution of the British Army, 1860–1920.* Abingdon: Routledge.
9   Putnam, R. 2007. E Pluribus Unum: Diversity and Community in the Twenty-first Century: The 2006 Johan Skytte Prize Lecture. Nordic Political Science Association. https://eportfolios.macaulay.cuny.edu/benediktsson2013/files/2013/04/Putnam.pdf
10 Jacobs, Jane. 1961. *The Death and Life of Great American Cities.* New York: Random House. p65.
11 Montgomery, Charles. 2013. *Happy City.* London: Penguin.
12 Bregman. ibid.
13 Harford, Tim. 2016. *Messy.* London: Abacus.
14 Sennet, Richard. 2018. *Building and Dwelling.* London: Penguin.
15 Huizinga. ibid.
16 Grant, H. & Michael, C. 2019. Too poor to play: children in social housing blocked from communal playground. *The Guardian.* 25 March 2019. https://www.theguardian.com/cities/2019/mar/25/too-poor-to-play-children-in-social-housing-blocked-from-communal-playground/
17 Wong, H. 2016. *Being Chinese.* Wellington, New Zealand: Bridget William Books.

18 Rose, Jonathan. 2016. *The Well-Tempered City.* New York: Harper. pp365–6.
19 Paluck, E. L. & Shepherd, H. 2012. The Salience of Social Referents: A Field Experiment on Collective Norms and Harrassment Behaviour in a School Social Network. *Journal of Personality and Social Psychology* 6(103) pp899–915.
20 Sakulku, Jaruwan. 2011. The Impostor Phenomenon. *The Journal of Behavioral Science*, 6(1) pp75–97. https://doi.org/10.14456/ijbs.2011.6

Chapter 5: Easing yourself back into play

1 Employment New Zealand. 2021. Hours of Work. Ministry of Business, Innovation and Employment. https://www.employment.govt.nz/hours-and-wages/hours-of-work/
2 Britain comes in 15th. Measures average work weeks including part-time and full-time workers. https://time.com/4621185/worker-productivity-countries/
3 Barnes, Andrew. 2019. The Four Day Week. Auckland: TED.
4 Wigley, Tom. 2005. The Limits of Rationalism: satisfaction without joy. Unpublished thesis. Wellington: Victoria University.
5 Brown. ibid.
6 Booker, Christopher. 2007. *The Seven Basic Plots.* New York: Continuum.
7 Chen, Angela. 2017. Neuroscientist David Eagleman and composer Anthony Brandt explain how creativity works. *The Verge.* 5 November 2017. https://www.theverge.com/2017/11/5/16597660/david-eagleman-anthony-brandt-runaway-species-creativity-neuroscience-psychology-design-interview

Chapter 6: Play and pleasure

1 Hogarth. 1732. Ridotto al Fresco. Washington: Library of Congress. https://www.loc.gov/resource/cph.3b36768/
2 Legge, Kylie. 2013. *Future City Solutions* Sydney: Place Partners.
3 Krishnamurthy, Ravindra. Vertical farming: Singapore's solution to feeding the local urban population. Permaculture Research Institute. https://www.permaculturenews.org/2014/07/25/vertical-farming-singapores-solution-feed-local-urban-population/
4 Curry, Andrew. 2008. Gobekli Tepe: The world's first temple? Smithsonian Magazine.

5   McGonigall. ibid.
6   Rose. ibid.

Chapter 7: Play in the city over time

1   Bregman. ibid.
2   Tannahill, Reay. 1989. *Sex in History* London: Sphere.
3   Bregman. ibid.
4   Gilbert, Dan. 2012. The surprising science of happiness. TED. https://www.ted.com/talks/dan_gilbert_the_surprising_science_of_happiness
5   Pruitt, Sarah. 2018. 8 winter solstice celebrations around the world. *History*.https://www.history.com/news/8-winter-solstice-celebrations-around-the-world
6   Huizinga. ibid.
7   Zeldin, Theodore. 1994. *An Intimate History of Humanity*. London: Harper Collins.
8   Johnson. ibid.
9   Hibbert, Christopher. 1987. *The English. A Social History*. London: Harper Collins.
10 Pincus, Steve. 1995. "Coffee politicians does create": Coffeehouses and Restoration Political Culture. *Journal of Modern History*. Vol. 67, No. 4 (Dec., 1995), pp807–834
11 Johnson. ibid.
12 Royal Society of Arts. 2018. Oceania.
13 Floud. ibid.
14 Floud. ibid.
15 Derby, Mark. 2013. Cards, board games and puzzles – Maori use of games. *Te Ara – the Encyclopedia of New Zealand*. https://teara.govt.nz/en/cards-board-games-and-puzzles/page-1
16 Schrader, Ben. 2016. *The Big Smoke*. Wellington: Bridget Williams Books.
17 Jacobs. ibid.
18 Gill, T. 2017. Building cities fit for children. UK: Winston Churchill Memorial Trust.
19 Gehl, Jan. 1987. Life Between Buildings. New York: Van Nostrand Reinhold.
20 Friedberg. ibid.
21 The Project for Public Space. 2021. New York. https://www.pps.org/

22 Alexander, Christopher. 1977. A Pattern Language. New York: OxfordUniversity Press

23 City of Vancouver. 1992 (2020). High-density Housing for Families with Children Guidelines. https://guidelines.vancouver.ca/guide lines-high-density-housing-for-families-with-children.pdf

24 Jacob, Allen & Appleyard, Donald. 1987. Toward an Urban Design Manifesto. Journal of the American Planning Association. 53(1). p112–120

25 Speck, Jeff. 2012. *Walkability*. New York: Farrar, Strauss & Giroux.

26 Florida, Richard. 2002. *The Rise of the Creative Class*. New York: Harper Business.

27 Montgomery. ibid., p137.

28 Stevens, Quentin. 2007. *Ludic City* London: Routledge. p218.

29 Jane Jacobs. ibid. & Tim Harford. ibid.

30 Sudjic, Deyan. 2017. *The Language of Cities* London: Penguin. p33.

Chapter 8: Winners and losers

1 Rich, Benjamin. 2009. *Whitopia*. New York: Hyperion.

2 https://edition.cnn.com/2020/09/12/us/freedom-black-cooperative-toomsboro/index.html

3 Jacobs. ibid.

4 Schulze, Elke. 2017. Beloved and Condemned: a cartoonist in Nazi Germany. *The New York Review*. New York. https://www.nybooks.com/daily/2017/09/14/beloved-and-condemned-a-cartoonist-in-nazi-germany/

5 Gladwell, Malcolm. 2014. The Crooked Ladder. *New Yorker*. 11 August.https://www.newyorker.com/magazine/2014/08/11/crooked-ladder

6 Groskop, Viv. 2020. It's just a joke comrade. London: BBC Radio 4. https://www.bbc.co.uk/programmes/b097zv5d

7 Brown. ibid.

8 Minton, Anna. 2011. *Ground Control*. London: Penguin.

9 Lange, Alexandra. 2018. *Design for Childhood*. New York: Bloomsbury.

10 Bird, William. 2007. *Natural Thinking*. UK: RSPB. http://ww2.rspb.org.uk/Images/naturalthinking_tcm9-161856.pdf

11 Derbyshire, David. 2007. How children lost the right to roam in four generations. *Daily Mail Australia*. https://www.dailymail.co.uk/news/article-462091/How-children-lost-right-roam-generations.html

12 Bird. ibid.

13 Alexander, Christopher. 1977. *A Pattern Language*. New York: Oxford University Press.

14 Swarbrick, Nancy. 2011. Road accidents – Promoting road safety. *Te Ara – the Encyclopedia of New Zealand*. https://www.TeAra.govt.nz/en/road-accidents/page-3

15 Worpole, K. 2003. *No particular place to go? Children, young people and public space*. Groundwork.

16 Skenazy, Lenore. 2015. 'I let my 9-year-old ride the subway alone and I got labeled the world's worst mom. *Washington Post*. https://www.washingtonpost.com/posteverything/wp/2015/01/16/i-let-my-9-year-old-ride-the-subway-alone-i-got-labeled-the-worlds-worst-mom/

17 Jansen, Tiffany. 2016. The preschool inside a nursing home. *Atlantic*. https://www.theatlantic.com/education/archive/2016/01/the-preschool-inside-a-nursing-home/424827/

18 Hoy, Selena. 2015. Why Japanese Kids Can Walk to School Alone. *Atlantic*. https://www.theatlantic.com/technology/archive/2015/10/why-japanese-kids-can-walk-to-school-alone/408475/

19 Smith, M. K. and Doyle M. E. (2002). 'The Albemarle Report and the development of youth work in England and Wales', The encyclopedia of pedagogy and informal education. https://infed.org/mobi/the-albemarle-report-and-the-development-of-youth-work-in-england-and-wales/

20 Ward, Colin. 1978. *The Child and the City*. London: Random House.

21 Booth, Robert. 2019. Youth club closures put young people at risk of violence. *The Guardian*. https://www.theguardian.com/society/2019/may/07/youth-club-closures-young-people-risk-violence-mps

22 Manaugh, Geoff. 2016. *Burglar in the City*. New York: Farrar, Strauss & Giroux.

23 Of the top twenty most surveilled cities, eighteen are in China; number sixteen is Hyderabad, a tech hub in India. https://www.comparitech.com/vpn-privacy/the-worlds-most-surveilled-cities/

24 Minton. ibid.

Chapter 9: Conceptualising the city as a game
(that is good to play)

1 Smith. ibid.

2 Hrubi, Denise. 2015. Why rich people in Austria want to live in

housing projects. *The World*. 26 October 2015. https://www.pri. org/stories/2015-10-26/why-rich-people-austria-want-live-housing-projects

3   De Botton, Alain. 2006. *Architecture of Happiness*. London: Vintage.

4   Sherwood, Harriet. 2018. Religion: why faith is becoming more and more popular. *The Guardian*. 27 August. https://www.theguardian.com/ news/2018/aug/27/religion-why-is-faith-growing-and-what-happens-next

5   CNN. 2020. Hurricane Katrina Statistics Fast Facts. https://edition. cnn.com/2013/08/23/us/hurricane-katrina-statistics-fast-facts/index. html

6   Anwar, Linya. 2015. In New Orleans' Hardest Hit Neighbourhood, a Recovery – By Sheer Will. US: National Public Radio. https:// www.npr.org/2015/08/21/432922681/in-new-orleans-hardest-hit-neighborhood-a-recovery-by-sheer-will

7   Craig, Eric. 2016. First laundry facility opens in Lower 9th Ward. Curbed New Orleans.

8   Cassidy, John. 2011. Save Our Shops. BBC. https://www.bbc.com/ news/business-13568374

9   https://www.fosterandpartners.com/projects/trafalgar-square/

10 https://www.trafalgarsquare.com/v/festivals/

11 https://www.landscapeperformance.org/case-study-briefs/sundance-square-plaza

12 Shelly, Brian. 2011. *Money, Mandates and Local Control in American Public Education*. Ann Arbor: University of Michigan Press.

13 Fox, Kate. 2005. *Watching the English*. London: Hodder & Stoughton.

14 Hawkins, T. T. 1942. *The Pub and the People: A Worktown Study*. London: Victor Gollancz.

15 Flood, Joe. 2011. *The Fires*. New York: Riverhead.

16 Politics.co.uk. Public Libraries. https://www.politics.co.uk/reference/ public-libraries

17 Central Office of Information. 1971. No Two the Same. Pace Makers. London: British Film Institute https://player.bfi.org.uk/free/film/ watch-lady-allen-1971-online.

18 Allen of Hurtwood, Lady. 1968. *Planning for Play*. London: Thames & Hudson.

19 Play England. 2015. Adventure playgrounds. http://www.playengland. org.uk/wp-content/uploads/2015/11/Adventure-Playgrounds.pdf

20 Association of Voluntary Organisations Wrexham. 2021. Play provision. https://avow.org/services/play-provision/

21 Friedberg. ibid. p47.

22   www.shorejunction.nz

23   Young, Emma. 2017. How Iceland got teens to say no to drugs. *Atlantic*. https://www.theatlantic.com/health/archive/2017/01/teens-drugs-iceland/513668/

24   Kershaw, Baz, Whalley, Joanne 'Bob' & Lee, Rosemary. 2011. Practice as Research: Transdisciplinary Innovation in Action. *Research Methods in Theatre and Performance*. Edinburgh: Edinburgh University Press.

25   Friedberg. ibid.

26   Speck. ibid.

27   Jacobs. ibid., pp120–1.

28   Sennett. ibid., p.211

29   Sennett. ibid., p.214.

Chapter 10: Planning the playful city

1   https://www.mercer.com/newsroom/2019-quality-of-living-survey.html

2   Doyle, Caroline. 2017. Perceptions and realities of violence in Medellin, Colombia. *Crime Justice Journal 8.2*. pp149–66. file:///C:/Users/bonhama1/Downloads/1010-Article%20Text-4112-1-10-20190507.pdf

3   Fabricant & Kuang. ibid.

4   Sadik-Khan, Janette. 2016. Streetfight. New York: Penguin.

5   Reid, Carlton. 2019. Closing central Madrid to cars resulted in 9.5% boost to retail spending, finds bank analysis. Forbes. https://www.forbes.com/sites/carltonreid/2019/03/08/closing-central-madrid-to-cars-resulted-in-9-5-boost-to-retail-spending-finds-bank-analysis/; Greene, Tommy. 2019. Madrid's new mayor is trying to scrap the city's traffic reduction scheme. It's not going well. *City Monitor*. https://www.citymetric.com/horizons/madrid-s-new-mayor-trying-scrap-city-s-traffic-reduction-scheme-it-s-not-going-well-4717

6   Ross, Nicola, cited in Skelton, Tracey. 2009. Children's Geographies/Geographies of Children: play, work, mobilities and migration. *Geography Compass* 3.4. pp1430–48.

7   Gill, Tim. 2018. The City that Got Serious about Child-Friendly Urban Planning. Rethinking Childhood. https://rethinkingchildhood.com/2018/04/03/ghent-serious-child-friendly-urban-planning/

8   Friedberg. ibid.

9   Stevens. ibid. p218.

10 Stevens. ibid. p211.

11 He was echoed recently by Miguel Sicart (Sicart, Miguel. 2017. *Unplayable Cities. Making the City Playable* Bristol: Playable Cities. https://vimeo.com/244818275).

12 MacGuill, Dan. 2015. A Welsh town has appointed its first resident jester in 700 years. *The Journal.* https://www.thejournal.ie/conwy-wales-town-jester-erwyd-le-fol-2250793-Aug2015/

13 Beekmans, Jeroen. 2011. Slide to the train. Pop up City. https://popupcity.net/observations/slide-to-the-train/;https://www.archdaily.com/153118/slide-to-the-train-station-with-the-transfer-accelerator-by-hik-ontwerpers

14 Duffield, Benjamin. 2018. *Megalodemocrat: The Public Art of Rafael Lozano-Hemmer.* Montreal: Fierce Bad Rabbit Pictures

15 By Hilary O'Shaughnessy and Matthew Rosier, 'Shadowing' started as a response to the 2014 Playable City Award in Bristol.

16 O'Shaughnessy, Hilary. Shadowing – five years on. Playable City. https://www.playablecity.com/news/2019/12/20/shadowing-five-years-on/

17 Montgomery. ibid.

18 Blainey, Geoffrey. 1990. Australian Rules Football. National Museum of Australia.

19 Sandseter, Ellen Beate Hansen & Sando, Ole Johan. We don't allow children to climb trees: How a Focus on Safety Affects Norwegian Children's Play in Early-Childhood Education and Care Settings. *American Journal of Play 8.* pp178-200. 2016/01/01. https://www.researchgate.net/publication/309770624_We_don't_allow_children_to_climb_trees_How_a_Focus_on_Safety_Affects_Norwegian_Children's_Play_in_Early-Childhood_Education_and_Care_Settings

20 Ball, David, Gill, Tim & Spiegal, Bernard. 2012. *Managing Risk in Play Provision* London: National Children's Bureau. The work was endorsed by Play England, Play Scotland, Play Wales & Playboard Northern Ireland.

21 https://texas.growingamerica.com/news/2013/08/update-worlds-15-largest-seed-banks/ Nevertheless the process is criticised for commodifyingseeds://regenerationinternational.org/2020/11/01/one-empire-over-seed-control-over-the-worlds-seed-banks/

22 https://www.kew.org/wakehurst/whats-at-wakehurst/millennium-seed-bank

23 https://safeswim.org.nz/

24 https://www.doc.govt.nz/news/media-releases/2020-media-releases/
    korora-live-cam/
25 Atkinson, Simon. 2012. Offices stand empty in tallest tower the Burj
    Khalifa.BBC.https://www.bbc.com/news/world-middle-east-18929271
26 Huizinga. ibid, p61.
27 Rose. ibid.
28 Sydney decided to develop Darling Harbour in 1984. It was opened
    in 1988 – with an aquarium.
29 Gu, Kai & Xie, Philip Feifan. 2015. Reid, Carlton. 2015. The
    changing urban morphology: Waterfront redevelopment and event
    tourism in New Zealand. Tourism management perspectives. 15.
    p105–114.
30 Ravenscroft, Tom. 2017. The Weird World of China's Copycat
    Architecture. https://www.youtube.com/watch?v=Qs940x0DDZ4
31 The Art Story. How a NYC Department Store Launched Warhol and
    Friends. theartstory.org
32 Bindelglass, Evan. 2019. The real story behind Philippe Petit's World
    Trade Centre high-wire stunt. *Curbed*. https://ny.curbed.com/2015/9/
    30/9916096/world-trade-center-philippe-petit-the-walk

Chapter 11: How you can bring more play into the city

1   Ramsey,Andrew.2014.Thestorybehindthebirth ofT20.Cricket.com.au
    https://www.cricket.com.au/news/the-story-behind-the-birth-of-t20-
    cricket/2014-07-21

Chapter 12: Reconnecting to nature in the city

1   Wigley, Jenny. 2018. Paddleboarding to work. Jesse Mulligan
    in the afternoon. RNZ National. https://www.rnz.co.nz/national/
    programmes/afternoons/audio/2018669512/paddleboarding-to-work
2   Friedberg. ibid.
3   Atkinson, Olivia. 2016. A pop-up sauna is coming to Auckland's
    waterfront.*UrbanList*.https://www.theurbanlist.com/nz/a-list/a-pop-up-
    sauna-is-coming-to-aucklands-waterfront1
4   Matthews,Carys.2020.Wild swimming in Britain: best places to swim,
    water safety, and how to get started. Countryfile. BBC. https://www.
    countryfile.com/go-outdoors/get-active/wild-swimming-in-britain-
    the-best-places-to-swim-water-safety-and-how-to-get-started/
5   Locker, Melissa. 2018. People skiing to work because trains were

canceled redefine limitless living. *Time*. https://time.com/5179041/people-ski-to-work-in-snow/

6   Auckland Council. 2021. Tupuna Maunga significance and history. https://www.aucklandcouncil.govt.nz/about-auckland-council/how-auckland-council-works/kaupapa-maori/comanagement-authorities-boards/tupuna-maunga-tamaki-makaurau-authority/Pages/tupuna-maunga-significance-history.aspx

7   Japan Guide. Sapporo Snow Festivals. https://www.japan-guide.com/e/e5311.html#:~:text=The%20Sapporo%20Snow%20Festival%20was,Japan%20and%20across%20the%20world.

Chapter 13: Your play personality in the city

1   Neira, Juliana. 2020. Anonymouse installs miniature, mouse-themed music store in Sweden. *Design Boom*. https://www.designboom.com/art/anonymouse-miniature-mouse-houses-07-18-2020/

2   Wollaston, Sam. 2019. Four men with a ladder: the billboard campaigners battling Brexit. *The Guardian*. https://www.theguardian.com/politics/2019/feb/07/billboard-campaigners-brexit-led-by-donkeys

3   Cascade Bicycle Club. 2021. Create your own DIY event. https://www.cascade.org/connect-bike-everywhere-month-find-bike-everywhere-month-event/create-your-own-diy-bike-event

4   Bonnett, Alastair. 2014. *Off the Map*. London: Aurum.

5   Hansford, David. 2017. Secret Passages. *NZ Geographic*. Issue 148. https://www.nzgeo.com/stories/secret-passages/

6   Proctor, Alice. Uncomfortable Art Tours. https://www.theexhibitionist.org/

7   Longwell, Karen. 2019. When a newspaper struggles you don't have to close it – you can give it to its community. 6 November. Niemanlab. Massuchessetts: Harvard. https://www.niemanlab.org/2019/11/when-a-newspaper-struggles-you-dont-have-to-close-it-you-can-give-it-to-its-community/; https://the-gleaner.com/

8   Krause, Nick. 2018. Communities choose their local papers. *East Auckland Times Online*. https://www.times.co.nz/news/communities-choose-their-local-papers

9   Wynn, Jonathan. 2005. Guiding Practices: storytelling tricks for reproducing urban landscape. *Qualitative Sociology 28.4*. pp399–417.

10   https://www.streetfilms.org/

11   Christian, Donna. 2016. Singing the praises of choirs. *NZ Herald*.

https://www.nzherald.co.nz/entertainment/news/article.cfm?c_id=
1501119&objectid=11764026

12 Siegle, Lucy. 2011. Totnes: Britain's town of the future. *The Guardian*. https://www.theguardian.com/environment/2011/feb/06/totnes-transition-towns-ethical-living

13 https://transitionnetwork.org/stories/lambeth-local-entrepreneur-forum-london-england/

14 https://www.thewarren.nz/

15 https://www.deveron-projects.com/projects/

16 http://www.pop-upscience.com/

Chapter 14: Playing on the edge

1 Acconci, Vito. 1969. Following Piece. Museum of Modern Art. New York. https://www.moma.org/collection/works/146947

2 https://assassins.soc.srcf.net/FAQ3.html

3 https://www.cluedupp.com/

4 https://www.landscapearchitecture.nz/landscape-architecture-aotearoa/2018/9/25/parking-day-2018-in-pictures

5 McHardy, Emelyn. Mystery surrounds painter responsible for faux zebra crossing at school. *Stuff*. https://www.stuff.co.nz/national/106839518/mystery-surrounds-painter-responsible-for-faux-zebra-crossing-at-patumahoe-school

6 Ryan, Belinda. Former Crewe headteacher arrested during climate change protest. *Cheshire Live*. https://www.cheshire-live.co.uk/news/chester-cheshire-news/former-crewe-headteacher-arrested-during-17064666#:~:text=A%20former%20top%20Crewe%20headteacher,being%20released%20under%20police%20investigation

7 Dixon, Haley. 2019. Former Senior Police Offers Risk Arrest to Join Extinction Protest. *The Telegraph*. 6 October 2019. https://www.telegraph.co.uk/news/2019/10/06/former-senior-police-officers-risk-arrest-join-extinction-rebellion/

8 Finnegan, William. 1995. Peculiar Precautions and Rigors of Guerilla Bungee Jumping. *New Yorker*.

9 Holmes, Brian. 2012. In Thompson, Nato (ed.). *Living as Form*. New York: MIT Press.

10 Hall, Peter. 2000. Creative Cities and Economic Development. *Urban Studies*. *37.4*. pp639–49.

11 http://dunedinstreetart.co.nz/artworks/

Chapter 15: Playing together nicely

1   Dean, Miriam, Martin, Doug & Auton, Leigh. CCO Review 2020. Auckland Council. Review of council-controlled organisations (CCOs) (aucklandcouncil.govt.nz).
2   https://kaboom.org/play-everywhere/gallery/yellow-brick-road-play-street
3   https://playingout.net/play-streets/playing-four-simple-steps/
4   http://www.hackneyplay.org/playstreets/preparing/
5   Hammond, Robert. 2011. Building a park in the sky. TED. The men recommend that other people embarking on a big project should start fundraising as soon as they can, not just to raise money, but also to create the community buy-in needed to see the project through. https://www.ted.com/talks/robert_hammond_building_a_park_in_the_sky
6   https://www.artshouse.com.au/ourprograms/refuge/
7   https://transitionnetwork.org/stories/ungersheim-village-transition-france/

Chapter 16: Levelling up

1   Gilbert, Dan. 2014. Ten years later: Dan Gilbert on life after 'the surprising science of happiness'. TED Blog. https://blog.ted.com/ten-years-later-dan-gilbert-on-life-after-the-surprising-science-of-happiness/

Acknowledgements

This book would not have been possible without the existence of many other books and articles written by other people. My apologies for any errors or misinterpretations. For those who want to find out more about play, I have particularly been guided by *Homo Ludens* by Johan Huizinga, *Work* by James Suzman, *Play* by Stuart Brown, *Sex in History* by Reay Tannahill, *The Ambiguity of Play* by Brian Sutton-Smith, *Messy* by Tim Harford and *Reality is Broken* by Jane McGonigal. For the intersection between cities, play and quality of life I have been inspired by Charles Montgomery, Jane Jacobs, Richard Sennett, Jonathan Rose, Quentin Stevens, Ben Schrader, Janette Sadik-Khan, Jan Gehl, Geoff Manaugh, Christopher Alexander, Niki Harré, Nato Thompson, Fran Tonkiss, Peter Hall, Deyan Sudjic and Anna Minton. Thank you also very much to Jimi Hunt for allowing me to quote your wise words.

Nor would this book have been possible without the support of lots of people. I acknowledge my debt to my publisher Duncan Proudfoot, and Rebecca Sheppard of Constable, my editors Sue Viccars, Ellie Kivinen and Romy Hume. Thank you to Sue Bonham and Benjamin Teh for reading different versions at various times and to Helen Coyle and Jacqui Lewis for your help from the start. Thank you to Andy, Olivia and Charlie, for all the good times and for allowing me the time and space to get this done. Thank you to Laura and Rob Windsor, Amber Burlinson, Lucy Dixon and Kate Allen for the awesome parties, and Dad and Katie just because. Thank you to Tom and Jenny Wigley who have shared their work and have always held the bar high and to Emma McInnes, Ellie Craft, Miriam Moore, Natalie Donzé and all those at Women in Urbanism and Auckland Free Walking Tours from whom I have learned so much.

Thank you to Auckland's mayor, councillors of all political stripes, the Independent Māori Statutory Board and fellow board members in Waitematā and across the whole region for all they do to make Auckland a great place to live. Same goes for Mik Smellie, Antony Phillips, Michael Richardson, Irene King, Dirk Hudig, Don Mathieson, Viv Beck, Mark Knopf Thomas, Suzanne Kendrick, Sarah Smuts Kennedy, Grayson Goffe, Christy Tennant, City Mission, Lifewise, Karangahape Road Collective, Sustainable Coastlines, Low Carbon Network, Protect Our Gulf, Million Miles, Transition Town Point Chevalier, Grey Lynn 2030, Greater Auckland, Lawyers for Climate Action, the Urban Farmers Alliance, school strikers, the youth providers network and all those who do amazing *mahi* in the community, sometimes paid, often not. Go Chloe Swarbrick, MP/drag king *extraordinaire*, Eugenie Sage and Julie-Ann Genter who get it. Kudos to Ngati Whatua, Ngati Paoa and your mana whenua and pakeha allies for bringing nature back in to Waitematā. Thank you Trina Thompson, Carlos Rahman, Caroline Teh, George Weeks, Marieke Neumann, Frith Walker, Arash Barzin, Shamila Unka, Leanne Roche, Adrienne Young Cooper, Barbara Holloway, Patrick Cummeskey and all the staff at Auckland Council who get good stuff done and have shared their wisdom along the way. I am sorry I cannot list everyone.

Finally, thank you always to my teachers, fellow students and supervisors at Auckland University: Murray Edmonds, Tom Bishop, Ira Seidenstein, Denise Boucher, Alys Longley, Mark Harvey, and Ralph Buck.

Index